**FRANCIS CL**

28.

15

-4.

-4.

28. N

10. JAN. 19

-3.

DESIGNED FOR RECREATION

# DESIGNED FOR RECREATION

A Practical Handbook for all concerned with
providing Leisure Facilities in
the Countryside

## ELISABETH BEAZLEY

Drawings by

### DESMOND THOMAS

FABER AND FABER

24 Russell Square

London

*First published in 1969*
*by Faber and Faber Limited*
*24 Russell Square London WC1*
*Printed in Great Britain by*
*Ebenezer Baylis & Son, Ltd.,*
*The Trinity Press, Worcester, and London*
*All rights reserved*

SBN 571 08948 8

This book is based on work done on
a Royal Institute of British Architects'
Research Award
1966–67

© *Elisabeth Beazley 1969*

To James and Roland

# Contents

## Contents

# Contents

# Illustrations

*All plates are at the end of the book*

## Site use

1. Watching the World Cup
2. Picnicking by the car
3. Cars absorbed in parkland
4. Small picnic pull-offs
5. Chestnut paling for dune-fixing forms picnic places

## Information Centres

6 and 7. Wildfowl Trust Information and Research Building
8. Hopewell Village
9. Culloden Information Centre (1967)
10. The Wright Brothers' hut
11. New Grange Information Centre
12. A Blue Ridge Parkway Visitor Center
13. Fishbourne Palace: North Wing shelter

## Signs

14–18. Yorktown Battlefield
19–20. Timber signs made up of separate planks
21. Grouped signs
22. Sign fixed to a tree
23. Worboys directional sign
24. Passing place post
25. Worboys type *toilets* sign
26. P.B.
27. Saying it twice
28. Water Authority multiple signs
29. Nature trail numbers: on stone
30. Nature trail numbers: on laminated plastic on timber post

# Illustrations

## DRAWINGS

19

## Illustrations

# Acknowledgements

This book is based on work done on a Royal Institute of British Architects' Research Award for which I am most grateful. Much of it would be of little value if it were not for other people's practical experience and ideas. I would like to thank them for their exceptional generosity in terms of both their time and knowledge.

If the book is even a quarter as useful as the collecting of its material has been enjoyable, their efforts will be justified. This is also a chance to thank again many of those on the list below and their wives for hospitality during the tours made in Denmark, Holland and Germany as well as the U.S.A. and U.K. Special thanks are due to Mrs Paul Carlisle and Miss Olive Kitson who so tolerantly accompanied me on camping trips (consumer research).

For all this help I am particularly indebted to the individuals and members of organisations listed below:

Mr. Robert B. Adams; Mrs. Kathleen Ashcroft; Mr. John Barrett; Miss Mary Burkett; Mr. Peter Bond; Mr. C. Bonsey; Mr. F. Breman; Mr. Victor Brown; Dr. Buchwald; Boy Scouts Association; Department of Recreation and Conservation, British Columbia; British Visqueen Ltd.; Bureau of Public Roads, U.S.A.; Mr. Jorgen Christensen; Mr. Simon Conolly; Mr. Neville Conder; Caravan Club; Camping Club of Great Britain; Council for Nature; Mrs. Dalrymple; Mr. J. Donovon; Mr. Michael Dower; Duinswaterleiding Van, the Hague; Mr. M. J. Dunn; Elsan Sewage Systems; Viscount Esher; Mr. Bill Everhard; Forestry Commission; Mr. John Foster; Mr. Frederick Gibberd; Glasdon Signs Ltd.; Mr. Frederick Gutheim; Lt.-Col. Grant; Mr. W. Grant; Mr. J. Hansen; Mr. David Harrison; Dr. J. C. Heytze; Vic Hallam Limited; Mr. Vic Hallam; Mr. R. J. S. Hookway; Miss Marie Hartley; Highway Engineer's Department, Maribo; Col. G. Haythornthwaite; Miss Joan Ingilby; Keep Britain Tidy Group; Mr. R. Illingworth; Koninklijke Nederlandsche Toeristenbond; Mr. G. Kragh; Skrodiver Ladefoged; Dr. David Lowenthal; Mr. Ira B. Lykes; Mr. Hew Lorimer; Mr. Henry Makowski; Mr. R. McKinstry; Mr. Ellis Miles; Miss Mary Mitchell; Mrs. Betty Moira; Motor Caravanners Club; Ministry of Public Building and Works—Ancient Monuments

21

Department; Ministry of Transport; The National Trust; The National Trust for Scotland; Natural Environmental Research Council; National Caravan Council; Countryside Commission; National Park Service, U.S.A.; Mr. Martin Orrom; Mr. Philip Oswald; Public Sanitation Advice Council; Public Health Inspectors Association; Mr. R. M. H. Purnell; R. H. Name Plates Supplies Ltd.; Mr. J. M. Richards; Mr. D. W. Riley; Mr. Ron Reid; Mr. Per Rundberg; Mr. Walter Roth; Resin Maps & Signs Ltd.; Dr. Roderkerk; Mr. Peter Scott; Mr. Roger Sidaway; Mr. David Stabb; Brigadier Sparrow; Staffordshire County Council Planning Department; Snowy Mountains Hydro Electricity Authority; Mr. H. Schmidt; Mr. James Stormonth-Darling; Mr. and Mrs. Frank Tindall; Architects Dept., Tennessee Valley Authority; Transatlantic Plastics Ltd.; Mr. Anthony Tynan; Wildfowl Trust; Mr. J. W. Zaaijer.

Thanks are due to the Architectural Press for permission to use part of the material on car parks which has already appeared in *The Design and Detail of the Space between Buildings*, and to the Editor of the *Architectural Review* for material in chapters 14 and 15 which has appeared in that Journal in a slightly different form. A small part of chapter 7 has appeared in *Country Life* and a few extracts from 1, 2 and 7 in the *Guardian*.

The American National Park Service continually publishes an excellent series of Information Sheets, *Design*, in its *Parks Practice Program*. Permission to use parts of these is much appreciated (pages 103, 104, 106, 118–121, 133, 139, 150, 164).

I am most grateful to Mr. Desmond Thomas who made the drawings with such care and imagination.

Lastly, Mr. Martin Orrom must be thanked both for reading the typescript and making many useful comments; and Mrs. Fuselli and Mr. Francis Gottesman for so patiently typing it.

# Acknowledgements for photographs

I am most grateful to the following for permission to reproduce photographs:

Miss Olive Kitson,1, 90, 94, 95, 108, 123, 124, 127, 131; Mr. Frank Tindall, 5, 79; Messrs. Hughes and Bicknell, 6, 7; The Wildfowl Trust, 61; American National Park Service, 8, 12, 57, 75; Mr. Sam Lambert, 11, 128; Mr. E. Reeve, 13; Mr. R. McKinstry, 22; The Netherlands-staatsbosbeheer, 20; Mr. J. H. v. Schuppen, 36; Mr. F. Thompson, 37, 39, 46, 47, 67, 98; Central Electricity Generating Board, 41; Mr. R. Whistler, 45; Mr. Frederick Gibberd, 56; Miss Hartley and Miss Ingleby, 62, 63; British Columbia, 70, 71; Kon. Ned. Toer Bond. A.N.W.B., 72; Mr. R. G. Sanzen Baker, 80; Dr. Roderkerk, 81, 114; Miss Mary Mitchell, 86, 112, 113; Messrs. Adamsez, 91, 92; Mr. Philip Jebb, 93; Tennessee Valley Authority, 96; Messrs. Vic Hallam Ltd., 97; Crown Copyright, 107; British Visqueen Ltd., 110; Fairey Marine Ltd., 116; Conveyance & Fork Trucks Ltd., 117; Cresta Marine, 118; Mr. Raglan Squire, 119; Mr. Harry Merrick, 120; Messrs. Palfrey, 129; National Trust for Scotland, 134; Nat. Foto Persbureau, 115; (other photographs are by the author).

# Author's note

**Metric system**

At the time of going to press neither the British Standards Institution nor the trade associations and manufacturers had completed their conversion to the metric system. The conversions given in this book are therefore included for interim guidance only.

Figures in square brackets throughout the text give equivalent dimensions in the metric system. Conversion is either to the nearest centimetre or to the practical working dimension in the particular case, whichever seems most useful: e.g. 1′ 0″ is converted to 30 cm., a round figure for site work, while a 12″ × 10″ sawn timber becomes 30·5 × 25·4 cm. But approximate figures are converted to the nearest round figure likely to be used: e.g. 'approximately 50 yards' becomes 'approximately 45 metres', not 'approximately 46 metres', although the exact conversion is 45·72 m. As a general rule, conversion of manufactured objects is made to the nearest millimetre. All metric dimensions on drawings are in centimetres.

**Materials**

This book is not intended to provide information on proprietary materials, but occasionally where trade names or particular descriptions make the text clearer, they have been included. This does not imply that no other material of the same type exists. Products may have been modified since the time of writing.

**Prices**

Occasionally approximate prices are quoted in the text. It is fully realised that these will be out of date before the book leaves the press, but it is felt that in a few cases it is helpful to the reader to have some idea of the cost of an article; to know whether it is pence, shillings or pounds.

# Introduction

'"But you get so tired with nothing but scenery all the time."
"Yes, but you get even more tired and bored without any scenery."
"Well, I guess so. But I like it better when there's mostly landscape and not much scenery."
"Well, I guess so. But then most of the scenery was gone when we were there. There was just mountains and things."' Post-vacation dialogue between two secretaries reported in the *New Yorker*.[1]

People go into the country for an extraordinary variety of reasons. Some with a specific aim: to climb, fish, sail, walk; to look at buildings, birds or beetles. . . . Many go for scenery and many more just for a change of scene, or to enjoy themselves in pleasant surroundings. Quite a number, like those bemused but honest girls quoted above, may not be quite sure why they go, but they will go on going (in search perhaps of a classical landscape, improved by man with human touches, rather than a romantic wilderness?).

Because there are vast and growing numbers of us wanting to do all these things in a countryside, much of it already intensively used for farming and forestry, we are faced with the problem of providing for informal recreation on an unprecedented scale. Problems that once looked after themselves can no longer be left to chance. Where there were five cars on an August afternoon, fifty or five hundred may now come. The few who explored stately homes and ancient monuments in the thirties were the vanguard of tens of thousands.

The idea that anything to be enjoyed with spontaneous informality must be planned is itself alien. The problem is made more subtle because many of us want to find the country 'unspoilt'; we want, anyway, the illusion of catching it unawares, getting on with its own affairs, rather than decking itself out as a tourist attraction. To design for a change in primary use (for example to establish a new ski-ing centre) can be far easier than welding some single intrusive element connected with tourism into fine countryside or coastline. An enormous variety of buildings and services is needed: information centres, camp sites,

[1] Quoted by Dr. David Lowenthal in *Is Wilderness 'Paradise Enow'*, Columbia University Forum. Spring 1964.

picnic places, boat harbours, observation hides, to name but a few; and all the impedimenta that must go with them to service the tourist :car parks, public lavatories, litter bins, signs and notices. . . .

Most of the small buildings and artefacts now springing up to serve this need are insignificant in themselves. They often have little design energy spent upon them simply because it is not available. Yet the quality of our environment depends enormously on these things whether they are in the agricultural countryside or the wild. Their visual impact is partly due to their repetition: one sign post or stile may be repeated on 20 miles of cliff path; one litter bin throughout a county. This is not an argument against standardization: rather, it is essential that we use the advantages of standardization and miss its pitfalls. Standardization is recognized as an essential tool even in the American National Park Service, with its immense (to us) resources in terms of design energy. More time is then available for the equally important and difficult problem of siting, which must be unique in each case.

This visual impact, which is out of all proportion to the intrinsic importance of much 'service paraphernalia', also stems from the fact that it is useful only for a limited part of the year. The public lavatory graces the castle wall or the litter bin the moorland lay-by when the holidaymakers are snugly home once more. They can look even more forlorn in December than in June.

The object of this book is twofold. First, to give background information which might be useful to anyone interested in the future of the countryside and particularly to those who have to work out the design brief whenever a new project is mooted: clients, committee members and the professional people involved. It is an extraordinarily difficult and time-consuming job to discover what is wanted, let alone how to provide it. This is as true of siting (e.g. what might be the side effects of a new boat harbour) as of function and character of an actual building. It may be necessary to look at a lot of existing examples; if these are few and far between the whole exercise may be out of the question in terms of time and cost.

Second, at the other end of the scale, is the actual provision of a signpost, or a picnic barbecue, a bench or a litter bin. This may be the lot of an already overworked warden or natural historian; or of a draughtsman in a local authority office. It may well be a problem new to him and it is very difficult to turn to any source of information on these small but important artefacts. It is hoped that this book, by elucidating some of the principles and searching out some good examples, may at least save him the time of going through the same process. Incidentally, an important point that has emerged during the search for good examples and interesting solutions is that cost of product (as against cost of designer's time) is not necessarily related to its success. Some of the best examples, both from the point of view of function and integration with the land, are the cheaper, and the reverse is true. This applies both to buildings and artefacts.

Much design now necessarily results from hand-to-mouth expediency and there is little material generally available for reference. 'Advice and comment' may be forthcoming over some major matter but what seems to be needed is down-to-earth information for those who have to get on with the job.

In optimistic moments it is my hope that this book goes a little way towards providing both this and some of the background information that may be useful in the preparation of the countless design briefs which will be needed in the next decade. It if does, it is thanks to those who have already constructed or provided some of the 'leisure paraphernalia' involved, or who are responsible for their management. I am very aware of the book's shortcomings; these are to some extent inevitable in a subject which is expanding so rapidly.

It is also hoped that those who may read the book will bear in mind what it is really about because this is seldom mentioned in the text: spring moorland and August beaches; mountains; wet pebbles; open down; blades of grass; October woodland and new plantation; laid out farmland and miniature reed-shaken wilderness; canals; castles, cowsheds and spidery suspension bridges; . . . and in all this, people. Fifty-five million of us of even more diverse character than the country we have inherited.

*London*                                                                                    E.B.
*February* 1968

# I

# Behaviour patterns and site use: picnicking and camping

## The problem of the day outing

We are repeatedly told to expect a fourfold increase in the number of cars in twenty years. Statistics of this magnitude generally numb. But one thing is clear: any solution of this enormous traffic problem automatically creates another. For an ever-increasing number of car owners the only chance to exercise this expensive and prized possession is the weekend jaunt (incidentally, a fact which is recognized to be of prime importance to the success of the American out-of-town supermarket). Such jaunts must have an objective and for the family outing high priority must be given simply to finding 'somewhere nice to picnic'. This is in itself the real objective of most such outings; its identity is a secondary consideration. Second perhaps only to the Persians, the British are the most avid picnickers on earth. It seems right that the townsman should enjoy this harmless occupation: his daily grind in office or factory contributes to the countryside's very existence.

The snag, of course, lies in our overwhelming numbers. The would-be picnicker, often in desperation, must opt for almost anywhere. Thus the day outing, with its demands on the countryside in terms of access, has become one of the most difficult things to integrate into the existing pattern. The pressure on the countryside from motorists who simply want to park and picnic is fast wrecking it.

## Distinction between ways of enjoying the country

Before deciding what we want in terms of access to the countryside, the different ways in which we want to enjoy it must be analysed. Most of us want different things at different times. A very real distinction must be made between enjoying the country for its own sake and enjoying it as a background to enjoying ourselves. It is essential to be clear about this because there is so little country to spare. In the first category come all those places to which we go because they are what they are. Unique bits of Britain ranging from lonely coastline to man-made park and garden. These are 'one-off' places, most of them utterly unsuited to large crowds. Their character can vanish through over-accessibility (e.g. the car park sited just where loneliness is everything), or through sheer erosion (the lawn at

31

Chartwell became nearly bald from the feet of 145,000 people soon after it was first opened). More subtly, the character of a place can be lost because it was originally designed to be in scale with relatively small numbers of people. Here democratic compromise can be disastrous; both experience of the effect of crowds and acute sensitivity to places are needed to gauge the answer.

There is also the country to which we have no access but from which enormous satisfaction is derived just because it is there and in good heart: well-farmed country and healthy woodland which we drive through, or see from a train or aircraft.

The need to distinguish between our motives for wanting access to one sort of country or another is relatively new. Until recently there were too few of us, sufficiently mobile, to create a problem. Such confusion is now very dangerous: without a clear picture of what we want to enjoy in the country, it is impossible for the country to survive. The pressure on it is too great: it is as simple as that. We must therefore siphon off some of the millions from the rare and precious, and from the working country, by providing the right setting for those whose first object is to enjoy themselves in pleasant surroundings, rather than in a particular place. As a background, provided certain criteria are satisfied, one 'beauty spot' may do as well as another.

The Americans who, it might be imagined, have few problems of overcrowding, are in a remarkably similar position to ourselves: too many people want to go to the same place at the same time (for recent observations on camping in National Parks, see Chapter 8). But this situation is enormously eased by the long-established recreational parks of a very high standard which are primarily intended as a background for day outings. These are set up by individual states and counties. Some of the best are in the equivalent of English parkland, lightly wooded. They may be relatively small; others are several thousand acres in extent. The country chosen for these parks is pleasant, but is *not* of unique landscape or historic value. Millions of Americans enjoy such parks on any public holiday.

## Behaviour patterns

In Britain, with less land to spare and great pressure on it, it is vital that every inch is used to the best advantage both for the sake of the landscape and of the user.

Little research on human behaviour in informal outdoor recreation has yet been carried out. For example, just how do people react when given the choice of precisely where to picnic, camp or park their car within a given area? However, although formal research[1] is in its infancy it is confirming the observations already made by those practically concerned. The guide-lines are established. In so many departments of planning we are unsure: the cost of making mistakes is enormous. In this field the cost of dilatoriness will mean bankruptcy in environmental terms. We must go ahead now, fast.

What do people *want* when they go out into the country? When we are on the move,

[1] Notably by Dr. J. C. Heytze, a sociologist working for the Netherlands Staatsbosbeheer.

walking, riding or motoring, many of us choose the wide open spaces: the exhilaration of immense seas and skies, of open down or moorland, of being at the top of a hill with the world at our feet. All these give a tremendous sense of release, particularly after being cooped up in a town, quite apart from the visual satisfaction enjoyed.

But few people want to linger in the middle of these empty spaces. To camp or picnic we want some sense of enclosure; there seems to be a primitive fear both of being far from cover and of not being able to watch the immediate approach to our lair. Regardless of practical need of shade or shelter, few would choose to picnic in the middle of an empty moor or beach. We prefer to be on one side of the bay, close to the rock outcrop, or under a dune or breakwater. We picnic against the moorland wall or better still in the angle between two walls whether or not we need shelter from the elements. We instinctively want some protection, something bigger than ourselves, partially to enclose us and to weld us to the terrain. The same instinct applies equally strongly when camping: we prefer a defined space.

## Space and sense of enclosure

This instinct, reduced to its simplest expression, is illustrated by a journey I once made across barren country. We were travelling reasonably fast and each evening looked for somewhere to camp just before nightfall. The country was flat and featureless; one stretch of camel-thorn being about as hospitable as the next. If there was an outcrop of rock, we made for it; usually there was nothing. Then our camps seemed remarkably lonely and vulnerable, pitched just anywhere, with nothing to anchor us in the immense landscape. But as soon as the sun had gone, the whole feeling of the place was transformed. Space was limited to the light of our lamp, the darkness beyond seemed a protective enclosure. We had a warm sense of belonging to this small spot of earth. But later, when the moon had risen, the whole landscape stretching for mile upon mile was lit by its pitiless white light. The immenseness of which one was again a part was suddenly frightening. There was nothing bigger or more permanent than a Land Rover to secure us in this seemingly limitless space.

## Sense of territory

Man's very strong instinct concerning space and his conception and appreciation of it are, after all, the concern of all architecture: then it is a matter of contrast, size, volume and proportion. But space is also an unarchitectural matter of territory and of territorial boundaries. We seem to be happier the moment these are established, and boundaries are naturally easier to establish when they already take physical shape on the ground. Our territorial instinct is quickly activated: we stake our claims in railway carriages astonishingly fast, and seem to have a moral superiority over newcomers, even when we ourselves have only been in the compartment for a matter of minutes. This sense of territory may be one of the factors determining the success of high-density camp sites: there is a strong invisible line of demarcation between pitches which is mutually respected.

It is possibly a combination of these strong feelings about space and territory, coupled with our practical needs of shelter from the wind and a place in the sun, that lies behind the behaviour pattern which is typical of most of us in the countryside. Given any stretch of country it is not difficult to predict where people will choose to camp or picnic.

## Choice of picnic or camp site

1. *Edge or fringe giving partial enclosure.* We choose first the fringe, preferably a *re-entrant angle* in the fringe, when we want to linger; the line where one ecological pattern changes for another; or where generally flat terrain is interrupted by a tree or rock; the hedge of the meadow or woodland; the bank of a stream; the fringe line of the forest or the woodland glade. Incidentally, this observation is corroborated in the brief given to supermarket designers who are instructed to plan to counteract our tendency towards 'perimeter shopping'. Another everyday example is our preference for corner tables or, failing that, tables against the wall in a restaurant. Many restaurants are planned in snug bays. In both Germany and Holland planners of picnic places and camp sites have made maximum use of the acreage available by designing with as much 'edge' as possible between, say, woodland and open meadow. The edge of the cover is planned in a series of bays of a size to take a family picnic. Numerous small bays may also be formed when a gravel pit is converted to a picnic pool.

2. Reinforcing this instinct to settle on the edge is our *primitive fear of forest and deep woodland.* Recognition of these two factors is the greatest boon when planning for the multipurpose use of forests. By planning for, rather than against, these instincts as little as 5 per cent of a productive forest may be used for recreation although the public have access to the whole. Conversely a forest whose timber is at a relatively non-vulnerable age can be made attractive for recreation if it has been planned with both forestry work and recreation in mind.

3. The other certain behavioural pattern is our reaction to *water* either in the town or country. It is the infallible lure that draws all of us and, as a magnet, is probably the strongest tool the planner possesses. Best of all is water where people can swim or boat. But water where only fishing is allowed, attracts non-fishermen. Its very presence gives peace and a sense of space far greater than that to which there is access. There is the endless fascination of watching the shifting light upon it. Our ancestors knew all this: there can be few lakes in England which are entirely natural. We make relatively little use of our knowledge. There are brave exceptions of wet gravel pits converted to recreational needs, but the amount of access allowed to reservoirs varies enormously. Given the right conditions small lakes are easy to form. Nothing else is needed to underwrite the success of camp ground or picnic place.

34

## Behaviour patterns and site use: picnicking and camping

This was underlined recently in a census taken of lengths of stay at three different types of site in New Hampshire, U.S.A.: lakeside, riverside and waterless. The counts were made when the sites were new and again after four years' use. It turned out that lakeside sites were considerably more popular than riverside. New visitors to a new waterless camp ground stayed on average only one day. At the opposite extreme they stayed an average of ten days on a repeat visit to a lakeside site.

Length of visit of repeat visitors and first-time visitors, according to age of campground development and on-site attraction, is shown in the following table:[1]

| Age and attraction of development | MEDIAN LENGTH OF VISIT | |
|---|---|---|
| | Repeat visitors Days | First-time visitors Days |
| 1 to 4 years | | |
| Lake | 9 | 3 |
| River | 4 | 2 |
| Non-water | (x) | 1 |
| Over 4 years | | |
| Lake | 10 | 3 |
| River | 5 | 3 |
| Non-water | 3 | 1 |

(x) Insufficient responses to analyse.

4. *Gregariousness.* Our innate gregariousness is another tool which can be invaluable to planners particularly in the conservation of a sense of solitude in wild places. Anyone doubting this instinct might watch what happens when a lone car is parked in a large lay-by. The next car to arrive will frequently be parked adjacent to that already there, regardless of the rest of the space. Camp wardens have expressed the difficulty they find in persuading campers to spread throughout a camp site when it is first opened; the tendency is to congregate in one part, usually near the entrance.

There is no doubt that picnicking and camping are to a great many people sociable occupations. Obviously this pattern is not universal. Others want to walk and to get off the beaten track on their own. Recognition of the gregarious instinct of the majority will mean that all kinds of people may get a chance to enjoy what they want: sociability or solitude.

5. The question of *cars and car parking* is perhaps the biggest single planning problem connected with countryside leisure. But where people have come primarily to enjoy themselves, that is, to picnic or camp rather than to enjoy fine scenery or an ancient monument, there are sites which can be planned so that people need not be separated from their cars. Some tidy-minded planners refer disdainfully to places 'which have become

[1] LaPage, Wilbur F., *Successful Private Campgrounds.* U.S. Forest Service Research Paper NE-58, 1967.

glorified car parks'. Given the right terrain these can be an excellent solution in both landscape and individual terms.

6. *Sun* is of such importance to any picnicking or camping expedition in the U.K. that we must guard against being misled by publications even from North European countries where it is taken for granted.

Kevin Lynch[1] has pointed out the vital connection between slope and climate, particularly in middle latitudes. 'The word climate is in fact derived from the Greek for "slope". . . . Maximum direct radiation is received by the surface which is perpendicular to the direction of the sun.' This can be easily tested by moving your arm through the arc of the sun's rays. It is considerably warmer when it is exactly at 90° to them. This is why most vineyards are sloped and is one of the reasons why some allotments on railway embankments grow such good vegetables. Lynch has calculated that 'a 10 per cent slope to the south will receive as much direct radiation (and to that extent have the same climate) as flat land 6° closer to the equator'. This is the approximate difference in latitude between south Pembrokeshire and Trieste, or Penzance and Genoa, or Aberdeen and Dover. There are many other factors to be taken into account, including air movement and frost pockets and, of course, the sun's altitude is itself constantly changing. But from pragmatic observation, slope might usefully be taken into account when selecting or shaping new camp or picnic sites.

7. *Shade.* The possibility of some shade, particularly the dappled shade which comes from deciduous trees, is necessary even in England. In more sophisticated arcadian settings and on sites near buildings slatted fencing or partial roofing can be used to shade a picnic area.

*Summary.* The patterns which emerge from these empirical observations suggest that the planner, by planning for rather than against our inclinations, has a splendid tool kit with which to lure us into those parts of the country which can absorb us in quantity by providing what we want when we get there.

The site we seek out for a picnic or camp will have certain characteristics. It is very difficult to place them in order of preference but both the lure of water and an aversion to being separated from our car certainly have high preference. The instinct of settling on the edge, on the ecological fringe with partial enclosure, is usually the easiest to satisfy.

1. *Water,* even if only a pool to look at.
2. Taking *the car* to the actual picnic/camp pitch.
3. A sense of *partial enclosure,* usually on an *ecological fringe* (e.g., a glade or the edge of woodland).
4. *Shelter* from the prevailing *winds.*
5. *Sun* and the chance of *shade* (hence the value of glades).
6. *Gregariousness.* Many people like to see others already using a picnic place.

[1] Lynch, Kevin, *Site Planning*. MIT, Press, 1962.

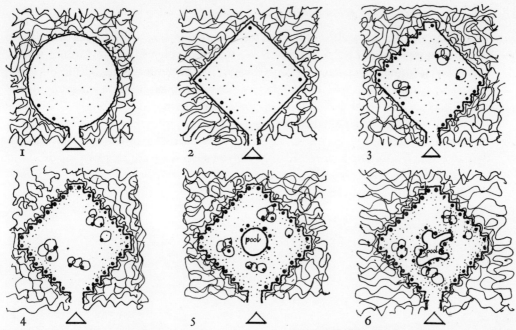

*Use of a picnic ground:* Sketches 1–6 are intended to show in diagrammatic form the probable use by picnic parties of an area of, say, 2–3 acres. This might be a woodland clearing or a hedged meadow. Without increasing the acreage of land set aside, or the facilities (other than the addition of the pool in the last two diagrams), the potential of the site can be enormously increased by the way the edges are treated and the space itself is planted (or cleared).[1]

The use of any site first depends on weather conditions: sun, shade, shelter. But, in addition:

1. The first arrivals may find it difficult to decide where to picnic since there are no corners and no focal point. Probably the first to arrive will settle fairly near the entrance and it is likely the second will follow near the first.

2. The corners are most likely to be taken first.

3. Angled sides will enormously increase the potential of the site.

4. Trees are of equal importance. They make the whole site more attractive visually and give anchorage in the middle 'no man's land' for more picnic parties.

5. Water is a magnet to all picnickers. The site as a whole will become instantly more popular. Even an exposed pool will attract some to picnic by it. Others will prefer to picnic in the sheltered edges.

6. An irregular pool with planting which provides more picnic corners will be popular with picnickers. This has the possible disadvantage of crowding the banks and making the pool less accessible to children.

This pattern holds true whether or not cars are allowed on to the site. But if two picnic grounds were available in the same vicinity one with separate parking and one on which cars were allowed, the majority of picnickers would almost certainly opt to stay with their cars even on a dull ground (e.g. 1 or 2) rather than use 3 or 4. This can be a valuable tool in providing for the tastes of different picnickers (gregarious: more solitary). But in all cases water is likely to be the deciding factor.

[1] Dr. J. C. Heytze's scientific work seems likely to confirm these empiric observations.

37

7. *A view* and particularly a short view is an ideal 'extra' but other factors seem to be rated of more importance. A view is often a neighbouring attraction; it is not strictly necessary to munch and stare simultaneously. The exception is the scenic overlook car park, particularly popular in winter, where people eat a sandwich lunch in the car. Many successful camp sites have no view but are inward looking.

8. *Picnic and camp furniture*, i.e. tables, benches and water points, can be useful on certain sites, but their intrusion may very easily ruin the character of others. They are the last and least important factors necessary to the success of the majority of sites, but are valuable in certain places (see page 100).

# 2

# Information on the spot: information centres

The tastes of today's tourists are a good mixture of those of their predecessors'. Some squirrel for the rational information hoarded by eighteenth-century travellers; geological and archaeological facts; number of peasants per hovel. Many more are swept up by the picturesque, thirsting for the awful and melancholy in mountain and glen, no legend too gloomy. Others imbibe history with a Victorian thirst. Others, beer; some both. Many of us would be content to sleep in the sun, but information is a more dependable tourist attraction than good weather.

The overwhelming majority of people going into the country for leisure are now town or suburb based. There is a widespread belief that they will not only enjoy what they see more, but will do less damage to it if they are given information about what they are seeing, when they are seeing it. Giving 'information on the spot' is the policy, maybe unconscious, of countless individuals and organizations in the U.K. In the U.S.A., it is a very conscious policy of the National Park Service. The policy of *Interpretive Planning* is the mainspring of all activities concerning Visitor Reception. Since the NPS has so recently given the subject a long hard look and as a result has reinterpreted many of its techniques, a lot can be learnt from its experience. This may throw different light on some of our own practices and problems.

**American National Park Service**

It must at the same time be remembered that debate over the rival claims of conservation for the 'enjoyment of future generations' and public access is as keen in the U.S.A. as it is here. The dilemma there is surprisingly familiar although in the U.S.A. it is the preservation and definition of wilderness which is the main concern. But where the problem is less acute and the NPS has decided to allow the car-borne visitor access it has a definite policy concerning his reception.

**Interpretive Planning**

*Interpretive Planning* is the key to this policy. The park must be interpreted to the visitor so that he can enjoy it for what it is, a National Park, rather than merely a recreational park.

The area has been selected for its outstanding natural or historic significance and this the NPS is determined that the most fleeting visitor should have a chance to grasp. If his curiosity can be provoked to look further so much the better.

This idea works at every level from the individual contact with the ranger-wardens (obviously highly important) to the audio-visual programmes (film, slides with sound-track, etc.) which run in many of the new Visitor Centers. Two actual examples of Visitor Interpretation follow here, in order to make the interpretation policy clear before going on to consider how it is implemented in the NPS.

The NPS has more historic sites in its care than natural parks and therefore much of the interpretive work is concerned with these. Of particular interest to us is the treatment of relatively modern sites where the architecture may be of low grade; not the stuff of splendid ruins. The event which took place is eminently worthy of commemoration; the idea is heroic but its physical remains mundane.

## Interpretation of architecturally low grade sites (Example: Ellis Island)

Ellis Island is a good example of this type. It was the first landfall of the vast surge of immigrants who sailed into New York Harbour around the turn of the century. Between 1890 and 1954 sixteen million immigrants passed through its Registration Hall. Few places could mean more in terms of hope or dread to these immigrants to whom the decision of the immigration officer decided whether this was the beginning of a new life or the dismal return to the old. It was the source of life-blood for much of the nation. In 1965 it was decided that it should become a historic monument (architect: Philip Johnson) in the charge of the NPS. A magnificent idea but not a magnificent site. 27·5 acres; flat; straggling undergrowth; wire fencing; red brick blocks with red tile roofs, 1905 on. The dejected smell is deeply depressing however stirring its emotional impact.

Probably the impact of Ellis Island lies in the intensely personal nature of the drama re-enacted seemingly time without number on this small plot of land. It would seem impossible to get this idea across in architectural terms. But the fact that each one of the immigrants is known by name has been grasped to produce what should be a monument of compelling simplicity: the survival of the ships' manifests listing all those who sailed steerage into New York Harbour during this period has made possible the idea of *The Wall of the Sixteen Million*: a round tower which is to be built overlooking the harbour; its walls will be covered with photocopies on metal of all these ships' manifests and a great ramp will climb past the sixteen million names so that visitors will find themselves on pilgrimage.

The rest of the scheme is equally imaginative. The Ferry Slip where the immigrants landed and the original Ellis Island Ferry boat still lying there at her moorings will be preserved. The Central Registry Hall, unpromising 1900 brick and tile, but with a vaulted roof, and a part of the hospital are to be converted into thorough ruins by the removal of timber and windows. Vines, ailanthus, poplar and sycamore will grow rampant among them. Visitors will wend their way through this haunting wilderness on concrete walkways. At night *son et lumière* programmes will remind them of the noise and confusion of immigration in action.

All other buildings will be demolished and a stepped viewing pyramid will be built on the tip facing Manhattan. To complete this recreational outlet for New York, for that is part of the objective, there is a ceremonial field for spectacles and parades, a picnic grove and an off-shore restaurant. A Museum of Immigration is now being constructed within the star fort which forms the base of the Statue of Liberty (also in the keeping of the NPS), so none need be provided on Ellis Island; trips to the two islands will form part of the same outing.

## Interpretation of scenically mediocre sites (Example: the Wright Brothers Memorial)

The site of the Wright Brothers Memorial contrasted in every way with Ellis Island. Empty and clean as a whistle; nothing but the surf booming on the Outer Banks a few hundred yards to the east and a long ribbon of road joining the straggling settlements of summer shacks. Here the NPS was faced with the problem of making something from nothing. Interpretive policy was to provide a Visitor Center which provokes human interest as well as scientific curiosity. There is plenty to inspire the aeronautic engineer but photocopies of the Wrights' correspondence bring the enterprise alive even more vividly than do their own vintage photographs (e.g. of the bicycle shop which was their base before they moved out to Kittyhawk). The focal point of the exhibit is the space under the shell concrete dome in which are the exact replicas of their two flying machines; these have that taut unreliable air and seem utterly authentic. Outside lies the grassy land over which the Wrights flew. There is nothing to obscure the view except two dull huts unaccountably left behind (by the building contractor?). These turn out to be copies of the Wrights' hangar and the shack in which they camped. Thanks to their addiction to photography it has become possible to reconstruct the interiors (Plate 10): even the canned food is accurately period. The stove made out of a kerosene tin; the heaps of driftwood; the bunks in the roof-space; all looks splendidly snug. But ideas of cosiness are instantly dispelled by the audio device installed for interpretive purposes. It starts, not with the reverend and awestruck voice to which one becomes accustomed in the U.S.A., but with the sound-track of a moaning wind. Few devices could change the scene so instantly from a summer outing to December 1903.

Architecturally the Visitor Center (architects Mitchell and Giurgola) forms a sophisticated background to what is being shown. It shelters the exhibits and that is its job. But even such details as the fencing or the scale of the benches outside the building have been thought out with great care; there is nothing trite or half finished.

The NPS probably owns many more magnificent sites than mediocre, but whatever the site the success of its interpretation derives from a great deal of background work following a standard pattern.

## Techniques of briefing

During the last few years hard thinking has been going on not only about interpretation itself but about the design policy which is all important to it. This is not so much talked about but the results are clearly visible.

The key to the success of this programme probably lies both in the careful instructions given to members of the Interpretive branch on the *briefing* of their architects and other designers, and in getting the whole design team together at an early stage. It is stressed that the man on the spot knows what his park has to offer, but the professional is needed to put it across to its best advantage (architect, landscape architect, engineer, exhibit designer, film maker, script writer . . .). He, the park interpreter (naturalist, archaeologist or historian), must plan ahead by deciding what he wants to communicate and preparing from this an Interpretive Prospectus: this proposes what is to be interpreted; it may suggest how in the broadest terms.

'Because interpretive planning has lagged behind the development program, visitor centers have been programmed, designed and placed under construction before the interpreter has presented a reasoned statement of the interpretive function of the building. Because of this planning lag a tighter programming procedure has been adopted. Unless Interpretive Prospectuses are completed on time, construction projects will be removed from the program and funds will not be scheduled.' Stern stuff indeed. Only when the Prospectus has been approved by all those concerned (remembering that the NPS is a branch of the civil service) can the Project Construction Programme go ahead, and the project be fitted into the Park's budget.

## Visitor Centers

The principal interpretive building in most parks is the *Visitor Center* or information centre. Its general siting will have been decided when the Master Plan for the park was worked out; detailed siting will obviously wait for the project design team. Centers are sited to be readily available to anyone wanting a quick idea of what the park has to offer, but *not* so that all visitors must pass through them. To have 100 per cent visitor attendance would be absurd if a percentage of these people were merely getting in the way of those who really wanted information. 20 per cent attendance may be a reasonable figure in some parks.

A Visitor Center usually consists of:

1. A large lobby which functions as a general milling space and gathering area for tours. In it will be the information desk; sales department (literature and maps); perhaps an information desk for concessionaires dealing with accommodation enquiries, concessionaires' tours etc.

2. An exhibition area which usually will be an extension of the lobby; sometimes it is a separate museum, conventionally indoors or out of doors as part of the landscape which is to be explained (e.g. battlefield, rare flora).

3. An Audio Visual Room for cinema or slide show.

4. Ranger offices. (The administrative offices of the park may also be combined with the Visitor Center building.)

5. Public lavatories.

Every Visitor Center is a one-off job. In some places the site is everything: the visitor to Grand Canyon, for instance, may learn a lot about its natural history by visiting the Center but nothing else in the world matches the experience of the Canyon itself. At Kittyhawk on the other hand there was nothing to see except the flat ground over which 'man first flew'. In such circumstances the Visitor Center is everything: the Wright Brothers Memorial and the Center are synonymous.

The most successful Visitor Centers have various qualities in common. These give clues to the approach to the design of Information Centres in the U.K.

1. Humility on the part of the architect in *making the building a tool of the main idea;* it must serve the Park rather than vice versa. There are, however, places where it is the function of a Visitor Center, in visual terms, to make a more dynamic contribution to a drab scene (e.g. the projected tower on Ellis Island).

2. *Siting.* Exceptional skill in the siting of the building and its relationship to the landscape which it is interpreting is essential. The fact that it is intrusive and is foreign to the landscape or event to be interpreted makes this all important. Great sensitivity on the part of the designer to the *genius loci* is essential. It may be necessary to break down the elements of the design so that the size of the building does not impose itself too boldly on the scale of the landscape (e.g. this has been done with great success at Fort Raleigh, by means of a series of pavilions instead of one block of buildings).

3. *Design and materials.* During its early days and particularly in the thirties, the NPS design policy has been described, rather unkindly perhaps, as stonsey-woodsey. This at its best was very good indeed. Building in natural materials with great simplicity and boldness of scale its structures fitted admirably into the landscape, weathered well and needed little maintenance. Like the parkways and other great schemes of the thirties much of this was achieved by the Civilian Conservation Corps which turned to such admirable use the unemployment of the depression. Inevitably, after the war, as traditional materials became prohibitively expensive and the vast labour force disappeared with full employment, such building was no longer possible. Nor, as might have been hoped, was it replaced by modern prefabricated timber systems.

The NPS now has three big design offices (Philadelphia, San Francisco and Washington, DC) with teams of architects, engineers and landscape architects working in conjunction with its Department of Interpretive Planning. Numerous private firms of architects are also employed: a formidable accumulation of design energy. Their programme includes the structures necessary to the day-to-day life of any park: employee housing, roads, bridges, camps and picnic places, as well as on an average fifteen museums a year (and these represent only one part of the interpretive programme). Now the NPS looks for the best which modern architecture can offer.

4. This attitude to design is beginning to permeate *all external details*. It can be seen in light fittings, notice boards, paths and benches, and is to be found in overlooks, self-guided trails and all other extensions of the interpretive programme. Consultants were recently invited to consider graphics and lettering of NPS signs and notices.

An approach similar to the NPS interpretive policy could be enormously helpful in the U.K., both for the interest it could provide in its own right and as a tool to regulate tourist pressure. It has been pointed out that pressure in the countryside in terms of leisure will shortly be so great that almost any outlet will be popular. The immediate problem is to make new parts interesting and attractive to tourists. Certainly the ancient monuments, stately homes and recognized scenic attractions must be thoroughly efficiently managed and planned to meet the onslaught. But they can only provide for a fraction of the demand, unless their intrinsic character is to be drastically altered.

In Britain there is an enormous untapped potential in land which is not necessarily top grade scenically. History, both natural and human, is everywhere. No government department yet budgets for its interpretation although a number of farsighted individuals have done so with astonishing success.

Closest to the NPS pattern is that of the National Trust for Scotland, in establishing a chain of Information Centres which may explain a historic event (e.g. Glenfinnan) or act mainly as a source of information on the tourist attractions in the neighbourhood (e.g. Dunkeld). The NTS has been particularly successful in the re-use of old buildings. Their choice of humble cottages of no great individual importance architecturally but of immeasurable value in the overall townscape has saved buildings which elsewhere would probably have been demolished.

Re-use of existing buildings in open country has also made it possible to provide a focus, both visually and practically, without the intrusion of a new building, which, however well designed, may not be an asset to a particular site. Culloden, for instance, one of the most emotive place-names in Britain, could be a let-down as a site: open moor is expected rather than grass and conifers. The NTS Information Centre[1] gives the scene of the battle a strong focal point. Its collection of relics and, particularly, facsimiles of documents instantly evoke the battle and its awful aftermath while the inside of the cottage fades into the background without intruding itself on the mind's eye, which wanders far beyond the actual geography of this scenically not very distinguished site.

Contrast this with the equally successful but utterly different solution provided by the small Bird Migration Museum at Oland, Sweden (architect, Jan Gazelius). Here there was nothing but sand, sky and a great lighthouse. The shipshape timber structure of the spic

[1] For reasons of space, a new information centre is now being considered.

and span museum unassumingly answers its purpose and provides a focal point to visitors as they arrive on a site where they might unwittingly do damage if they wandered.

Both the Forestry Commission and the Nature Conservancy do what they can on minimum funds (information not being included in their budget). The Forestry Commission's small deer museums, excellent in content, variable in presentation, have made notable forays in providing information *in depth* (as well as provoking curiosity: the NPS policy). They are as popular with school outings as with experienced stalkers and naturalists. Its observation towers (pages 173–174) are enormously popular with photographers and naturalists. Such hides give enormous pleasure and can limit damage which might otherwise be caused by over-enthusiasm.

The Wildfowl Trust, on the other hand, has proved that there is enormous public interest to be tapped and that the public is willing to pay for expert presentation. The Information Centre at Slimbridge (architects, Hughes and Bicknell) with its Wildlife Exhibition, lecture theatre and laboratories has much in common with American interpretive planning plus research in depth for those interested. Its artificial pools have also been expertly handled (designer, Peter Scott). Planning and management mean that what was recently a damp field and a stretch of salting (scenically dullish, except to addicts) now attracts 200,000 visitors annually. More important, the goose, its *raison d'être*, returns undeterred.

The Beaulieu Motor Museum, the Aircraft Museum and St. Fagan's Folk Museum have also proved to be magnets. The proposed Museum of Industrial Archaeology is likely to be equally successful.

The Council for Field Studies in its Field Centres has also provided a unique opportunity for serious study of information on the spot (chiefly of natural history), which is independent of any examination curriculum.

## Siting

An Information Centre, the function of which is to provide information about anything *which is itself a landmark*, must be played down visually if it is not to compete or even create a duality with the object to be interpreted. This problem should first be considered from the visitors' point of arrival: usually the car park. After leaving the car or bus he will make for the strongest visual magnet at that point. If both Information Centre and monument are visually equally 'important' he will probably make for the thing itself. (Size, distance, colour, as well as access, all count here.)

It must therefore be decided whether or not it is essential that the tourist goes to the Information Centre and if he should visit it *before* going to the site. This will depend on both the site itself, the type of display and information given, and whether the Information Centre is also a ticket office. Any ticket office must be sited so that it is *easier* to go through it on the way to the objective than to by-pass it. Planning failures can always be detected (too late) by the extra direction notices stuck up by despairing wardens.

Provision of an Information Centre for an archaeological site in open country can be particularly difficult. It will almost certainly be out of scale with the landscape and detract from the sense of solitude and dramatic isolation of the site itself. Earth moulding or planting may help here. Better still is the withdrawal of the Information Centre some distance if possible into a clump of trees (as at Newgrange, plate 11). At the other extreme, the site itself may need protection. In this case a workmanlike building of shed or hangar character will probably fit better into the landscape than anything more grand.

## National Trust for Scotland Information Centres

The NTS has planned a variety of Information Centres in both converted and new buildings. They usually consist of an information room which in addition to the information and sales desk and maps exhibition space provides window seats and/or small tables and chairs where visitors can look at literature, or write postcards (a most important holiday occupation). It is difficult to gauge the size necessary for the information room; influxes of bus loads cause short term overcrowding which would be extravagant to budget for and, in terms of space, could make the room seem impersonal and over large for non-peak periods. A room 50 × 20 feet catered for 90,000 visitors in a summer season. A

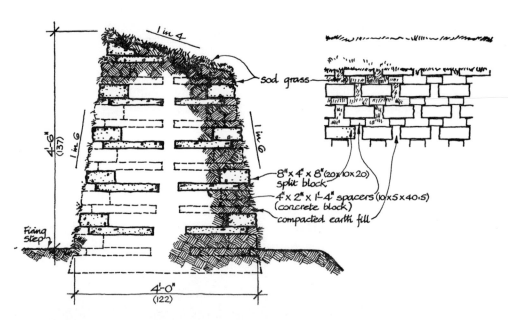

Historical interpretation. Reconstructed earth embankments of fortifications are unlikely to withstand the onslaught of small boys. The parapet shown here is reinforced with concrete blocks which will gradually be overgrown by grass. (National Park Service, Fort Carolina, Florida.)

46

domestic scale and friendly atmosphere is characteristic of these centres. A warden's office, store and public lavatories are also included. A generous covered area with coin-operated machines for hot coffee etc. is sometimes provided; at other centres there is a separate café.

## National Park and Forest Centres in the U.K.

Buildings such as those of the Brecon Beacons Mountain Centre and the David Marshall Lodge in the Queen Elizabeth Forest Park provide a cross between an Information Centre, tea-room, and a picnic place. The idea has proved attractive chiefly to the motoring public in search of 'somewhere to go'. In future centres a good deal of thought could go into the general character of the building and its interpretive function, when the architect is given his brief. The gentility of one of these buildings and the canteen-like atmosphere of the other might be replaced by something more robust and in keeping with the idea of a mountain or forest centre. Provisions include:

1. Large car park.
2. Reading/lounge/information room with exhibits/tea-room.
3. Terrace for sitting out.
4. Brew-up space with gas rings and sink for picnickers.
5. Lavatories.
6. Warden's office (and accommodation).

The siting of centres should be considered with regard to the very heavy motor traffic they will almost certainly cause. Anything which provides a new objective for the touring or Sunday afternoon motorist is likely to be popular. If narrow lanes and by-roads are to be used it must be possible for a one-way system to be adopted at weekends.

## Mobile vans

Various organizations[1] have used mobile information vans with considerable success. They cannot provide a substitute for a full-scale Information Centre where visitors may spend twenty minutes to an hour, but they are a useful stop-gap and can be valuable in planning the siting of future Information Centres. Their temporary character makes them acceptable where a permanent building would be an intrusion.

## Summary
In the U.K., generally speaking, we pay homage to the idea of information on the spot, but leave it to the idealists to put it into practice on what is, too often, a nearby non-existent budget.

[1] e.g. The National Trust; National Trust for Scotland; National Parks Commission; motoring organizations.

Experience from both the U.S.A. and the U.K. underlines the following points:

1. The possibilities of making dull terrain fascinating. The potential of relatively dreary landscape in both visual and historical terms if it is given a focal point for the visitor's interest.

2. The importance of design and technical expertise in putting information across to the public. We (in the U.K.) have the expertise but few public bodies are in a position to budget for it. Fees are a small percentage of the cost of any scheme. Professionals may be responsible for economies (we are not as renowned for this as we might be). The public is now accustomed to quality in the exhibition world; even a display of charity Christmas cards is produced with polish. Being conditioned to good design there is a natural tendency to suspect the product if its display is not shipshape.

3. The positive results in physical terms of the hard thinking in the American NPS which has produced both a design and an interpretive policy.

4. The great possibilities of providing information in depth on a relatively narrow front. This tends to widen interest in a way that general information cannot do.

5. Private enterprise in the U.K. suggests that there is an enormous scarcely tapped potential public willing to pay for the expert presentation of interesting information on site.

6. Skilful planning and management can make it possible for a large number of visitors to enjoy some sites without destroying what they have come to enjoy. This applies particularly to those described in paragraph 1 above. Established attractions are usually those where the site 'speaks for itself': these are often much more vulnerable.

7. It is important that the tourist should know what attractions a region has to offer. Each Information Centre should not only give full coverage of its region but it should also pass the tourist on to the next Information Centres in the network. A national system of signs could be worked out, which would form part of the traffic sign system, directing tourists to Information Centres. If agreement could ever be reached on what to include these directions might also include sites of national importance.

# 3

# Signs and notices

Any organization whose work entails much signing will consult an experienced graphics designer. Even so this section may be of value as background information when his brief is discussed. Others, responsible perhaps for only one site, may not be able to afford this service. (*For illustrations please see Plates* 14–35).

New signs are now being erected throughout rural Britain with a zeal which often astonishes and frequently dismays. The official road signs derive from the publication of *Traffic Signs Regulations and General Directions*, 1964, which results from the work and report of the committee, under the chairmanship of Sir Walter Worboys; thus they are commonly known as Worboys signs. In this book it is not intended to discuss traffic signs which are the responsibility of the ministry or local authority except where they affect the visual enjoyment of remote country, off the major roads. But these signs have already had an immense impact on the countryside and there seems to be a lot to be learnt about more humble signposting from them: its scale, colour, siting, repetition, wording. . . .

The section is chiefly concerned with signs put up both on the highway and elsewhere in the countryside to direct tourists who are walking as well as those who are motoring. It is tremendously important that signposting is not overdone, particularly on footpaths. The character of the countryside could be wrecked by too zealous and systematic an attitude to a common-sense problem.

The first function of any sign is to provide a visual target so that it is quickly seen; the second, to convey a message. An additional objective of the kind of sign to be considered in this section is that it should impinge as little on its surroundings as possible while fulfilling the first two requirements. To take an extreme example: a sign on a motorway can provide visual interest on what may be a dull drive; that kind of visual interest is not wanted on a bridle-path. Since circular signs provide the best visual target, the Worboys signs reserve these for those that are mandatory. Whether or not confusion would follow if circular signs were used for non-mandatory signs (e.g. for an informatory pictogram) is obviously open to question. But it would certainly seem that if the visual impact of a circular sign is notably effective, it might be extremely useful in 'countryside leisure' signs where maximum efficiency with minimum intrusion is the ideal. The small NO ENTRY signs used on the Continent are an example of the visual efficiency of circular signs; a small circular pictogram blazing the trail to a tourist attraction might prove both effective and reasonably sympathetic to its surroundings.

## Wording

Brevity is essential. Wording has been cut from the majority of Ministry of Transport mandatory and warning signs. The less said the clearer the message is likely to be. Unnecessary words should be cut: 'to' is superfluous if the sign itself acts as a pointer. 'Public Footpath' is usually unnecessary, but in certain cases where confusion with a bridle-path is possible, it has legal implications; where a path is obviously only for the use of those on foot word the 'footpath' might be omitted. Like roads, a signed path might be assumed to be public unless it is otherwise described. 'CURB YOUR DOG and help keep New York clean' is a nice example of American directness (New York City, 1967). In actual content, precision can be salutary even at the expense of brevity: 'KEEP YOUR HEAD, ARMS & FEET INSIDE THE CAR' (the Expo Mini Rail, Montreal 1967).

Some signs seem to spawn. Often, as in women's letters, 'the pith is in the postscript'. When a place is newly opened to the public it may be useful to use temporary notices only, so that these can be edited for maximum clarity with a minimum number of words, when experience has suggested exactly what is needed.

## Lettering

Lettering alone can have an immense effect on the mood created by the sign. All lettering has character of some sort whether or not this is intended: traditional; fashionable; sophisticated; straightforward; fussy; sturdy; bold; timid; prim; flamboyant. . . . The public soon recognizes a sign and connects it with the owner or organization concerned. This serves not only to advertise. It can also be useful in maintaining standards. For example: knowing this is X's property, people may care more how it is treated as a result of their opinion of X. If it belongs impersonally to 'them' land tends to be less than cherished.

Lettering on the kinds of sign considered here should generally steer clear of fashion: it cannot afford to date. For 'do-it-yourself' lettering the answer for non-experts probably lies either in wielding a paintbrush quickly and confidently (painters often dash off WET PAINT with considerable aplomb so long as they do not try), or in using stencils or transfers (see page 58). The golden rule seems to be to *fill the space available*. This not only looks better; it conveys a sense of purpose.

Simplicity both in lettering and the sign itself is the basis of most modern design. The notion that Nature must be signed with rustic art still prevails in parts of the U.K., greatly to the detriment of the countryside. But the general shift in opinion since the thirties is well illustrated by the two most useful publications associated with the American National

Park Service. In 1938, when 'The urge to capture naïveté and rusticity in a park sign'[1] was still felt to be a laudable aim, the reader was warned against 'using letter forms not readily legible'. In 1967 those responsible for another NPS study[2] found it necessary to point out that 'Letters should convey a message and not attempt to compete with the landscape', a warning occasionally needed here. Incidentally, some of the 'naturalistic' timber signs of the earlier publication may seem to suggest perches for hefty gnomes or launching pads for leprechauns but many also have a toughness which is invaluable to the maintenance man and a boldness of size in scale with the surroundings of wild country.

The *Canadian National* railway gives the following table for guidance of those using their signs in both capitals and lower case (alphabet used is *Standard Medium*) when deciding size of letter in relation to distance of viewer.

| height of letter (or of x height[3] in lower case alphabet) | | Distance | |
| inches | mm. | feet | metres |
| --- | --- | --- | --- |
| 1 | 25·4 | 25 | 7·62 |
| 2 | 50·08 | 50 | 15·24 |
| 3 | 76·2 | 75 | 22·86 |
| 4 | 101·6 | 100 | 30·48 |
| 6 | 152·4 | 150 | 45·72 |
| 8 | 203·2 | 200 | 50·96 |

It may be difficult for sign writers to make letters which are smaller than 1½ in. [38·1 mm.]. This also applies to some manufactured signs. (N.B. The typical London BUS STOP sign has letters 1½ in. high.)

## Symbols and Pictograms

In graphics language symbols may be abstract signs; pictograms attempt to portray. The word symbol is used for both types here.

Symbols should replace words whenever possible. Many, like the camp site pictograms, are now internationally recognized. Others could be invented. Their meaning should be instantly guessed. They must be direct, and each should convey only one message. Where two pieces of information are needed, two symbols can appear on one sign. They are usually more satisfactory both visually and practically if they are circular, polygonal or square, rather than long shaped or rectangular.

## Siting and height of signs and notices

Multiplication of signs is all too common. Many notices seem to be erected on the principle

[1] *Park and Recreation Structures*, 1938.

[2] *National Capital Regional Sign Study*.

[3] x height is the height of the letter x in a lower case alphabet. Metric conversion in this table is by the author.

which guided the snark hunter: 'What I tell you three times is true', but those desperate notices put up by despairing curators and wardens often originate from some basic planning mistake, in, for example, the siting of a ticket office.

Wherever possible signs should be fixed to existing walls rather than new posts.

Siting of statutory traffic signs is laid down in the *Traffic Signs Manual* which may be useful for reference. For those dealt with here common sense mostly answers. Low signs are easiest to read from cars and are unobtrusive in the landscape. 3 ft. 0 in. [91 cm.] is the dimension given to the *bottom* of a motorway directional sign; 3 ft. 0 in.–5 ft. 0 in. [91 cm.–1·52 m.] for warning signs on other roads; 4 ft. 6 in. [1·37 m.] to the centre of the sign is likely to be convenient for many of those covered in this section (4 ft. 9 in. [1·45 m.] for notice boards) unless other vehicles or planting are likely to obscure them. Any sign under which people may walk should give 6 ft. 9 in. [2·06 m.] clearance. 18 in.–24 in. [46–61 cm.] horizontal clearance is usual between the kerb and the sign.

*Position and speed* of the reader. Both these aspects need consideration. Some of the new footpath signs (with their 2 in. [5 cm.] x-height of letters) seem to be designed to be read from a car travelling at 20–30 m.p.h. (The Worboys footpath signs are no longer statutory.) Some traditional signs still in production which are intended to be safely read by car drivers are better suited to those in pony traps.

## Official traffic signs (Worboys signs)

The Worboys signs have rationalized many anomalies. They are perhaps at their best in the sophisticated traffic conditions such as those imposed by the motorways and they seem to be visually more in tune with urban rather than rural conditions. It has to be admitted that the high standards of design brought about by the introduction of many of the signs has been counterbalanced at the other end of the scale by the visual havoc wrought in some of our best country; particularly in small scale landscape intersected by many small lanes. This apparent blindness both to the scale of the country itself and, often, to the scale of the problem which is to be solved is the inevitable result of a standard answer which has not been made in a sufficiently wide range of sizes, and perhaps of the man on the spot being given insufficiently wide discretion in the interpretation of regulations. Examples abound: giant directional signs sited where small lanes join primary roads; the size and number of GIVE WAY signs where lanes join roads[1].

The Traffic Signs work to a system which is touched on briefly here since it explains some of the signs which inevitably follow in remote rural areas.

COLOURS are not chosen 'because they are pretty'. It is cheaper to produce a white reflecting letter on a coloured ground than *vice versa*.

[1] M.o.T. Circular, *Roads* 11/68, amends the *Traffic Signs Manual* (Table B, Ch. 3), proposing that a 27 in. high triangle 'be used on all rural roads where the 85 percentile speed of free running traffic is less than 40 m.p.h. and where the carriageway width does not exceed 20 ft.'.

*Blue*   The existing Ministry of Transport Blue was chosen (0–013).[1] This is used for motorways (fine) and all informatory signs (in urban areas this is excellent; it is less sympathetic to the green of the countryside). It is interesting to compare this blue with that used by the National Trust for Scotland, 7–085. The lettering in both cases is white. 7–085 contains some yellow which gives what is normally a cold colour a warmth sympathetic to the countryside. It is not aggressive and can be easily read. The M.o.T. blue is particularly unfortunate when combined with red and white in a reflective finish (e.g. as in the *No Through Road* signs which now appear on quiet farm roads).

*Red*   Red is traditionally associated with danger. This ruled out the agreeable Venetian reds used on some rural directional signs in Denmark (similar to 1–024). Reds can be tricky under artificial lighting conditions, but these are unlikely in remote country.

*Green*   It was decided that primary routes should be marked differently from motorways. The much criticized green (6–074) resulted from this decision.

*Grey*   Signposts and backs of signs are grey (9–101)—a warm grey very sympathetic to the countryside.

*Green and Cream*   The traditional combination of green and cream used by the Ministry of Public Building and Works to signpost ancient monuments is particularly unattractive. This is underlined in those regions where individual initiative has substituted deep blue and white or black and white on their standard cast aluminium signs with most satisfactory results[2].

SHAPES: Circular signs are mandatory. Triangular signs are for warning. Rectangular signs are for information.

*Informatory Signs for Use on All Purpose Roads* (H.M.S.O. 1964), Section VIII, Miscellaneous begins: 'There are several other informatory signs which require little comment. Normally such a statement would be read with relief and acclaim. Unfortunately, some of the signs which cause most dismay in rural areas come under this heading.

(80) *Passing Place*   For many years the great majority of passing places were effectively marked by a 3 in. [8 cm.] diameter post, tall enough not to be buried in snow. In some areas a plain white diamond topped the post. The 18 in. × 18 in. [46 cm. × 46 cm.] white diamond bearing the words PASSING PLACE shown in the Schedule (1 Part IV 822) does the job no better. Long experience has proved words to be superfluous. This sign impinges unnecessarily on the landscape and is particularly ostentatious in open country where it is most likely to be used. The economics of its installation (it must usually be repeated frequently on a stretch of road) might also be considered.

(84) and (85)   These *No Through Road* signs now appear on remote farm roads. The only size available is 21 in. × 21 in. [53 cm. × 53 cm.]. This with their background colour, blue, combined with the red and white seems stridently aggressive in such situations.

---

[1] Colour reference numbers from British Standard 2660; see Chapter 11.

[2] Black and white are excellent colours in the countryside. They show up without being discordant. It would be interesting to substitute black for M.o.T. blue and green as a background to signs in rural areas.

(78) '*Unsuitable for motors*' is a nicely spaced sign but since it is again likely to be used on farm tracks it is a pity that its colour is inevitably this particular blue. The same criticism applies to (83) the *bicycle* sign in rural situations. In this kind of position the use of a bronze green (e.g. 4–050 from BS 2660) would be a tremendous improvement. (It has been used most effectively on Boundary signs in the Peak District National Park.) 16 in. [40 cm] is unnecessarily high for most bicycle trails, although suited to A roads.

## Worboys camp signs

*Informatory Signs for Use on All Purpose Roads*, Section VI, page 40, shows camp and youth hostel signs. (N.B. they are not included in *Traffic Signs Regulations and General Directions*, 1964.) These signs are not prescribed. Authority to use them should be sought through the Divisional Road Engineer. Those for camping sites (signs 69–71) can only be used with the approval of the British Travel and Holidays Association. These signs seem to have been swept in at the tail end of the system. Following the rules which regulate the general signs, consistency has dictated that they should be rectangular with a blue edging. The symbols themselves (tent and caravan as used on the Continent) are neat and explicit but the background rectangles with uneven blue frames seem awkward and over-large away from primary routes for the majority of sites where they may be used. 24 in. is the standard height. Smaller signs are now seen. A bronze-green background colour would be much more attractive in rural areas.

Since few of us are aware of the rules which govern the shapes of signs it might cause no confusion if the same standard symbols were used on circular signs. A 19 in. [48 cm.] diameter sign comfortably carries the tent symbol shown in the 24 in. [61 cm.] high rectangular sign. This size could usually be further reduced.

The *advance directional* sign (73) includes the symbol and distance; it is a clear design which is likely to be very useful. It can be used without the permission of the British Travel and Holidays Association.

## Directional signs to tourist attractions

The question of signposting to tourist attractions in the countryside reduces many of us to a hopeless state of ambivalence: although the landscape is cluttered enough without the addition of still more signs yet there are too many places which the tourist has the greatest difficulty in finding. He has been lured by the travel blurb from Tennessee or Teheran to seek aristocratic enterprises (ancient and modern) or famed beauty spots; these prove to be frustratingly elusive as he approaches his goal. We, the British, are often equally foxed when within a mile or two of our objective: ditherers at cross-roads inevitably endanger other road users. Yet the intentions of the planning officer to preserve the countryside are as laudable as those of the owner or curator who wants to guide not only the dedicated sightseer but also the Sunday afternoon motorist who is wondering where next to stop.

54

There are several ways of alleviating if not of entirely solving the problem of these directional signs, bearing in mind that it is usually the additional, separate object rather than the idea of the sign itself which most offends:

1. It might be assumed that the tourist will know the name of the nearest small town or sizeable village that might be marked on a motoring organization or petrol company map. He needs help from this point.

2. Here signs made to match the standard Ministry of Transport directional signs could be fixed to the same posts. Thus, at a cross-roads, CROTCHET CASTLE would simply be added to the other place-names on the existing post. It would also have the function of providing an advance warning to the impulse sightseer.

3. Where there is no signpost to which to add, the sign might be fixed to an existing wall; it could be equally legible but far less obtrusive in landscape terms.

4. If the distance is given, it is likely that fewer signs will be needed. Strangers naturally want frequent reassurance if they are given no indication whether their destination is to be discovered within 500 yards or 5 miles. It was common practice to give distances on all signposts until 1940.

5. At junctions on minor roads closer to the objective small pictogram signs should be enough to give clear and instant direction. When people are already on the look-out and are travelling relatively slowly on minor roads quite a small sign, say, 6 in.–8 in. [15–20 cm.] should answer. A system might be devised of very simple signs containing *only* a symbolic silhouette of the castle, abbey, country house etc. for which the visitor is looking.[1] If there is any chance of confusion between two similar attractions the initials of the name could be included. The system might be extended to include silhouettes of birds or beasts for nature reserves, boats for harbours, a pony for polo. A sign indicating *Information Centre* (not included in the Worboys Signs) is badly needed.

6. Temporary signs put up by the AA or RAC can be exceptionally effective provided their use is limited.

## Information boards

At the entrance (which is often at the car park footpath exit) to an ancient monument, picnic place, self-guided trail etc. an *information board* should include the following:

1. The *name* of the place.

2. A *map* showing where the visitor is now and marking other local places of interest, say, within a 15 mile radius. Ordnance survey maps unfortunately usually fade quickly.

3. A *plan or diagram* on a larger scale showing what is to be seen here with a *brief* description. The plan of a castle, trail, or a section through a building (e.g. mill, explaining

---

[1] The British Travel Association has now published *Informatory Signs for Historic Houses open to the public.* These are based on well designed pictograms but all include the name of the property and are therefore large: 26 × 19 in. [66 × 48 cm.] *minimum*; 52 in. [132 cm.] high for fast roads.

its working): this can also be reproduced in guide books which means a considerable economy in design time. For a local map the $2\frac{1}{2}$ in. to 1 mile O.S. map is useful, if fading problems can be overcome.

4. Seasonal information.

5. It may be essential to display the *local bye-laws*. It is anyway often useful in augmenting the authority of car park attendants, wardens etc. Bye-laws are often fixed to the back of a board where they are less aggressive. 'It is forbidden' is a daunting start to an outing (if it is read at all). On the front of a notice board, a brief summary, explaining the reason for the bye-law and its main point, should be more effective than the small print.

Information boards are best sited under cover but where this is not possible care should be taken to prevent puddling of the ground in front of the board. Where it is not already paved it should be a well-compacted gravel graded to fall away to the surrounding surfaces.

Texts: information boards are often read in non-ideal conditions such as in wind, rain, a crowd, a hurry. Diagrams are more useful than words. Size of print must be related to the distance of the reader who is standing 1 ft. 6 in. to 3 ft. 0 in. away. Spacing is equally important. Expert advice should be sought. Fixing: wherever possible the information board should be fixed to an existing wall. Failing this it can be erected on stout timber posts (say 4 in. × 4 in. [10 × 10 cm.]), steel tube (3 in. [8 cm.] diameter is common for minor traffic signs), or fibre glass posts. Reinforced concrete is likely to be too heavy for the job and pre-stressed posts giving a slender section are difficult to find. Posts will be carried into the ground to a distance necessary to give stability against both wind pressure and minor vandalism, say, 18 in.–36 in. [45–90 cm.] depending on size and situation of sign. The posts should be bedded in concrete; the holes finished in well-rammed soil.

## Grouping of signs

Even three signs fixed to one post can look thoroughly trim if they are the same width (Plate 21), but are inevitably shoddy where their width varies. Two signs will nearly always look better if their width is constant but variation is possible in certain cases.

## Signs fixed to trees

Notices on trees are usually frowned upon both by the landscape architect who does not wish to see a tree maimed and the timber producer who knows that no merchant will consider a tree which might have a nail in it, out of respect for his band-saw. But there are exceptional cases when a well-designed notice, (Plate 22) may look better on a tree than on yet another post, and the tree itself may not lose by carrying a sign. Fixing for a notice of this kind can, in fact, be designed to 'grow' with the tree.

**Types of signs:**
**Gouged timber boards**

The Netherlands Staatsbosbeheer has developed a very successful sign using standard lettering gouged from $1\frac{3}{8}$ in. [3·5 cm.] planks of marine plywood (see Plate 20). It has several particular advantages:

1. Its robust, straightforward design is in character with the forest without being bosky: shipshape but sympathetic to the landscape.

2. Colour: White lettering on deep brown stained wood reads clearly but is not obtrusive.

3. Each notice is made up of the required number of horizontal planks, usually spaced at about $\frac{3}{4}$ in. [2 cm.] intervals. This means that the landscape can be seen *through* the sign. The sign is clear, but it does not dominate its surroundings as would a solid sign of similar area. It also offers less wind resistance. Planks can be added if there is more to be said.

The Staatsbosbeheer specifies a special quality of marine plywood $1\frac{3}{8}$ in. [35 cm.] thick with a highgrade veneer which allows for engraving. The wood is treated before the letters are cut with two coats of *Kleur-Copperant* preservative stained dark brown. The letters are cut with a pantograph machine and are then filled with white *Aircraft Lacquer*. It is important that the timber is treated with preservative before engraving; otherwise the preservative may flow into the engraved letter and mix with the white paint. The American National Park Service uses a similar system on solid timber—e.g. redwood.

**Branded signs on timber**

Repetitive signs can be cast in iron. (See Plate 35 for example from the Aarhus Forest Park.) Timber can then be branded in a matter of minutes. This is a very cheap method of reproduction provided sufficient notices with the same wording are needed to justify the cost of the original casting.

**Carved signs on timber**

One-off signs carved in oak perhaps have a greater potential corniness than other types. On the other hand a first-class designer/craftsman can carve simple signs of great distinction. Mass produced signs with the lettering raised and their background cut out are less successful. Carved timber signs can look very out of place in treeless country.

**Carved signs on slate**

The tradition of slate engraving, closely associated with the splendid lettering on slate graves, is very much alive and is particularly useful where a first-class name sign is needed. It is clear, maintenance free and has a seemingly infinite life.

## Stencilled and transferred lettering

Good sign writers are thin on the ground. Many of those faced with the problem of producing notices on a low budget have used drawing office stencils and other aids.

*Packing Case Stencils* (in capitals) which can be bought from builders' merchants (and drawing instrument shops) provide a quick answer which proves very effective once the knack of letter spacing has been worked out. To remain trim boards will need repainting at least every other year if not each spring.

*Letraset Letters*, originally designed to be transferred on to drawings, are used for timber signs. They should be sealed with clear varnish. Sheets of letters and signs can be bought at most art shops.

An alternative use of Letraset has been devised by the Hancock Museum for producing cheap, well designed signs on nature trail leaflet dispensers. A black and white notice was designed with an emblem and Letraset lettering. This was photographed on white paper, stuck on a wooden leaflet dispenser which had been painted white, and protected by mipofolie (a transparent sheet with adhesive on one side). This gives the impression that the lettering and emblem have been expertly painted on the box itself (a very laborious procedure). The result is a thoroughly professional looking job which can be reproduced any number of times at low cost. It is for use in sheltered positions.

## Cast Aluminium

The Royal Label Factory[1] now manufacture their signs in cast aluminium instead of cast iron. As in the case of all castings it is uneconomical to have much variation in the style of lettering. The factory produces Roman and Ministry of Transport block lettering. The Roman gives a sense of tradition and permanency. Repainting is necessary if the sign is to remain spic and span but rust is no problem provided fixing is with rustproof screws.

## Map and drawing display

Traditional forms of map mounting out of doors have presented problems: glass breaks; colours fade. Maps themselves may need to be brought up-to-date, so economy is important. There are several new methods which promise well though none has been on the market long enough to give much idea of its life span.

## Maps encapsulated in resin[2]

The map or drawing is impregnated with polyester resin and backed with glass-fibre; in the process the article becomes homogeneous. This means that it can be cut or drilled

[1] Royal Label Factory, Stratford-upon-Avon.
[2] Resin Maps and Signs, Crondall, Farnham. Kenneth Wardle Ltd., Millthrop Mill, Sedbergh.

either in the workshop or on the site without impairing its waterproof qualities, nor does the edge have to be sealed. Since the map or sign is itself impregnated it should be on paper rather than card. Tests should be made to check that the ink or paint is itself impervious to the process and will not run (resin based inks may react): When treated in this way, one-inch Ordnance Survey maps seem to be less sharp than Bartholomew's $\frac{1}{2}$ in. to 1 mile series. The maximum size available is 4 ft. 6 in. $\times$ 3 ft. 0 in. [137 $\times$ 91 cm.]. Gloss and matt finishes, and iron-filled encapsulations (for use with magnets) are available. Prices: say 15/- to 20/- per sq. ft.

## Laminated signs[1]

PVC laminated signs come in various qualities. The printed paper is laminated between a clear and opaque sheet of PVC. The paper is kept a $\frac{1}{4}$ in. [0·5 cm.] clear of holes and cuts since exposure to moisture could cause creep and delamination. The laminated sheet is best fixed to a rigid backing. Screws should be slightly smaller than the holes in the sheet to allow for thermal movement. PVC laminates of this type are cheap: say 3/- per sq. ft.

Tougher and correspondingly more expensive laminated signs are also made. The paper can be impregnated with resin. It is sandwiched between melamine (clear thermo-setting plastic lacquer) for weather protection with a layer of phenolic (thermo-setting resin plastic) toughened paper for rigidity. Sheets can be mounted on aluminium etc. Signs are best drilled in the factory but manufacturers do not expect deterioration to result from site drilling since the paper itself has been impregnated.

## True-to-scale prints on cartridge paper

The Planning Department of East Lothian County Council has produced a number of information sheets which provide interpretive information on lay-bys, nature trails and in places of historic interest. An ordinary ink drawing on tracing paper is reproduced by 'true-to-scale' process (approximate cost: 5s. for 30 in. $\times$ 20 in. [76 $\times$ 51 cm.] sheet). This is pasted on copal varnished $\frac{1}{2}$ in. marine quality plywood with lap cold water paste and finished with copal varnish. Very attractive displays are thus reproduced at low cost; the drawing itself can also be used in guide books, etc. The two essentials are: someone with the ideas to be put across and a first-class draughtsman to produce the original drawing. Examples to date include:

1. Lay-by information. Standard bill-boards are used in pairs, horizontally. On one board information on hotel and tourist facilities is given; on the other, a pictorial description of things of interest in the immediate locality (e.g. local traditions of farm building and agricultural practice). Advertising pays for culture.

2. On a geological trail. This trail starts in a lime kiln which shelters the information

[1] Manufacturers include: Glasdon Signs Ltd., Blackpool. Transatlantic Plastics Ltd., Surbiton.

board. A sectional drawing showing how the kiln once worked is displayed with the trail map and other information. See drawing on page 65.

3. A horse-mill has been restored beside a new petrol station. A similar sign describes the working of the mill.

## Engraving on aluminium

Maps, diagrams and lettering can be quickly engraved on aluminium sheet by the following method (demonstrated in the Yosemite National Park. Plate 35):

1. A line drawing is made on tracing paper of the map or sketch which is to be engraved.
2. An ordinary architectural dye-line reproduction is made of the drawing (Cost: approximately 2 shillings for a 30 in. × 20 in. [76 cm. × 51 cm.] sheet).
3. The dye-line is pasted on to a $\frac{1}{4}$ in. [0·65 cm.] thick aluminium sheet.
4. It is coated with shellac to protect it from the oil which is used on the cutter.
5. The sheet is engraved through the drawing with an electric engraving tool.
6. Lettering is engraved by means of a pantograph, approximate spacing being indicated on the dye-line drawing; final spacing is designed by the operator.
7. It is sand-blasted.
8. Powdered chalk is rubbed into the aluminium sheet where shading is needed (e.g.: to give a three-dimensional effect to hills).
9. The whole is coated in latex.
10. The aluminium sheet is mounted on marine plywood and framed in aluminium channel.

Natural aluminium can be clearly read out of doors. Its matt silvery-grey finish does not stand out obtrusively in a natural setting.

## Photographing on metal

Diagrams and maps are photographed on to anodised aluminium sheet.[1] This process has been used extensively in the U.S.A., particularly for the description of view-points and natural phenomena. The image seems to be permanent; the aluminium is claimed to be impervious to sea corrosion. 6 gauges of sheet are produced. Sizes: up to 24 in. × 20 in. [61 × 51 cm.]. The sheet itself is sold for use in customers' own dark rooms in sizes up to 24 in. × 40 in. [61 × 102 cm.].

## Signs on foot trails

Numbered signs on trails can be made of or fixed to anything to hand except living trees or plants. Plates 29 and 30 show some possibilities. The size of figure depends on both the

---

[1] Information supplied by R. H. Name Plates Supplies Ltd., Winchester.

distance of viewer and the scale of surroundings: 2 in. [5 cm.] for close viewing; 6 in. [15 cm.] or so at, say, 20 yards [18·3 m.]. Types of marker include:

(a) Walls or rocks boldly painted: white on natural stone or white on black paint.

(b) 2½ in.–3 in. [6 cm.–8 cm.] diameter, barked posts 18 in.–24 in. [45 cm.–60 cm.] high, driven into the ground. Weathered top marked with colour code of trail.

(c) 2½ in. × 2½ in. [6 cm. × 6 cm.] weathered posts. The weathered top can itself be numbered or a piece of laminated plastic on which the number has been painted can be screwed to the post. Alterations can very easily be made on the site if plastic is used. One inch [2 cm.–3 cm.] of the top of the post should be squared off to take mallet blows.

(d) Circular metal markers.

## Guides and leaflets

Many *guides and descriptive leaflets* seem to be written to be read at home in a comfortable chair. This should apply only to the souvenir guide; or that produced for specialists; not to the document which is to be used by everyone on the spot. The guide must be designed for quick reference. The reader does not want to be lost in its text when he might be looking at the place he has come to see. This is true whether he is in a stately home in June or propped against the gargantuan gothic heating system of a cathedral in mid winter. It is even more important to the multitude of guides now being written for self-guided trails in the country. These are more likely to be read in competition with a gusty wind, persistent drizzle or midges, to children some of whom may be keener to contribute than to listen.

On the spot guides are not the place for conventional literature. They should convey as much information as possible by means of clear annotated line drawings. Good bird's eye views mean more than plans to most people. Incidentally, these may be the same drawings as those used for an information poster, reduced to a different scale. Text should be terse and telegraphic. Expressions like 'it might be fun to. . . .' or 'on the hillside towards which you are looking. . . .' are best avoided. Any words not specifically to the point should be ruled out: this does not exclude relevant information.

The length of a guide will, to some extent, depend on the length of the tour. An excursion of perhaps 1–3 hours can obviously carry a longer guide, not only because there may be more to say but because people will make one or two longer halts and probably picnic during the trip. But it must still be light and easy to carry.

## Typography and spacing

These are very important. It must be simple to relate the text and the object at a glance. Expert advice should be sought.

A particularly effective idea, common in the U.S.A., which helps enormously in

61

THE
# GRAND CANYON
## VISITORS'
# ALMANAC

*A COMPENDIUM OF*
NEW, USEFUL, AND ENTERTAINING MATTER
Concerning Nature's Crowning Splendor.

PRINTED FOR THE VALLEY NATIONAL BANK
GRAND CANYON, ARIZ.
And offered with their compliments to travellers,
visitors, wayfarers, &c.

A current publication of the NPS.

creating the mood of the place is to produce a guide or leaflet whose typography is contemporary with either the discovery of the exhibit or the exhibit itself. For example, that for Grand Canyon is rich nineteenth century; for the Wright Brothers Memorial, Art Nouveau; Williamsburg, late eighteenth century.

## Size of guides

Guides should be small enough to be thrust in the pocket and tough enough not to disintegrate in gentle rain. One of the most effective house guides seen consisted of a double folded sheet $8\frac{1}{2}$ in. $\times$ 8 in. [22 $\times$ 20 cm.]. The brief text was divided into 3 sections: *the Man*, *the House*, and *the Gardens*, with two plans. This seemed to contain exactly the right weight of information for the ordinary visitor and allowed him time to concentrate on the building itself. More detailed guides can be provided for specialists and enthusiasts.

# 4

# Self-guided trails

A trail is a planned route from which the significance of various features which are visible from it is interpreted to visitors. This is usually done by means of a written guide which refers to numbered points along the trail. It is designed with this function first in mind but allowance must also be made for the group conducted by a warden.

Most trails are designed to be followed on foot. Motor trails are becoming more common. Pony, bicycle and canoe trails are all popular.

From the conservation point of view a trail can be of great value in directing people where they will not cause damage or undue erosion. It discourages indiscriminate wandering but provides a path to places which might otherwise be inaccessible. On the other hand a badly routed trail can be extremely hazardous to the terrain. Where two or three people might wander, several thousand may be directed along a single track; the risks are obvious. Even a well sited trail is open to over-use but this can be prevented by management and timing. A sequence of trails can be put into operation as seasonal interest and use demands. This will also be worked from the conservation point of view: for example, it may be necessary to avoid nesting areas during the breeding season. Trails can be temporarily closed so long as there is an alternative.

## Types of trail

Trails can be general or specialized; they can deal with man-made things or natural history or both; most deal with both in a fairly general way. In the U.K. it is very difficult to be without one or the other and it is their interaction which makes for some of the most interesting interpretation. Many of this type are lumped together under that rather depressing and uninformative title, Nature Trail.

1. *Land-use* trails explain forestry, farming, village settlement, local industry (e.g. iron foundries/charcoal burning) and their influence on the countryside.

2. *Natural history* trails may concentrate on identification (dullish) or they may have an ecological basis. It is essential that they should be devised with the seasons in mind.

A print of Catcraig lime kiln, East Lothian, fixed inside the kiln, explains how it worked (actual size, say 2 × 3 ft. [60 × 90 cm.]).

3. *General trails* may also include sites of *happenings*, both present and past, local history or recurring events.

4. *Specific trails* can be of great value. Dealing with one subject, they can take it in greater detail and depth. This tends to broaden general interest rather than narrow it. Specific trails also avoid the dangers of repetition which may be inevitable between one general trail and another. Examples: geological, botanical, archaeological, canal or railway development, irrigation and drainage. A specific trail such as a geological trail could link the geology of the region with a local industry such as lime burning (see above). A motor trail exploring churches dedicated to a particular saint can provide wide architectural and topographical interest.

5. *Coastal paths* make a very useful basis for a general trail. *A Plain Man's Guide to the Dale Peninsula* (John Barrett) gives an excellent idea of the potential of a path of this kind (history, ancient and current; geology; flora and fauna . . .). Coastal paths often offer the enormous advantage of already being in existence on the ground.

6. *Day Field Centres* in or near centres of population or industry are an extension of the trail idea and they usually include trails. A valuable lead has been given by the Central

E

Electricity Generating Board and the Nature Conservancy on power station sites in the Midlands.[1] (Plate 41). These have the following major advantages:

(a) They make use of what is virtually 'amenity sterilized' land, usually within the perimeter fence, by turning it into what has been described as a 'controlled wilderness'.
(b) They are easily accessible to a relatively large number of schools.
(c) Their location underlines the fact that an interest in the environment and field study is very much a part of everyday life and not merely something that happens on a special occasion in remote country.

7. *Trails with blind people in mind* can also be devised. They should not be exclusively for the blind, as people do not appreciate being lumped in separate categories. Labels in braille, an emphasis on sound, scent and touch, and carefully planned paths free of hazards are needed. A change of texture of the surface of a path at junctions with loop trails is useful as is some form of edging or kerb, particularly at changes of direction, for a blind person's stick.

8. *Trails for those in wheel chairs.* Some of the notes in (7) above equally apply. Gentle gradients should be aimed for; steps are obviously out. At pausing places allow space for two or three wheel chairs as well as a bench.

## Foot trails

*Length and route*: The National Audubon Society recommends $\frac{1}{2}$–1 mile with about 10–12 stations or 30 items. At a picnic place on a highway a 10–15 minute trail may be quite long enough. It is probably better to indicate the time likely to be taken rather than the length of a trail.

Stations should be slightly closer in the first half when interest is fresh. But actual distance is likely to be governed by topography, e.g. a trail round a lake. Flexibility of length is obviously useful: hence, figure-of-eight trails. Trails with loops or spurs have the additional advantage of allowing the main stream to by-pass and leave undisturbed features which are of specialist interest. Seats (logs or benches, not municipal seats) can be sited on these spurs or loops. People are apt to forget that they are likely to see far more wild life when still.

Winding trails give an illusion of remoteness: one party stands less chance of seeing those ahead or behind. This can also be achieved in more formal layouts. A path planned for viewing pens or enclosures can be scalloped on plan to this end. It is important that it should be curved so that there is a view down the whole length of the pen on approach. Fencing of back-to-back pens will run through in straight lines (economy in erection and

[1] See *Field Studies on a Power Station Site*, a Nature Conservancy/CEGB paper by Philip Oswald and Ray Shekell.

ease of maintenance); a scalloped path can run round the double block of pens. Paths would naturally deviate in sympathy with local topography and planting, and the length and rhythm of the scallops can be varied to avoid monotony.

In all cases the car park should be lost from view as soon as possible.

*Width*: The general aim should be to allow two people to walk comfortably side by side. The actual width which allows this depends on whether or not the path is enclosed or across open ground; say 3 ft. 0 in.–5 ft. 0 in. This should only be taken as a general guide. In places it may be single file; in others cart track width. Nothing is duller than a path that does not vary in sympathy with the terrain. Long stretches of narrow trail are awkward when groups are being taken round (e.g. school parties): a single line means a long straggle. Where possible trails should widen slightly at pausing places so that children can gather for discussion and explanation.

*Gradient*: Trails should avoid long steep runs. The trail will be more interesting and less tiring if gradients vary. The NPS recommends a maximum gradient of 15 per cent (1 in 6·6). Halts should be more frequent on uphill pulls.

## Motor trails

The speed of traffic on a motor trail will depend on the road: its plan, section and its surface. Speed should be in sympathy with the interest and scenic excitement of the views from the trail. Otherwise slow speeds can be frustrating. But trails which provide plenty of interest both to driver and passengers can be designed for speeds of as low as 10 m.p.h. in places.

The motor trail through Cade's Cove, a pioneer settlement in a remote valley in the Great Smoky Mountains, is designed for speeds of 10–20 m.p.h. The one-way road twists through woodland and pasture with halts (average interval, $\frac{1}{4}$ mile) at pioneer buildings (farms, chapels etc). At the most distant point from base a group of buildings has been restored; this includes a working mill. The group gives a focal point to the expedition where visitors are likely to stop for half an hour or more.

The trail starts at a car park. Here in an open shelter is a large map showing the trail; information about what is to be seen; and a dispenser for leaflets. Points of interest are identified on the map, leaflet and on the ground by the same numbered symbol. On the trail itself this symbol (an outline of a bird containing the relevant number) is painted on a blackboard fixed to a short post (see Plate 42).

*Width of trail*: although some road engineers might recommend a minimum width of 13 ft. 0 in. it should be borne in mind that there are still very attractive and driveable one-way roads with grass down the middle with an overall width of 7 ft. 6 in. Ten feet seems a likely width for one-way traffic at low speeds with passing places at draw-offs for points of interest. This width should discourage overtaking elsewhere.

Motor trails are also being devised on established roads, e.g. that with its emphasis on forestry and landscape by the Duke of Atholl on the Atholl Way. In such cases co-operation with the road authority on the use and siting of lay-bys is essential. Winter use of motor trails is likely to increase. Detailed local knowledge of frost and snow conditions can help in avoiding places which tend to become impassable before conditions are generally severe. A short stretch will put the whole trail out of use. Tourists will be less experienced than locals in negotiating bad patches.

## Bicycle trails

As roads become more deadly to cyclists, bicycle trails are likely to increase in popularity. Already some of the roads in New York's Central Park are closed to motorists and given over to bicycling on Sundays.

Bicycle trails will usually be made out of existing tracks so design will depend on what is already there (Plate 36).

One-way traffic is the ideal. Design for viewing the country, not speeding; long downhill stretches are irresistible. Meandering trails are usually (but not always) more interesting and they cut speed. Bicycling can provide an ideal speed for exploring forest tracks.

Trails must be long enough to be worth taking: around 5 miles minimum. A figure-of-eight plan again has advantages for small children.

Old railway tracks are ideal, particularly embankments; the speed of a bicycle is in scale with the view. Canal banks give long level runs full of interest. Tunnels can be awkward since towpaths almost always stop short. Railway bridges on disused lines are seldom maintained. A light prefabricated bridge might be designed for foot and bicycle traffic only.

Trails should be wide enough for two abreast, say 6 ft. 0 in. (again much depends on the edge conditions). At halts there must be room for people with bicycles to stand around. Timber rails, 2 ft. 6 in. above ground level, made an effective bicycle prop in a Dutch National Park.

## Pony trails

There are few better ways of seeing the country than from the right sort of pony. To be that much higher off the ground and to move slightly faster for a lot longer than when walking is an enormous advantage, quite apart from the enjoyment of riding itself.

Pony trails will be devised by trekking organizations. Ponies naturally tend to churn up damp heavy soil and this has caused a certain amount of antipathy to trekkers, but common sense should produce treks which do not spoil the country for other users.

A successful trail will depend on detailed local knowledge. The following points may be useful:

1. Gates on trails should be openable on horseback. They must be properly hung and

have easy latches. Admittedly this is a counsel of perfection but it can be as helpful to farmers as riders.

2. Notices should be kept to a minimum but they may be necessary to give warnings of unsound ground and bogs, depth of fords, firing on M.o.D. property, etc.

3. Tethering posts or rails at recognized halts and picnic places must be very sound. Usual provision 8–12 ponies. Aim for some shade or shelter at halts, and a stream or drinking trough.

## Trail paraphernalia

At their start, trails need:

1. *A car park.* This can influence siting. If the car park can be combined with one used for some other purpose so much the better. Here, at the beginning of the trail, a certain amount of 'starting paraphernalia' accumulates (signs and notices, leaflet dispenser, litter bin, benches, etc.). It will be more useful, and look much better, if grouped rather than dotted round the car park. It will also mark the beginning of the trail.

2. A *shelter* to house this starting paraphernalia not only helps in giving visitors protection from the weather but gives visual cohesion to a clutter of objects, which can otherwise distract. There may be an existing building which can be used, e.g. the lime kiln or the old shed illustrated on Plate 40 both serve admirably; alternatively a simple lean-to might be constructed in the lea of a wall. Nothing grand is necessary.

3. *Name sign.* It may be considered necessary for the trail to have some sort of sign to announce its existence. The briefer the better but it is more useful if it is specific, e.g. geological trail; bicycle trail to——. It is not always easy to combine brevity with information; a simple symbol meaning 'self-guided trail' could save a lot of words: 'self-guided coastal path to——' is altogether too much of a mouthful. The sign (with an arrow where necessary) should be fixed to a wall or building, otherwise it is probably better omitted.

4. A *notice board* showing a map of the area, a plan of the trail, and a *drawing* explaining its main features. All information given here should be visual rather than literary.

5. A *leaflet dispenser*. It seems logical that leaflets should be paid for but the safe-keeping of the money box can produce both practical and aesthetic problems. In the north-west of Scotland (and other places) this has been practically solved by the provision of an old tobacco tin, emptied daily, in which the public put their money on trust. There it works well on the whole. Much will depend on the locality and the type of visitor. Where a safe is provided, the safe itself (only the size of a brick) must be built into something equally impregnable. If this can be a wall which has some fencing function the problem is solved. On the other hand a small brick pillar constructed merely to house the safe can look absurd and is expensive. Where no alternative to a special structure exists it looks much better if the safe is combined with something long and low, e.g. a bench (see Plates 38 and 37). Literature itself always seems to be available on trust. It must be sheltered from wind and

rain. A recess in a wall, which is deep enough to give this degree of shelter (but without a door which may be left open), has been found to be satisfactory provided it does not face the prevailing wind. The design of the dispenser is enormously simplified if no charge is made for the leaflet. Where there is no wall in which to provide a recess, timber boxes, like fly-catcher nesting boxes but with an 1 in.–1½ in. opening at the bottom of the front, could be useful. For outdoor use they must be thoroughly waterproof, probably with a felted top.

6. *Benches* can be helpful here: wardens may give introductory talks; Mum may like to sit while the family sorts itself out (she may like to miss the trail altogether so if this can be a comfortable place for her to knit or snooze in the sun, so much the better).

7. A *Litter bin*, provided it can be emptied often enough, may be useful.

8. *Paths, steps, stiles etc.* Sound construction with minimum fuss is a hallmark of traditional work in the country. Sloppy work devalues its surroundings. Owing both to lack of time and experience and of money to employ someone who knows, some of the tracks laid for nature trails are shoddy and out of key with their surroundings. Undue anxiety about 'natural' appearance can also lead to similar results.

If the path happens to run along a field bank or hedge, plants, etc. can be labelled with quite small—say 3 in. [7·5 cm.]—labels since they will be close to the viewer, maybe at eye level.

9. *Numbered signs* will mark the trail itself. To discourage souvenir hunters these must be relatively 'permanent', at least for a season even if the item numbered is only seasonably relevant for a few weeks. This can be noted in the leaflet. Clarity, maintenance, suitability to site, capital cost (in terms both of actual cost and effort on the part of the warden responsible) should be considered. Size will depend on the distance from which the sign is to be read. Where possible fix to or paint on an existing feature (e.g. fence).

10. *Half-way halt.* Where possible a trail should have some objective about half-way from base. A focus of interest is easily created if this can be at the highest point of the trail or by water. A shelter with a good view is ideal. Land use can be described. Simple benches can be provided.

11. *Elbow rests for binocular users.* A rail 4 ft. 6 in. [137 cm.] above ground level is very useful where no five-barred gate or wall happens to be available. These can be sited where deer, wildfowl, etc. may be watched or where there is a particularly fine view.

Trail design in the U.K. is usually done by wardens and naturalists. There is little doubt that someone with specialist knowledge of exhibition design could produce useful ideas on the techniques of trail interpretation. The following ideas have emerged from a variety of trails:

1. To use senses other than sight is desirable but has its limitations. Taste has obvious complication. Touch and smell lead to picking; this may be impracticable, even when only the commonest plants are affected, if a trail is likely to be visited by hundreds if not thousands.

2. Man-made permanent examples can be particularly useful on a natural history trail. Examples:

(a) Animal spoors cast in a concrete slab set near some muddy ground which animals tend to cross, serve both as guides to identification and provide an object of interest when the animals have chosen to walk elsewhere.
(b) A soil section (like an archaeological section) can easily be recut when it crumbles. The various layers can be labelled *in situ*.
(c) A sawn tree trunk, with dates and happenings on the annual rings, short-circuits time by showing an instant link between now and the historic event recorded.

3. An object finder (a fixed tube bearing on a particular point) is useful for picking out objects and concentrating attention. It has the added advantage of giving people something different to do.

4. Low level bridges, piling, or railway sleepers laid across swampy ground allow people virtually to walk through a marsh and to see its wild life at close quarters.

5. A board walk laid over dunes which have interesting flora or erosion problems not only provides access without damage, but gives the viewer the advantage of being a foot or two above natural ground level. It also allows him to view awkward terrain in comfort.

## Text of leaflets

The points discussed in pages 61 to 63 apply particularly strongly to trail leaflets which will often be read under conditions most inconducive to absorption of literary effort. Brevity and clarity are all important but a general introduction (with instructions to skip if desired) could be included for first timers.

## Warning

There is a real danger that trails may be overdone in the future. Much of the best country must be left unmarked if we are to escape spiritual claustrophobia.

# 5

# Access roads and car parks

Our attitude to our own car and to everyone else's is a well-known mid twentieth-century characteristic which is not always recognized as a planner's tool. There is a natural tendency towards we-and-theyness about the whole problem. Once in a car, most of us instinctively want to drive as near to our objective as possible. It is the ninety-nine other people with the same idea who are breaking the solitude, disturbing the silence and churning up the field track. We all have schizophrenic tendencies as we change positions from walking up to the car and driving it. But few of us can still be thinking back to the days when it was positive progress to get a motor car as near to its objective as possible, whatever the result.

The right siting of car parks is one of the most important and most difficult of all planning problems in the countryside. Their position and thus what focal points are to be seen from them will decide where a given number of people will descend on the terrain, what direction they are likely to take, and what they will do.

It is now also generally recognized that the car park may have to be a considerable distance from the place it serves if, by sheer magnitude, it is not to swamp the thing people have come to enjoy.

## Access to car parks

The question of access to the ancient monument or picnic-worthy bay, or to be precise to its car park, is of vital importance. Much of the quality and character of our country-side depends on the close-knit pattern of traditional hedgerows, walls or field banks. Any of these boundaries can now be bulldozed with astounding speed and ease. Their destruction can be as serious a blow to landscape as the felling of a fine tree or the demolition of a building, both of which can be legally protected. The work of generations can go in a morning by too zealous an attitude towards 'road improvement'. The absurd but tragic side to this situation is seen in those areas where the County Surveyor's Department is busily engaged in reinstating traditional walls and banks on the roads for which he is responsible; a hundred yards away down a side lane the Rural District Council is equally busily tearing down similar boundaries and replacing them by post and wire.

Obviously, then, access to car parks, particularly those used by motor coaches, is as important a factor in decisions concerning their siting, as is the visual effect of the car park itself.

## Access from car park to objective

There are still people who would enthusiastically site car parks as close as possible to the tourists' objective regardless of their visual result, or of the noise and smell inevitably engendered. Some of our most splendid monuments rise from a sea of shiny metal in season and of macadam out. But this policy is now less common and even the most optimistic of its supporters must suspect that in the long run it is the surest way to kill the goose.

## Internal public transport

Some sites are themselves too large to be appreciated entirely on foot. Others generate so much traffic that no amount of ingenuity, or of traffic engineering amounting to vandalism, could solve the problem. Here the only answer is to make adequate car parks at a distance and provide very frequent public transport, usually in small buses. The service is 'free', fares are usually covered by the entrance ticket to the site. This method caters for the millions who visit Williamsburg, Virginia, a town site. It is an equally valuable technique in the wilderness.

## Distance

The *distance* a tourist can reasonably be expected to walk from his car depends on what he is going to see and who will be walking. It is largely a matter of common sense in which committees may differ; fortunately it is usually finally settled by the site itself. Where one function of a building is indoor entertainment at a specific time people will be less happy to accept, say, five minutes' walk through the rain in concert going clothes, than perhaps one of ten to fifteen minutes if they are going to admire a ruin, itself open to the elements. It is often possible to use a one-way service road so that passengers can be deposited near the entrance.

## Service access

Most buildings need occasional vehicular access, either for servicing (including the Fire Service) or for occasional functions. From the tourists' point of view it is frustrating to see a road leading from the car park to his objective on which he is not allowed to drive: the car park should be seen to be at the physical limit of normal vehicular access. Beyond this point the route should be scaled down; perhaps wheel tracks only in a hard surface suited to pedestrians; or a 7 ft. 6 in.–10 ft. 0 in. width of drive.

## Crossings

If for good reasons the park is separated from the objective by a busy road, a footbridge (or even a tunnel) will almost certainly be needed since in tourism both pedestrian and vehicular traffic are likely to reach a peak simultaneously.

## Access paths

Much can be done to cheer the walk from car park to objective without necessarily incurring extra expense. But if the objective can be seen from the park the path must be reasonably direct unless there is some obvious, impenetrable obstacle in the way: a moat or wall or dense undergrowth. If it is out of sight, or if the position of the entrance is not obvious, the following ideas may be useful:

1. The path should follow a route naturally sheltered from the prevailing wind.
2. Shaded walks are helped by patches of sun. If through woodland, glades can be opened up. Provide a bench in the sun.
3. Glimpses both of the objective and the surrounding country may be slightly opened up.
4. Instant local history may encourage visitors ('Here X eloped with/ expired/ accepted the throne . . .').
5. The route may provide local information on geology, forestry etc. But if a fast circulation of visitors is necessary, this must be avoided.

## Design and screening

The car park must be subservient to what it serves; in certain notable cases it takes precedence: Tintern Abbey for instance, rising apologetically behind its vast macadammed forecourt.

Siting will take into account changes of level: a low wall may satisfactorily screen a park which is below the general level of the ground (see Plate 54). This is the greatest help in treeless areas.

Large areas of hard surfacing are intrusive in most landscapes and should be broken up. Trees are the greatest boon. Large car parks can be divided by strips or clumps of planting (see Plates 45, 48). This is now the practice of forward looking authorities. The possible nuisance of leaves is counteracted by the very real benefit of both screening and shade. Species with smaller leaves, or with leaves which decompose relatively easily, or with needles (conifers), cause least trouble. Shrubs (e.g. sea buckthorn) can be very effective. If a few trees or even scrubby shrubs already exist, they should be kept for at least a year, to see if they are not in fact an asset rather than a liability. Only species sympathetic to the regional landscape should be introduced; otherwise the screening itself becomes an intrusion.

## Collection of fees

If a 'Trust the Motorist'[1] machine is installed it must be in an obvious position at the exit which pedestrians use. (This system might be extended to the collection of entry fees.) There should be a machine for each such exit; this may mean limiting the exits. Where entrance tickets have to be bought in the conventional way it is essential that the layout allows ticket buying to take its natural place in the sequence of events. See page 45.

## Entrances

Sight lines are essential for safety. They also automatically destroy the scale and pattern of existing stone walls and hedgerows if an opening has to be made direct to a road. Therefore if an entrance to a car park can be set back from the road so that sight lines cross existing wide verges, much less visual damage will be done. (See Plate 51.)

## Kerbs

The *edge* of any surface, commonly known as trim, is as important to its successful design as the surface itself. This applies equally to roads, car parks, paths, paving, etc. A new access road edged with white concrete kerbs leading from a long established grass edged country road is a thoroughly depressing sight. It is all too common and usually stems from zealous but illogical application of a standard originally intended for urban or suburban use. The quality of the country is diminished by this unnecessary, expensive intrusion.

If edge strengthening is thought to be necessary, the foundation of the road can be carried beyond the surfacing, under the grass verge, to give a substantial edge. Kerbs are often laid with the intention of preventing damage to the grass caused by vehicles cutting the corner, or by deliberately pulling off to park. The occasional run off does not much matter. Some mud is more in character with the countryside than prim over-tidiness. If drivers intend to pull off, a standard 4 in. kerb will not deter them. It is quite negotiable by the toy-like wheels of a mini.

[1] A 'Trust the Motorist' box at Inverewe (National Trust for Scotland) collected £1,000 in one shilling fees during the 1967 season. 90,000 people visited the garden. These figures suggest that the system works well.

## Edge barriers to keep vehicles on road

Where it is necessary to deter vehicles from parking off the road, the following prove effective:

1. *A sizeable ditch* can be cheaply dug by ploughing a single deep furrow about 3 ft. [1 m.] in from the road. This is particularly useful where visual obstruction is to be minimized. The raw earth is soon naturally re-seeded, except on poor moorland soils.

2. *Big stones acting as bollards.* They must be heavy enough not to be shifted. Spacing depends on zeal of trespassers. A mini (narrowest likely vehicle) is 4 ft. 8 in. [1·42 m.] wide. (See Plate 51.)

3. *Pegs* of stripped timber, 2 in.–3 in. [5–10 cm.] diameter, projecting about 9 in. [25 cm.] at 4 ft. 8 in. [1·42 m.] from centre to centre are unobtrusive but effective against cars. (See Plate 52.)

4. *A small natural change of level* should look after itself but a bank liable to crumble can be reinforced when necessary with stone slab or brick without necessity of kerbing the whole.

5. *Posts and rail* of stripped timber approximately 8 in. [20 cm.] above ground. (See Plate 49.)

6. *Slate on edge* as a miniature retaining wall (See Plate 53.)

7. *Kerbs.* Where it is decided to use kerbs, granite is the best material but concrete (cheaper) is improved visually by the addition of lamp black pigment in the mix. The typical creamy white is too startling a contrast except where it is specially needed to shine at night. Logs or poles work well in car parks. (See Plate 50.)

## Surfacing of car parks

Choice of material depends on traffic load, natural ground conditions and the character of the place. British compromise would often produce the best answer; e.g. gravel chippings, only where necessary, on a thoroughly consolidated base. This sympathetic attitude is relatively easy where direct labour is employed but more difficult to administer where the work is contracted. Liability for future maintenance is also unconducive to this kind of design, e.g. where an exchequer grant is available towards capital costs but not for maintenance. For this reason, among others, many green fields have become macadam parade grounds.

In many instances it would be sufficient to surface *part* of a car park only for regular use. At peak periods (summer) cars can spill into the adjoining field. Early, wet Easters can cause trouble. It might be cheaper in cash as well as visual terms to hire a tractor and driver to stand by for such relatively rare occasions than to create sufficient hard surface for rare peak demands.

## Types of surface for car parks

1. *Grass:* on well drained soil where traffic is not heavy, it is often sufficient to gravel entrances and exits, places where vehicles tend to turn, and in bigger parks the roadways between parked cars.

2. *Hollow paving in grass:* for heavy occasional use or for lighter everyday use. Hollow concrete paving blocks (see Plate 55) through which the grass grows provide a 'reinforced field'. This is a most effective answer and has been used with success particularly in Denmark and Germany.

3. *Unsealed gravel or quarry chippings* can usefully be used for the whole parking space or in conjunction with a sealed surface where turning, braking or acceleration are likely.

4. *Gravel sealed with a cold bituminous emulsion.* The final coat of emulsion is covered with $\frac{1}{4}$ in.–$\frac{3}{8}$ in. chippings or clean washed shingle at about 130 yards per ton. This finish must be chosen to be in character with the surrounding terrain.

5. *Macadam:* a large smooth area of tar or bitumen macadam is difficult to absorb in the landscape pattern. It can be broken by planting and by varying the surface between macadam roadways and gravel parking lots. A surface dressing of $\frac{1}{2}$ in. chippings gives a more sympathetic finish than denser, smoother finish with smaller aggregate.

## Surfacing of access roads

Public roads are considered in other publications. An access road consisting of macadam wheel tracks with grass growing down the middle is exceptionally attractive (Plate 43). 2 ft. 0 in. [60 cm.] wheel tracks with a 2 ft. 6 in. [75 cm.] gap between are generally satisfactory for cars. (A 7 ton truck is under 7 ft. 6 in. wide so for occasional service vehicles a total width of 9 ft. 0 in. should be adequate.) Walls and banks should be kept clear of the immediate edges.

## Trees

The sealing of the surface of a car park may cut off the vital water supply of some existing trees, even if it does not cover their roots. The condition of trees should be watched for some time. Where a new car park includes trees, water must reach the limit of the root spread, which is at least as great as the branch spread. There may be a convenient water bearing strata in the soil. Unsealed gravel or tree grids provide other possible answers. The roots of such trees as beech, which grow near the surface, must be protected from traffic (e.g. by low post and rail).

## Falls

Paved surfaces should never be 'flat'. On flat sites the following falls are recommended to prevent standing rain water:

| | | |
|---|---|---|
| Gravel | 1 in 30 | |
| Bituminous or tar surfacing | 1 in 40 cross fall | 1 in 200 long fall |
| Paving slabs | 1 in 72 | |

## Marking of parking lots

If the general direction of parking lines is indicated at each end, and the angle of parking suggested, drivers can usually be relied on to make intelligent use of the space. It is extravagant to mark individual lots; space must then be allowed for the widest vehicle. Markers can be made by stones or bricks set nearly flush with the paved surface, or timber posts. Positions for coaches and motor cycles should be clearly marked. Most car parks, except the very smallest, need both an entrance and an exit even if these are close together, or are merely separate lanes. If it is necessary to mark parking lots in areas of blowing sand or where loose gravel makes painting on the surface impracticable, precast concrete beams can be laid on the surface and secured in the ground by bolts. Edges should be chamfered to avoid chipping. Old railway sleepers look much better and usually are very much cheaper.

## Economic parking plans

The following notes[1] may be useful for planning purposes:

*Angle of parked vehicles.* Where the angle of parking is not dictated by the shape of the site, the following points should be borne in mind:

(a) The width of the access road is related to the angle of parking. The visual impression of the road width may be more important than the actual width of the traffic lane. Therefore many people prefer 90° parking with a two-way traffic access road, to angle parking on a one-way road. Backing out is also easier.

(b) 0°, 30°, 60° and 90° angles are usual. For maximum economy of space, the choice lies between 60° and 90°.

(c) The only angle that can be economically arranged in a true herring-bone pattern is 45°.

*Projection of body beyond wheel base.* A car will probably be parked with its wheels resting against the kerb. Therefore it may project 3 ft. 6 in. [110 cm.]—or even more, in the case of certain American cars—over the verge or pavement. Whether it is parked nose in, or is backed against the kerb will also affect the extent of the projection. Allowances should be

[1] *Design and Detail of the Space between Buildings,* Elisabeth Beazley. Diagrams are given in this and other publications so are not repeated in this book.

made for this overhang, or a barrier (e.g. a timber kerb, or bollards more narrowly spaced than the cars) should be provided to prevent it happening.

## Overlooks

Most of this chapter is concerned with parking and access as a means of reaching an objective. Parking for the sake of a view has always been popular (cf. the front of any seaside town). In an American National Park the provision of overlooks is considered to be integral with the policy of showing the park to the visitor: when asked about the spacing of lay-bys it was an Engineer who patiently explained 'It's just a matter of Interpretation', meaning that the road engineers spaced them according to what was to be seen, not according to any book of rules.

Overlooks can be provided in several ways:

1. By providing pull-offs or lay-bys at strategic points. Motorists can then stroll to look down the valley/gorge/across the bay. These pull-offs can often be cheaply provided where the line of a road improvement leaves the old route.

2. By forming a lineal car park either on an old road or parallel to a new one. A one-way system and a shallow angle of parking (arranged to face view) means that the park can be quite narrow (only 21 ft. 0 in. [6·40 m.] for 16 ft. 0 in. [4·80 m.] long cars at 31°).

3. By providing a terraced car park so that cars can look over each other. This has the great advantage of reducing the scale of the car park. Banks between terraces can be planted with 'indigenous' shrubs, e.g. broom or gorse. An old quarry site might be found. This would have the additional advantages of screening the cars in the landscape and of giving them some shelter.

*Provisions.* Viewfinders and telescopes (6d. a look) are popular. They must not be sited where their view can be obscured by other tourists. Nor should litter receptacles be allowed to interrupt the view from parked cars; too often they are sited at the edge of the overlook. Benches in sheltered positions may be popular but people are likely to find that their own cars are more comfortable. Public lavatories should not be necessary, unless the overlook becomes a trunk road pull-off.

## Pull-offs

Small lay-by pull-offs are needed at frequent intervals on both motorways and trunk routes (particularly on trunk routes since these lack motorway service areas). Here tired motorists can have a nap or stretch their legs, or children can work off surplus energy. They are provided at three or four mile intervals on some Continental routes. The obstacle to their provision is that lay-bys tend to become fouled because there are so few public lavatories on trunk routes. But this makes the need nonetheless great. Someone driving under the influence of alcohol is a menace because his reactions are slow. A tired driver

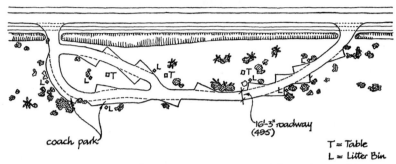

This site averages 200 × 45 metres. The picnic area is separated from the road by an embankment which makes it considerably quieter. Two parks are supplied for coaches, sited so that they will not block the view. (The Netherlands.)

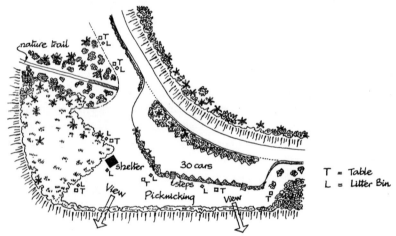

Parking space for about 30 cars. It is sited between the road and the picnic area which is at a lower level. A shelter and nature trail are provided. Benches have been designed to be light enough to be moved around so that picnickers can be in the sun or shade. (The Netherlands.)

can be more dangerous, both to himself and others; once asleep he will not react at all. A little Exchequer money might be usefully spent on this aspect of road safety.

One step towards solving this problem could be to provide pull-offs at, say, five mile intervals and public lavatories twenty-five to thirty miles apart. A notice could be fixed in lay-bys giving their distance and direction (this has been done by some RDC's).

The best pull-offs are separated from the road by a change of level and by planting which gives a sound baffle (again, retired stretches of road left behind by improvement schemes can be economically used). An old tree on which children can climb is useful.

Litter bins may not help the cleanliness of lay-bys; litter dumping can be a particularly difficult problem and some authorities prefer the take-your-litter-home policy.

## Control of access

As motorists penetrate deeper into the countryside and forestry land in search of somewhere to picnic or camp it becomes ever more necessary to find inexpensive ways of controlling access. The simple device of putting up a 'No Entry' sign which works well in some Continental countries is not yet accepted here in the remote country. Gates are expensive and often unnecessary.

*Booms.* Numerous designs for *booms* in both timber and steel have been worked out and are in common use on the Continent. A cheap, easily constructed timber boom could be very useful in the U.K. during the next decade. That shown here is one of the simplest designs seen; this example spanned 18 ft. 0 in. Sliding booms are inclined to jam and seem less satisfactory.

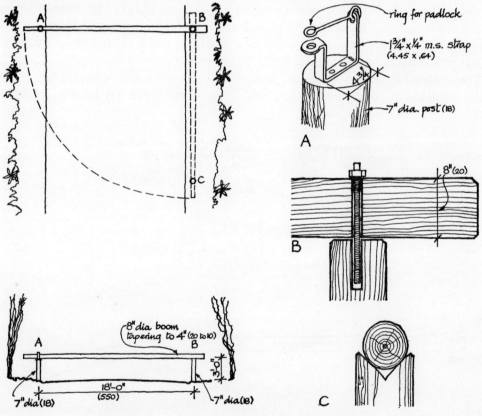

Boom across forestry road to control access.

*Cattle Grids.* The installation of *cattle grids* can save much frustration both to owners and drivers. Their provision for private roads is covered in detail in *Cattle Grids for Private Farm and Estate Roads* (Fixed Equipment of the Farm, Leaflet No. 7) H.M.S.O., 8*d.* A warning sign is sited to give due warning of the grid. It is common (if not universal) practice to site the gate for animals and horsedrawn vehicles directly beside the grid. In this obvious position it would scarcely be possible to miss it. Yet in the great majority of cases local authorities erect a second notice, following the warning, to direct those in charge of animals to the gate. Owing to an inconsistency between the *Traffic Signs Regulations* and the Worboys Committee *Report* on which they are based, and the *Traffic Signs Manual,* it is not clear whether local authorities have much choice in this matter. In the *Traffic Signs Regulations,* 1964, Schedule 1, Part 1, the caption under the sign which directs *Horse drawn vehicles and animals* (553) reads 'By-pass of cattle grid. Plate for use with sign in diagram 552 [i.e. the Cattle Grid warning sign]'. But in the Worboys Committee *Report, Traffic Signs* (1963), paragraph 117 notes 'If the by-pass to the cattle grid . . . is entered *at some distance* [my italics] from the grid we recommend that the sign be placed at the entrance and be supplemented by the plate at figure 63a [i.e. the directional sign]'. If this common-sense attitude could prevail much open country would be relieved of a double burden of signs. It would seem to be a matter on which a private road owner who allows public use of his road could use his judgment.

*Timber Guard Rails.* Guard rails on public highways do not fall within the scope of this book but there are situations where a timber guard rail (Plate 57) may be suited both

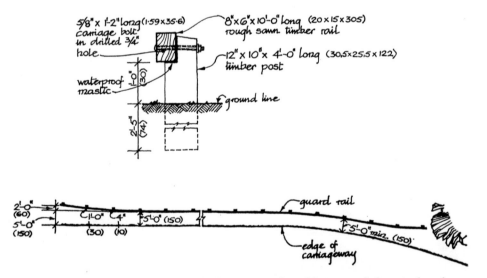

Sturdy timber guard rails are in scale and character with wild or wooded agricultural country.
For use when slow moving traffic is to be protected.

functionally and visually if traffic is slow moving: motor trails, forest roads, pull-offs and overlooks. That illustrated is on the Blue Ridge Parkway, U.S.A.: a 600-mile scenic drive on which commercial vehicles are prohibited and speeds are limited. Stump supports of the rail in the drawing are also provided to a similar section in reinforced concrete. Timber rails are not permitted on the U.S.A. Interstate system or on primary highways; on major, high speed and high volume highways the steel W-Beam is commonly used. On normal roads the clean lines of the steel barriers now available usually enhance rather than detract from the scenery.

A guard rail itself constitutes a hazard so should be used only where the result of running off the road would be worse than hitting the rail. Should impact occur, the vehicle should be redirected as nearly parallel as possible to its normal course to minimize the possibility of accidents from the rear.

# 6

# Links and barriers for people on foot

This chapter is concerned with provisions (other than paths) for access on foot. For motor vehicles please see Chapter 5. For footpaths, pages 66–67 and 74.

Access to the countryside means a multiplication of everything that must be provided to allow people to cross boundaries between properties or land of different use, or to negotiate natural barriers. These links include footbridges, stiles, flights of steps and gates. Fencing and barriers are also necessary to protect both the countryside from the public and sometimes to protect the public from its own enthusiasm.

Both walling and fencing and gates have been covered in considerable detail in other publications[1] (though seldom with particular reference to leisure in the countryside). Both are large subjects and too important to be skimmed over, but a few outstanding general points must be considered. Ways of negotiating walls and fences, other than by gates, seem to be generally overlooked in recent publications. Often these methods have been thought too insignificant to be written down and are now dying with the traditional craftsmen who practised such skills. The recording of new skills is also often overlooked.

## Lines of walls and fences

Traditional walls and fencing have a straight run of coping or top rail, broken only when some sudden change in contour dictates a break. New work looks far better when it follows this traditional practice. Occasionally artificial breaks are made in an attempt towards naturalness; the artistic result achieved is usually to be regretted. The exact position of a line of fencing, even a wire fence, can have an enormous visual effect on its surroundings not only on account of the fence itself but because of the grazing that will or will not take place on either side of it (the effect of rabbits and deer on woodland is particularly applicable here). Where ten to twenty yards can be spared at the edge of a road through forest it is often possible to create an entirely different illusion of landscape in that part through which the road runs, by setting the fence back this amount.

[1] See Bibliography.

## Protective barriers

It can be extraordinarily difficult to know where the public needs protection from the natural hazards of the countryside. Apart from any legal obligations, no responsible owner or warden wants to take risks; on the other hand the landscape can be wrecked by fencing and other barriers put up to protect those who have come to admire it.

No one would consider fencing the Pembrokeshire coastal path (except for the very occasional guard rail); despite its sheer drops and unquestionable hazards this would generally be considered an absurd undertaking. Grand Canyon is probably the classic example of the unfenceable tourist attraction. The principle on which the American National Park Service works here is that if the visitor is invited (by path or sign) to a view point, some form of protection should be given. Elsewhere he is free to fall in. Such happenings are very rare. From experience of this Park and other less dramatic examples, common-sense conclusions can be drawn which may be helpful to those who have to decide how to deal with particular problems.

1. 3 ft. 6 in. [1·067 m.] is a typical *height* for railings, etc. whether or not it is laid down as a required minimum in regulations. The width of the barrier (i.e. front to back) as well as its height gives a sense of protection and can also increase the actual protection given by the barrier. Where there is a sheer drop of great depth, immediately beyond the barrier, the height of the barrier may need to be increased beyond 3 ft. 6 in.

2. A protective barrier or handrail need not be provided throughout the length of a path because it is needed in certain places. Uniformity is no particular virtue. At Grand Canyon a single steel tube is fixed at tricky stretches (including flights of steps), on the paths which lead to the overlooks. This may be on either side of the path, according to need. It is seldom on both sides. Barriers on each side of a path are usually awkward-looking and heavy.

3. Places which are *obviously* dangerous are probably the most safe. People are geared to expect danger at, say, Grand Canyon; they come in that frame of mind and what they see out-reaches their wildest imagination. But there are people who seem to find certain places irresistible; particularly rocky banks of rivers near waterfalls. Even if they were protected by 'unclimbable' fencing, a way round would probably be found.

4. Townspeople particularly, but any who are not used to a particular sort of terrain, can easily be misled by seemingly gentle landscape, e.g. turf can be very slippery and consequently may be much more dangerous than sheer rock.

5. Today's tourist is motoring rather than walking and consequently is often inadequately shod to stray from the car park. Therefore places within, say, ten minutes' stroll of a car park may need to be more guarded than those further afield. The traditional walker will not thank anyone for too much solace in this respect. He wants the hills to remain empty.

6. Places where children are likely to run on ahead usually need to be guarded. The aim

should be to prevent them bounding over the edge before parents arrive on the scene. It is usually impracticable to attempt to provide a barrier they will not climb; even if it is possible the result is likely to be a hideous distraction. The barrier should be designed to halt a child running at full tilt.

7. Conversely, places which can only be reached slowly need less protection, e.g.: the parapet round the top of a church tower may cause comparatively little anxiety because in order to stand at the top of the tower it is necessary to climb through a smallish hole in the roof at the top of a tight spiral stair. (A stone parapet is also usually fairly wide).

## Stiles

Stiles should be considered wherever access for walkers only is needed. They can save the farmer a lot of worry about open gates; gates, too, however well treated, need more maintenance because they move.

The fact that stiles must be easier to climb than the wall or fence in which they are set might seem too obvious to be worth noting, but the reverse is not now uncommon. It mostly happens where a non-traditional timber stile is used in place of the traditional stone. This is a fairly common practice since labour is expensive and skilled masons are scarce. It is often forgotten that the two free ends of the wall or bank which has been cut to take the timber stile must be finished with workmanlike coins if they are not to disintegrate. Since it is a carpenter's job to erect the actual stile this masonry may be bodged or left undone; it is also often as difficult to get good corner stones for these coins as to find stone for a new traditional stile. But if the wall is not made good it soon deteriorates further, leaving the stile with a growing gap on each side of it, through which walkers push their way. (Plate 60).

A stone slab or step on the path at each side of the stile prevents puddling. When this is provided, dimensions should be taken from this level, rather than from the ground.

Whenever a new stile is to be constructed it would seem to be worth checking:

1. Whether any stile is now necessary. There are places (e.g. on some cliff paths) where stock is no longer grazed and the fields are fenced from the cliffs. Here a properly formed gap in a wall or bank may be all that is needed.

2. Where a mason is not available, a retired man might happily make one or two stiles when he could not undertake a whole wall.

3. Whether new techniques or those not traditional to the district are applicable. In stone wall or stone hedge country where sheep are to be grazed some of the very simple stone gap stiles, traditional to Yorkshire and parts of the Lake District and Derbyshire, might answer well (see Plates 62–63).

## Stone gap stiles

Dimensions (as shown in drawing, Plates 62–63) are critical. Those indicated come from stiles which have given good service for many years. They result from a mean between the minimum dimension which would stop a 6-month lamb (not a young one running with its mother) but would allow a comfortably proportioned farmer's wife to pass. The maximum width at around 15 in. [38 cm.] above ground level is 6 in. [15 cm.] (a 7½ in. [19 cm.] gap may let a full-grown lamb through). The restriction is often continued for about 9 in. [23 cm.] vertically in order to deter more persistent sheep. At 2 ft. 0 in. [60 cm.] it starts to flare out to allow for humans. In the Dales, stiles usually widen out at the bottom; others may taper to as little as 2½ in. [6 or 7 cm.].

Such stiles could be constructed with rough lengths of stone which happen to be close to the site. Where these are not available there seems to be a promising future for cast concrete slabs. These could be cast either on the ground beside the stile or be pre-cast. It is essential that the concrete should have a good rough textured finish: the actual aggregate is then seen. The colour of the sand and aggregate should be chosen to be in sympathy with the existing wall; the slab is then hammered over lightly while it is still green. This gets rid of the cement which normally collects on the surface giving the concrete a whitish look; it also prevents hair cracks due to surface tension.

## Timber stiles

Timber stiles are particularly useful in rabbit or sheep fencing where an open gate can be

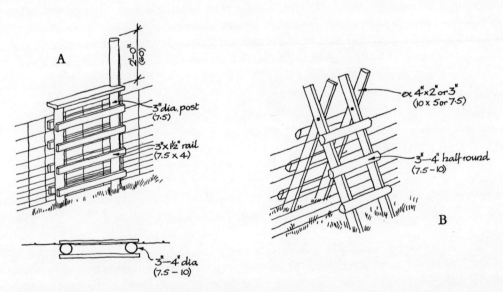

Two examples of the many traditional timber stiles in use for crossing wire fencing. (A) It is useful, particularly for elderly people, if one of the posts projects above the fence line as a hand-grip. (B) Planks (not shown) can be spiked to the top pair of rails to form a small platform. This is helpful for getting dogs over fences.

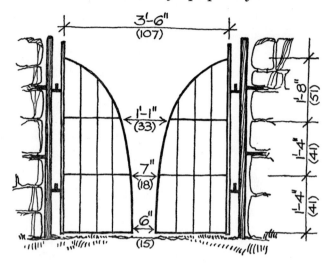

This iron gate is an example from the Lake District which works on the same principle as a stone gap stile but has the advantage of opening. It could be adapted for modern vehicles.

disastrous. There are numerous designs, locally traditional. Sizes of timbers will depend on the type of timber (hard or soft wood), its availability and the dimensions of the stile. Indications are given on sketches. A post taken up to a height of around 2 ft. 6 in. [75 cm.] above the top step makes a useful hand grip. A few shovelfuls of gravel or a stone slab set in the grass or path on each side of a stile prevents the inevitable puddling where an un-paved surface gets particularly hard wear.

*Types of timber:* sweet chestnut, oak and larch are all good for fencing without further treatment (except to butt ends). Many other home-grown species give good service if treated with preservative.[1]

*Treatment of timber:* all timber should be stripped of bark; if left it will soon begin to die and will form a trap for water. Butt ends of softwood posts in the ground and for 12 in. [30 cm.] above ground level should be treated with preservative. It is best applied hot by the open tank method. *The posts,* usually about 4 in. [10 cm.] diameter, will be taken 2 ft. 0 in.–3 ft. 0 in. [60–90 cm.] into the ground, according to the nature of the soil and their height. The holes (make these as small as possible) should be very well rammed when the earth is returned. Where soil cannot be consolidated or a deep enough hole be dug, posts are set in concrete (mix 1:10). It looks much better if the top few inches of the hole can be refilled with earth.

[1] See *Design and Detail of the Space between Buildings*, Elisabeth Beazley, for a short outline of preserving methods and a list of relevant publications.

## Openings in deer fences

A public path cutting a deer forest fence gives rise to particular difficulties: it is essential that no gate should be left open but stiles will be 7 ft. 0 in. [213 cm.] high. Solutions include:

(a) A narrow gate, 2 ft. 0 in. × 6 ft. 0 in. [61 × 183 cm.], held by a heavy (14 lb.) counter weight on steel wire and iron pulley wheel.

(b) Stiles of a similar design to that shown on page 87(B) but to clear a 6 ft. 0 in. [183 cm.] fence. It would be difficult to get a dog over this type of stile even if it has a boarded platform at the top.

(c) A cattle grid of normal length will almost certainly deter deer. A long narrow cattle grid—say 12 in. [30 cm.] wide—might answer on footpaths.

## Board walks

Board walks are of two main types:

1. Fixed walks usually constructed over dunes to prevent erosion. That in the photograph (Plates 58–59) is 4 ft. 6 in.–5 ft. 0 in. [1·40–1·50 m.] wide and is constructed of

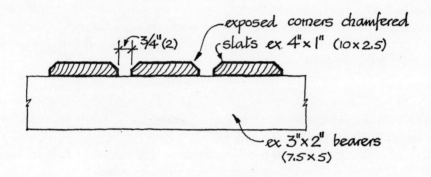

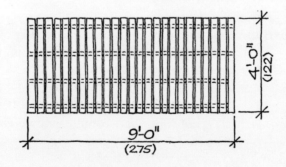

Duckboarding for crossing soft sand.

8 in. × 2 in. [20 × 5 cm.] untreated Douglas fir planks supported on three longitudinal bearers (also 8 in. × 2 in.) on timber piles are 8 ft. 0 in. [2·50 m.] from centre to centre. This board walk forms part of a Nature Trail through a sunken forest. It varies in height from ground level to 2 ft. 0 in. [60 cm.] above. At look-out platforms a handrail has been fixed.

2. Portable lengths which are laid on the soft sand above the high-water mark to ease the trudge up from the beach. The Dutch example shown in the sketch is 9 ft. 0 in. × 4 ft. 0 in. [2·80 × 1·20 m.]. 4 in. × 1 in. [10 × 2·5 cm.] slats are carried on 3 in. × 2 in. [8 × 5 cm.] bearers (3). A section of this size seems to be about the right weight and size not to be blown away in ordinary high winds. At the same time, it seems to be portable enough for beach wardens to move while not tempting those holiday makers who see some other potential in the structure.

Timber should be of a kind which does not splinter easily; both Douglas fir and Western Hemlock are good provided they have been rift sawn, that is, cut on the quarter to an angle between 90° and 45°. European redwood is suitable but is seldom obtainable rift sawn. To minimize risk of splintering, boards should be laid with the heart down so that the softer sapwood does not splinter off with the corners; all arrises and corners should be rounded or chamfered. Fixing should be by rustproof nails. Board walks, particularly on slopes, can be very slippery. It is important to have a gap between the boards, say $\frac{3}{4}$ in.; this allows the sand (which makes the walk slippery) to drain through it. It also gives a slight foot grip. Where this allowance has not been made, new paths are commonly seen in the marram *beside* the walk.

## Steps

Steps have been discussed elsewhere[1] but some examples of fairly primitive but very effective steps are shown in Plates 58 and 59.

The scale of steps out of doors is totally different to that indoors; treads are bigger and risers are usually smaller. This is borne out by the formulae which have been arrived at as a basis for staircase and step design:

where r is the rise or height of the step
and g the going (horizontal measurement from nosing to nosing of treads)

|  |  |
|---|---|
| indoors: | 2r + g = 23 in. (E.g.: 6 in. risers with 11 in. treads) |
|  | 2r + g = 58 cm. (E.g.: 15 cm. risers with 28 cm. treads) |
| outdoors: | 2r + g = 27 in. (E.g.: 5 in. risers with 17 in. treads) |
|  | 2r + g = 69 cm. (E.g.: 13 cm. risers with 43 cm. treads) |

In outdoor flights the formula is not completely comprehensive. The main point is that the rise is usually low (say 4 in.–6 in. [10–15 cm.]) and the going generous (say 19 in. or 15 in. [48 or 38 cm.]) in quite ordinary seeming flights.

[1] *Design and Detail of the Space between Buildings*, Elisabeth Beazley.

## Footbridges

Footbridges are one of the most difficult things to find information about since the small ones tend to be knocked up (very successfully) by an ingenious carpenter. These knowing men seldom work to drawings. Drawings, where provided, seldom survive.

## Suspension bridges

Some very attractive suspension bridges have been constructed recently; for spans above 80 ft. 0 in. [25 m.] a suspension bridge is likely to be the most economical form. Anyone interested might find the River Wye useful territory to explore. Here private land-owners have been slinging suspension bridges for many years. More recently, both the Radnorshire County Council and the Forestry Commission have constructed useful foot-bridges, whose spidery lightness enhances rather than intrudes upon the character of that very beautiful river and its wooded valley. They seem to net the space with a precision which makes one more aware both of its form and of the bosky trees, moving water and grassy meadows to which they make a perfect foil.

It is hard to think of a suspension bridge, great or small, that is not exciting simply to look at. Foot suspension bridges have the added advantage of being exciting to cross. Their transparency largely accounts for this; there is not much sense of separation from the river. These bridges are guyed laterally against sway, but the slight movement adds to

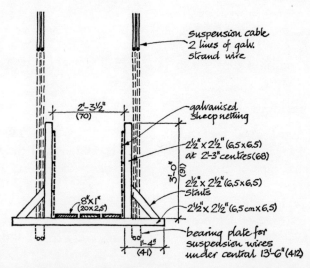

Section of a suspension bridge (Plate 65) indicates the economy of such structures. A wider bridge might feel unsafe since those crossing may want to be able to touch each side.

the immediacy of the experience which is rather akin to flying with an open cockpit. On one bridge where guys are removed in winter, since branches and flood debris might catch and break them, it is reported that energetic children have achieved a sway through 90°.

The dimensions which follow are taken from two particularly satisfactory Wye bridges. The widths of the footways (2 ft. 3½ in. [70 cm.] and 2 ft. 4 in.) may seem surprisingly small on paper; in fact they feel just the right width. If it were not possible to touch each side of the bridge, those crossing could feel unsafe.

*Cwm Coch Suspension Bridge* (near Rhayader). Designed and constructed by Mr. N. R. Hope, Building Contractor, Newbridge-on-Wye. See Plates 64 and 65.
Span: 108 ft. [32·76 m.]. Suspension cables: each consist of 2 galvanized wires.
Main posts: 7½ in. × 7½ in. [19 × 19 cm.].
Width of footway: 2 ft. 3½ in. [70 cm.].
Height of side fencing: 3 ft. 0 in. [91·5 cm.].
Walkway consists of three 8 in. × 1 in. [20 × 2·5 cm.] planks screwed to 2½ in. × 2½ in. [6·5 × 6·5 cm.] bearers at 2 ft. 3 in. [68 cm.] from centre to centre. Where the suspension cables run under the bridge (central 13 ft. 6 in. [4·10 m.] of the span) they bear on 4 in. × 3 in. [10 × 8 cm.] grooved runners. Sides of walkway are protected by 6 in. × 6 in.— 3½ in. [15 × 15–9 cm.] galvanized wire netting.

*Biblins Bridge* (near Symonds' Yat). Designed by the Forestry Commission Engineering Department. See Plates 66 and 67.
Span: 190 ft. 0 in. [57·91 m.].
Width of footway: 2 ft. 4 in. [71 cm.].
Width of footway at top of sides: 4 ft. 6 in. [137 cm.].
Height of sides: 3 ft. 6 in. [107 cm.].
Walkway and sides consist of 3 in. × 2 in. [8 × 5 cm.] × 3 s.w.g. Weldmesh sheets.

## Small timber footbridges

Some simple traditional small footbridges are shown opposite. Two general points, common to all bridges, can only be settled by site conditions and the amount and type of traffic: how much visual obstruction is desirable or tolerable, and what protection is necessary for the users.

*Handrails:* a low bridge with no handrail can be exactly in sympathy with its surroundings; for example see Plate 69. Nothing cuts across the lines of the trees and the water except the simple arc of the bridge itself. Where this is considered to be adequate, particular care must be taken that the bridge is wide enough as well as low enough to give no sensation of dizziness (width: around 4 ft. 0 in. [1.22 m.]; contrast with suspension bridges). Usually one handrail is necessary and is little detriment to the scene. On narrow bridges one rail usually looks much better than two (in fact; not on the drawing board when the

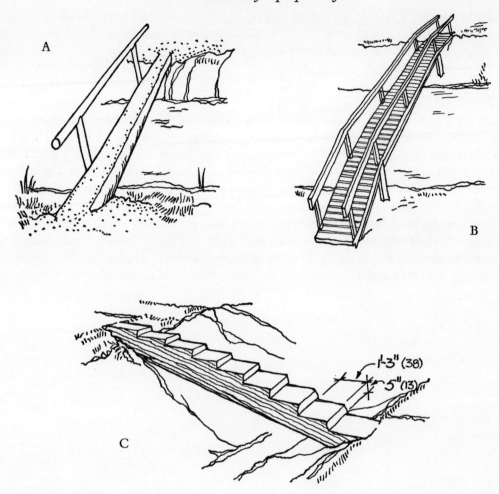

(A) A *half log* makes an adequate crossing. The top has been tarred and sprinkled with grit to prevent slipperiness.
(B) A small footbridge with *two handrails* may seem unnecessarily heavy.
(C) *Stepped bridge* cut from a log.

second disappears in the side elevation); many low bridges have given long service with one only. Over dangerous drops two rails with proper infilling below are obviously necessary.

*Non-slip footways:* timber footbridges, particularly those under trees, can become very slippery through damp encouraging mossy growth, and when wet planks become icy. This is often overcome by fixing galvanized chicken wire over the planks. It needs to be

93

fixed at frequent intervals to prevent picking up; mesh should be kept small to prevent the possibility of forming a trip. Another method, useful on solid baulks, is to coat the walkway in tar or bitumen and sprinkle grit before it sets (page 93).

## Piling causeways

Swampy places, too wet to cross without some sort of bridge or causeway, can be traversed by the age-old method of a causeway made of short timber piles (see Plate 68). These can be of varying diameter, around 6 in. [15 cm.]. Piles are driven home to form a solid walkway; length of pile will depend on local conditions. Suitable timbers include oak and ash (which have been used in Holland) and European larch. This sort of crossing, being at ground level, forms no visual obstruction in the landscape, a fact which can be a great advantage in certain circumstances. It also offers little obstruction to the water which can percolate between the piles. It is obviously only suited to swampy ground or slow moving streams where there is little change in water level. Perhaps for this reason, modern examples have only been seen in the Netherlands. Its wider application might be useful.

# 7

# Picnicking

## Cost

Even small picnic sites cost money: very little compared with the costs of other outdoor recreation, but picnicking, unlike camping, is of little benefit to the locality. Part of the operation is to stock up at home; this is an expedition to be provisioned at base. All that is likely to be contributed to the country is litter. It therefore seems quite unrealistic to expect the local authority to foot the bill alone. By the time this is in print it is to be hoped that picnic places, wherever sited, may be eligible for an Exchequer grant. This is vital. The present grant system whereby such provisions within a National Park may be eligible for a 75% grant, does little to ease the overall pressure on our finest country-side. If a substantial grant were available there would be incentive to upgrade those count-less dull or down-at-heel sites which are now little good to anyone. The only way to relieve pressure on the existing 'beauty spots' is immediately to create new ones: given modern techniques the most desolate site could be transformed in a matter of weeks.

The cost of wardening sites can be cut by making one warden, mobile in a Land Rover, responsible for several sites in one area. He can then show the flag as the site requires, maybe once or twice a day.

## Density and control of numbers

Work on likely acceptable densities for picnic areas is at an early stage.[1] 'Acceptable' must be considered both from the picnickers' point of view and that of his effect on the site. Intense gregariousness still surprises. On Milford Common, Cannock Chase, 700 cars were counted on six acres during a September Sunday afternoon ('65) although other nearby sites were available. Parking can be controlled in various ways but it seems likely that some picnic sites should be gated so that numbers can be regulated, and perhaps a picnic fee should be collected. Some sites in the U.S.A. are only available by advance booking; a procedure that could become necessary here.

[1] Following preliminary counts made in glades in the New Forest, R. P. Illingworth suggests that 10 cars (picnic parties) to the acre constitutes medium use; 5 light, and 16 heavy use.

## Siting

Experience indicates that there are few places five to forty miles[1] from the centres of population which are the 'wrong' distance for someone's day picnic. What is too near or too far from one town will probably be the right distance from another. Time on the road is perhaps a better guide: half to one hour is popular. The inexorable pressure building up suggests that any congenial site will become popular, but people will go much further for some unique objective (e.g. visiting a grandmother or an ancient monument) than simply to enjoy a pleasant picnic place. But the opening up of a new length of motorway can make the remote suddenly vulnerable; conversely a freeze could cut the range of the typical jaunt (the cost of petrol does not seem to deter people from buying cars, only using them; this experience holds good in both Holland and Denmark).

## Detailed site use

Please see Chapter 1, 'Behaviour Patterns', pages 32 and 38, where reactions of campers and picnickers to open space in the countryside are discussed.

## Terrain

1. *Light woodland and parkland* on well drained soil obviously make for ideal picnic grounds, but the ease with which soil can now be shifted and semi-mature trees transplanted has changed the whole time scale of providing shelter. It is not difficult to create the 'edge conditions' described in the first chapter.

Some of the most successful picnic places are small areas on the sunny fringe of a wood which take up to half a dozen cars. The felling of a very few trees can create open glades where cars can pull off the roads. The judicious tipping of a few loads of gravel can deal with damp spots if ground conditions are generally suitable.

At the other end of the scale, the enormous popularity of places like Clumber Park[2] (Plates 2 and 3), Nottinghamshire, derives from this same recognition of the reluctance of most people to wander far from their car, coupled with the right natural conditions. Here. over Whitsuntide, over 10,000 cars have been visually absorbed into around 3,000 acres [1,200 hectares] of eighteenth-century parkland landscape. The gregariousness of many

---

[1] See also *Public Recreation in National Forests*: A factual survey; W. E. S. Mutch. F. C. Booklet No. 21. Tables concerning recreational use of various forests are given. The figures below are from the New Forest.
day visit groups:  mean distance 38 miles
camping groups:  mean distance 95 miles
day visitors: more than 62% had travelled less than 25 miles
camping and caravan groups: 68% had travelled between 50 and 150 miles.
[2] Owned by the National Trust and financed by neighbouring local authorities.

people means that distribution is uneven, and some parts seem to be quite free of vehicles. The success of this technique has astonished those foreigners who stick to a separate car park/picnic place pattern.

At Clumber, cars can be parked anywhere off the road except in one part reserved for walkers only and also where there is young planting which would be damaged. Families return Sunday after Sunday with their children, grandparents and the family saloon. Some choose isolation; most are parked in small loose groups in open glades; others line grassy commons where spontaneous games of family cricket are earnestly pursued. Each car becomes the nucleus of a day camp; an extension of home. Chairs and tables, cushions and rugs and all the impedimenta of eating out are spreading around. Tremendous enjoyment is derived from the increasingly rare pleasure of being able to park and picnic wherever the spirit moves. It may seem a middle-aged pastime, but it is an ideal family outing. Babies can come in carrycots, children can roam around and join up with other families; mum can sit and knit; father can read the paper or tinker with the car. With young marriages, young families and more and more car owners who might once have opted for more active weekend entertainment, picnic places of the 'park where you like and picnic by the car' type are urgently needed.

Obviously this will only work where local conditions are suitable: the ground must be sufficiently light and naturally well drained to take cars. Equally important are the visual factors involved. Can cars be satisfactorily integrated into a particular stretch of landscape? This is usually only possible in wooded parkland.

2. *In forests.* It has been pointed out[1] that if forests are planned from the start for both timber production and recreation, recreational facilities may be included with little extra cost. The importance of *edge* is recognized.

'Compartment rides, forest roads and streams may easily amount to one mile of woodland edge per 100 acres [40 hectares]. Modest rideside improvements are often helpful to managements when they include such things as improved loading bays, and space on the edge of the compartment in which to work. A realization that these are places where the public might like to come will influence many factors in the planning of a forest all through its life, and yet have a minimal influence on costs.'

Numerous ways by which this quality could be implemented are suggested:

'(1) Consider the provision of car parks at all forest entrances when normal operations, such as roadworks and thinnings, are carried on near the entrance.
(2) Site rides to follow natural contours and features, and never to have straight lines for long distances. This precaution will avoid the "tunnel" effect which dense walls of conifers bring about.
(3) Accept relics of the old semi-natural hardwood woodland along new roads and riversides.

[1] *Recreation in British Forests,* M. H. Orrom, paper for Commonwealth Forestry Conference, India, 1968.

(4) Plant not only a mixture of species near rides, but start at an irregular distance from the ride centre.

(5) Try to arrange the inclination of the planting rows so that they cease to be obvious from the long view as quickly as possible. This may mean changing direction at contour rides.

(6) Use failed areas close to rides for picnic sites.

(7) Avoid a totally brashed (branches removed to a height of 6 ft. 0 in. [1·83 m.]) or pruned edge to compartments.

(8) Thin so that a ragged edge to a compartment is achieved.

(9) Consider the sunny sides of rides most carefully and plan picnic sites here rather than in the shade.

(10) Site loading bays so that a view is opened, and thus the bay can serve as a picnic site when not needed by the forest site.

(11) Put down an extra load of fine stone beside a bridge to provide a picnic site.

(12) Smooth rideside verges during road construction to provide grassy roadside paths where possible.

(13) Plan clear-felling in tiers, leaving the coupe (the strip to be felled) next to the ride to the last, and never clearing the rideside (windfirm) line but leaving this as a feature through which to view the new planting beyond.'[1]

3. *Water*. Pools, lakes (see Chapter 13 for construction notes) and streams are a certain magnet for both picnickers and campers. Wide use is now made of disused sand and gravel pits as the focal point of a picnic area. The feasibility of making such a pool in a sandpit depends on the height of the water table which is to be exposed.

The popularity of such pools for bathers has been firmly established in the Kennen-merduinen, Holland. When this area was turned into a recreational park there was much concern for the rare flora and fauna of two meres. To act as a counter-magnet, bathing pools within easy reach of car parks were created in the dunes. These pools are a few hundred yards from the sea. It has been found that the public not only gravitate to the new pools leaving the meres to the wildfowl, but choose to bathe in the pools rather than in the open sea, even on calm days. They seem to prefer not only the warmer water but also the sense of enclosure and protection given by the man-made pools to the wide expanses of the North Sea beaches. The only snag seems to be that the ducks like the new pools too and tend to foul them inconsiderately.

4. *Cindery wastes bordering estuaries and canals,* have great possibilities. They can be planned for both summer picnicking and as overlooks for cars in winter. The marvellous thing about water is that it can create the right conditions for a day picnic in semi-urban surroundings. Much of the seaside proves this. We squander wonderful industrial estuaries which could provide the Englishman with one of his favourite and least catered-for

[1] ibid.

spectator sports: ship-watching (the Dutch have popular picnic places for watching aircraft). Too often our estuaries, rivers and ship canals are cut off from the public by tantalizing cinderstrewn wastes where old cars disintegrate and willow-herb blows bravely over scrap dumps.

5. *Bridges.* The pleasure given by water can be immeasurably increased by bridges, even where they are not needed on any functional grounds. This is really another extension of 'edge effect' but it also means that people can have a much closer relationship with the water, whether only to look into it (as against at it) or to paddle or bathe from the bridge. A plank across a stream or a small footbridge across a bathing pool means that people can peer at fish, watch birds or just sit dangling their feet in the water.

Grander bridges which are no longer safe for modern traffic make admirable picnic sites. Incidentally, the seventeenth-century Kajou Bridge, in Isfahan, was designed not only to carry the road south to Shiraz but as a place to linger. Pavilions were constructed on it for the Shah and his court. From these he could enjoy the sound of the water, dammed by sluice gates which were also part of the bridge. They controlled the height of the river so that the gardens on either bank could be watered. The Shah could also enjoy watching his subjects picnicking on the buttresses between the sluice gates: after three hundred years the bridge is still the focus of the favourite Friday outing for the people of Isfahan.

6. *Flights of steps* make favourite places for office workers to eat their lunch-time sandwiches. There is no reason why they should not be popular where they happen to occur in the suburbs or more open country. Hard surfaces of steps or paving not only reflect the sun but being dry are much poorer conductors than damp earth or grass. Therefore their micro-climate may have a much higher temperature.

7. *Retired railway stations* linked already by their tracks to some of the best country could make excellent picnic places or camp sites. Many country railway stations have pleasant views and some are sited to command wide stretches of country. Unless of architectural value, most of the station buildings would be demolished, but some could be kept. It is valuable to have shelter available on any picnic site. Lavatories could be refurbished. Car parks are already provided.

8. *Unwanted farm or stable building* could form a nucleus for picnic sites. They are often in sheltered courtyards and may have some of the advantages noted under stations and steps.

## Lavatories

Please see Chapter 9. Whether or not lavatories need to be provided depends on several factors: (1) the length of time generally spent on the site (e.g. two hours or a whole day). (2) The terrain. (3) The density of people. Only knowledge of a particular site can decide whether lavatories are necessary. Obviously they must be provided on closely picnicked sites where people spend the whole day. Where picnicking averages two or three hours, they may not be necessary. The Netherlands Staatsbosbeheer were (1966) aiming to provide lavatories on day picnic sites where numbers reached a peak of 250 people.

Where lavatories are provided some form of wardening is also essential.

## Litter

Please see Chapter 16. A 'take-your-litter-home' system works on many sites. Elsewhere if the local authority collection is only made weekly the warden can replace litter sacks as necessary. Litter receptacles may be useful:

1. Where paths leave a car park.
2. At picnic pitches or groups of pitches, if they do not impair the character of the site.
3. Where any van selling ices or drinks may pull up. Litter receptacles look ridiculous and are of little use in the no man's land between car park and pitches.

## Picnic tables and benches

Picnic furniture is taken for granted in the U.S.A. where a sort of mystique about its provision has grown up. No pitch is complete without its own table, benches and fireplace. This idea originated before the days of universal motoring, and the easy carrying of aluminium furniture and camp stoves. It must be remembered, too, that the majority of American picnic sites are in woodland or forest shade, and that the ground under the trees is usually bare of grass and is therefore unconducive to the spreading of rugs and other picnic paraphernalia. It would in fact become either very dusty or very muddy. In the U.S.A., too, wild-life at ground level is often not the sort that can be sat on with impunity. In the U.K. picnickers seek the sun or partial shade so most sites are pleasantly grassed. It would therefore be absurd to introduce picnic tables here as a matter of course. Observation shows that even the Netherlands (more picnic table orientated than this country) rate the need for a picnic table low on the list of picnic amenities. Sense of enclosure, for instance, is more important.

However well designed the picnic furniture may be, there are many sites where tables and benches are quite out of character and have an urbanizing effect. On the other hand in more arcadian, as against rural or wild, settings where large numbers congregate, tables can be useful to the planner as well as the picnicker. A well sited table can act as a decoy and suggest to people where they might picnic.

Tables grouped near, say, a woodland shelter can give each picnic party a focal point. In this way gregarious picnicking can gain a sociable quality without a sense of overcrowding. In British Columbia, the Department of Recreation and Conservation has sites of this kind with as little as 10 ft. 0 in. [3 m.] between tables (see Plate 70). Sociable picnic groves can thus be planned at quite high densities.

## Picnicking

Picnic tables are particularly useful on lay-bys: few people want to picnic on grass at exhaust pipe level, nor do they want to unpack their own table and chairs for a short stop. Tables are unlikely to seem out of place in a lay-by setting.

But tables and benches dumped at random look absurd however suitable the site. The placing of picnic furniture is governed by much the same principles as the placing of garden or park furniture, but it is much easier to go wrong in the open country than in the enclosed garden or semi-urban town park. Benches scattered in the open with no relation to trees or planting, walls or buildings can seem ridiculously forlorn. The space needs to be furnished in scale with itself, with benches and tables related to other parts of the design; this usually means that something of much greater visual importance than a mere piece of picnic furniture will be needed to integrate it into the landscape (see page 74).

The furniture must also be big enough to be in scale with other natural features. For this

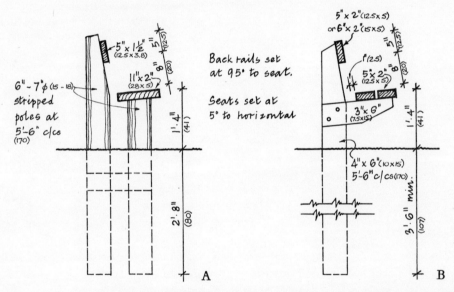

Benches on trails, at view points, in gardens, etc. often look best if they consist only of a single plank but they are much more comfortable if given a simple back board in the right position, i.e. low enough to support the spine rather than the shoulders. Those on the market tend to be either too expensive and sophisticated for this sort of setting, or they do not give support where it is most needed. Seats are often on the high side ( 18″ [45–46 cm.] is a typical height of a dining-room chair, rather than an easy chair). The designs shown here are based (A) on a design by Netherlands Staatsbosbeheer and (B) on a design produced by the Maine State Park Commission. (Heights of both benches and backs have been adjusted.)
(A) 6″–7″ [15–18 cm.] diameter rough poles stripped of bark, spiked together below grade for stability.
(B) The seat is cantilevered on bearers from the uprights.

reason, among others, a fallen log may look better under mature trees than a man-made bench.

Erosion and mud are likely wherever provision is made for picnickers since numbers of people are encouraged to picnic repeatedly on precisely the same spot. This can be mitigated by choosing the right site, seeing that surface water is not going to drain into it, and putting down a few shovelfuls of gravel below benches etc. where puddles are likely to form.

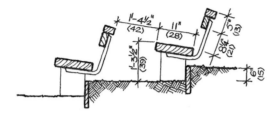

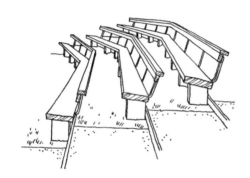

Seating in an open-air theatre which is particularly comfortable. The benches are supported on concrete stumps at 5′ 0″ from centre to centre. The backs are fixed on $1\frac{1}{2}$″ × $1\frac{1}{2}$″ [3·81 × 3·81 cm.] steel angle. (Roanoke, N. Carolina.)

In both cases the benches and backs project about 12″ beyond their supports. Span of seat will depend on the size of timbers.

## Types of furniture

1. *Timber benches and tables.* See opposite for a typical design, now widely used in North America and Europe. Suitable homegrown timbers include: larch, sweet chestnut, elm and oak. 6 ft. 0 in. × 2 ft. 6 in.–3 ft. 0 in. [180 × 75–90 cm.] is a usual size but tables up to 15 ft. 0 in. [4·5 cm.] long are popular for parties and for real feasts; the kind of meal a French family might consider picnicworthy. Table legs can be concreted into the ground where tables may be stolen, but many designs are so heavy that it is unlikely that they will be removed except by those so determined that legs would be sawn. The disadvantage of this type is that it gives no back rest, and the supporting rail of the bench has to be negotiated—a possible disadvantage to elderly people. If the bench plank projects well beyond this rail (14 in. [35 cm.] as shown in the drawing), there is space to sit on the outside of the rail. Tables and benches designed in other ways to overcome this problem tend to be awkward and cumbersome.

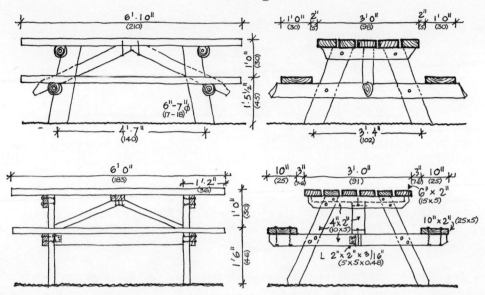

Numerous designs of this type have been produced. Some are light enough for the table to be shifted according to the weather; others have legs concreted into the ground. The bench and table tops should have a generous cantilever, at least 12″ [30 cm.], to allow someone to sit at the table without having to step over the rail. Rails set on the inside of the uprights would give more leg room. The edge of the table top should not be more than 3″ [7·6 cm.] from the bench for comfort. All edges should be chamfered. All joints are bolted with round headed bolts. Nuts are countersunk. Nail holes should be filled with mastic.

2. *Timber tables and benches as above but with tubular steel supports or concrete legs.* Both these types seem to be growing in popularity in the U.S.A. where they have some advantages which do not apply in the U.K., e.g. that the legs are termite proof; or that they are also less likely to be used for firewood than all-timber furniture (maybe more important in a campfire-conscious country). They seem to be suited to sophisticated settings. Steel must be galvanized or thoroughly painted, and maintained, and nothing looks worse than concrete which has been damaged or through which rust is beginning to stain; therefore very sound workmanship is imperative. Timber has the advantage of being amenable to first-aid repairs on the site. Tubular steel legs are usually chained to an anchor bar in the ground; the horizontal parts at ground level may trap litter. Concrete legs can be set in. All concrete designs (with timber seats in temperate or cool climates) have been developed. Finish and design of a high standard can produce a piece of equipment well suited to outdoor cafés and picnic places in urban or suburban settings.

3. *Timber tables and benches on pipe legs* (see page 104). This design gives minimum obstruction to users (see paragraph 1 Page 102), and has the advantage of an unobstructed ground area which provides no traps for litter etc.

This design gives minimum obstruction both to users and also at ground level where litter, dead grass, etc. may be trapped. 2″ × 2″ × ¼″ [5 × 5 × 0·64 cm.] L is welded to the 4″ [10·2 cm.] and 3″ [7·6 cm] internal diameter, pipes which are set in concrete.

4. *Log furniture* cut to form seats can have positively sculptural quality but is often reminiscent of gnomes. This may depend on scale as much as on the mood of the beholder. Logs can be chosen to fit all shapes and sizes of people. They also have the advantage of making looser circular clumps which may be more easily integrated into their surroundings than the rectangular slabs of the typical picnic table.

5. Tree stumps left in the ground can make excellent nuclei for picnics particularly if they are sawn off at an angle, sloping to the sun. Thoughtful foresters have been known to cut stumps to form back rests. These, and the items mentioned in paragraph 5 below, are good for the more lounging type of picnic favoured by many British.

6. Fallen logs and big boulders are very useful as back rests for picnickers. Both might be dragged a short distance to improve on their siting (e.g. for shelter/sun/view).

## Drinking water

Drinking water points: please see pages 147 to 148.

Water points may be expensive to provide. They are not essential but are useful to picnickers. If lavatories are provided a water point can easily be fixed on the outside wall. If a supply pipe crosses the picnic area, at least one drinking point, probably near its entrance, can be taken off it. If it is difficult to encourage the public to use the whole of the site a water point can be sited further in.

## Fireplaces and barbecues

Lighting a fire has never been an integral part of the typical British picnic as it is of the American. Now, in spite of bottled gas and vacuum flasks, a meal out of doors means a barbecue to countless American families so although the picnic fireplace might be seldom

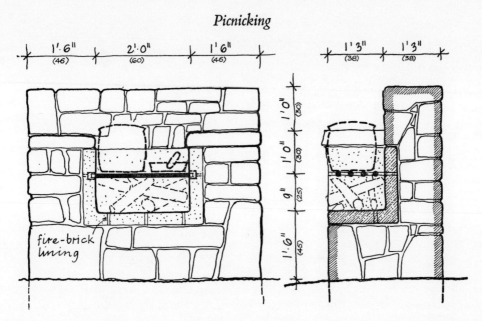

*Fireplaces* may be needed on group camp sites. Size will depend on the scale of cooking but in all cases protection at the back and sides is necessary if pots are not to be cooled by the elements as they heat from below. It might be difficult to find enough coin stones to build this type in stone unless there was a new ruin available to quarry. Alternatively brick could be used. Grate bars, say 1″ [2·5 cm.] diameter, should be in sleeves to allow for expansion. Alternatively they might be set in a very weak cement mix at one end.

used at roadside halts it is still very popular in recreational parks where people go for a day outing; probably very much more than in National Park picnic sites where people are on tour with the object of seeing the park. On the other hand, the NPS find that individual fireplaces are still popular on some longer stay camp sites where they are used to sit around in the evenings rather than for cooking. Campers invite each other to their fires and this casual entertaining can enhance the quality of a camping holiday.

In the U.K., concern about fire and lack of firewood combine with the weather and a natural inclination not to bother with picnic fires. At the same time the growing popularity of evening barbecues, both the neat charcoal grill in the patio, and the giant driftwood fires on the August beaches accompanied by guitars, indicates a trend to the camp fire as a form of spontaneous entertainment. Whether we will ever be willing to buy firewood or to bring our own charcoal as the Americans do is hard to predict.[1]

[1] The Forestry Commission has a barbecue site at Gortin Glen Forest Park which can be hired for £3–£5 for an evening plus 2/6 per car parking fee. It is limited to 120 people. Advance booking is essential as it is proving so popular. Charcoal is available on the site. This suggests that American practice has anyway reached Northern Ireland.

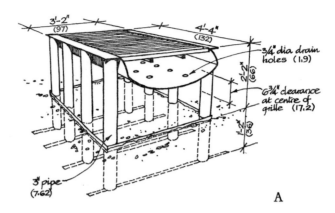

(A) Grill designed by Metropolitan Park Dept. Akron, Ohio, for large parties. Metal flats are welded to the pipes below ground level for rigidity, to prevent tipping and to prevent the grill from being removed.

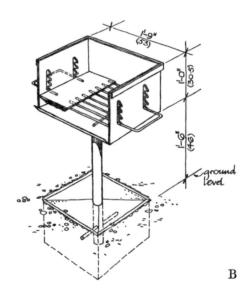

(B) Type now used by the American NPS. More foolproof and less liable to vandalism than its predecessor in which the grill had to be removed from the box in order to adjust its position (like the typical oven tray in a domestic cooker). A more sophisticated model allows for the pipe to turn so that the grill can be rotated according to the wind.

106

*Fireplace design* has altered considerably in recent years. It is now generally accepted that the cooking grill should be at the height of an ordinary kitchen hot-plate; say 2 ft. 3 in.–2 ft. 9 in. [75–85 cm.] above the ground. Squatting uncomfortably at ground level is considered archaic by most field cookers including the Boy Scouts Association.

The fireplace should face the prevailing wind so that smoke is not blown into the cook's face. Ground in front of the fireplace must be well drained if it is not to puddle. Gravel or chippings can be rolled in.

Camp fireplaces fall into two main types: the traditional wood fire and the charcoal-burning grill.

*Wood fireplaces:* In the British climate cooking out of doors, other than frying or grilling, is fraught with the fact that the weather tends to cool a kettle or cooking pot almost as quickly as a fire heats it from below. Thus fireplaces which give protection at the sides and back are much more efficient. That shown on page 105 has this advantage.

The sophistication of cooking at waist level obviously makes for much more expensive fireplaces. Good masonry practice is essential if they are not to look tatty and quickly disintegrate. Stone that will not expand and crack with heat must be chosen; even so a fire-brick lining is advised. Bars for the cooking grill must be fixed to allow for expansion or they may crack the stone. A sizeable slab to use as a work top beside the fireplace is handy since the ground is now at the wrong height to act as a table.

*Barbecue grills* are very popular on American sites, particularly those where little firewood is available. The NPS has worked out a design with manufacturers which consists basically of a shallow steel box with a metal grill which can be adjusted to different levels. This is mounted on a tubular steel leg which can be set in concrete on the site. In some more sophisticated models the box can be rotated to suit the wind. The main points of this design are that besides being efficient as a cooking stove it is very robust and reasonably inexpensive. Unfortunately although a variety of barbecue grills are now imported from Scandinavia and the U.S.A., transport costs make it uneconomic to import any but the more expensive 'fancy' types which are anyway not tough enough for public use. For large barbecue parties a long trough made of sheet metal provides an effective answer (see page 106).

*Gas fired barbecues.* In Canberra, Australia, a gas fired barbecue is being tried by the parks department. It consists of a brick housing 9 ft. 9 in. × 3 ft. 6 in. × 2 ft. 9 in. [3·0 × 1·07 m. × 84 cm.], in which are housed hot-plates and rings, which are available through a coin-operated meter. So far, no particular snags are apparent, but it must be kept clean.

# 8

# Camp sites

## Density

The *Model Standards,* Caravan Sites and Control of Development Act, 1960, lays down that on holiday caravan sites:

1. The gross density should not exceed 25 caravans to the acre.
2. Every caravan should not be less than 20 feet from any other caravan in a separate occupation.

These Model Standards do not cover tents but the Camping Club of Great Britain works to a maximum of 25 units per acre.

Experience both of European and American sites suggests that for many camps these figures are extravagantly lavish; on others, in the U.K. and abroad, far lower densities give the pleasant illusion to the camper that he is on his own. The weakness of our system seems to be that it tends to impose an average standard on everyone regardless of the inclinations of the camper and the type of camp. It has probably derived from the laudable aim of preventing slum conditions due to overcrowding and of giving the overworked planning authorities some kind of tool with which to work. Prevention of fire spread is of course vital and consultation with Fire Officers might produce interesting results. Density is discussed under types of camp site.

## Function

Camps vary enormously by reason both of terrain and *function* but here, in the U.K., an illogical prestige seems to have been bestowed by many of those responsible for camp layout (be they professional planners or club committee members) on the preference for camping on one's own, 'away from the crowd'. A curious snob-value is attached to this attitude. The result is a sameness of brief whether the camp is an overnight transit camp or is intended for one or two weeks' holiday. A pride in low density for its own sake is common.

## Camp sites

This state of affairs has probably been furthered by the fact that the majority of those connected with camp organizations themselves prefer it that way. I must admit to being one who, in remote country, would spend a long time searching for an empty place where a dormobile might be tucked away on its own overnight, but this aim for solitude gives no right to any sense of superiority. It is not even particularly civilized: to the Greeks of classical Athens it would probably have been incomprehensible. The countless caravanners who have taken the golden road to Samarkand would have been equally mystified, and it is doubtful whether those nobles and gentlemen who camped on the Field of the Cloth of Gold would have thought much of the densities laid down by Model Standards of 1960. Camping for these people provided a chance for that most civilized of all human occupations: exchanging ideas and stories with their fellow men.

Quite elementary observation of human behaviour suggests that we have not changed much: it is a great mistake to imagine that the majority of those who choose a camping holiday do so in order to escape from other people, or that solitary minded campers cannot enjoy the more 'urban' type of camp on occasion. Incidentally, some of the senior members of the American National Park Service are among the first to recognize the social element of camping: that for the great majority it has little to do with getting into backwoods on their own.

People camp for an extraordinary variety of reasons. That most commonly given is economic. The cost of taking a family with, say, only three children to a hotel or lodging is prohibitive to most. The cost of camp equipment can also be high, but it is considered as capital expenditure; it can be used again and again.

Of equal, and to some of even greater importance, is the sense of freedom. Get up when you want; meals when you want; informality of dress or non-dress; domestic chores to a minimum and anyway different (camping has this advantage over most holiday houses). It is at the opposite pole to the seaside boarding house, with its inevitable anxieties about children's behaviour and punctuality for meals.

### Planning brief

Perhaps one of the most re-creating things about family holidays is not only for dad to see the kids each day all day but for everyone in the family to be able to find kindred spirits with new ideas and occupations: yogi, or canoeing, or a Provençal variation of Lancashire hot pot. Somewhere on the site such people will exist and for the typical family, often routine bound, casual meetings and time to follow them up may be one of the chief pleasures of the holiday. Camp sites should be designed in such a way that chance encounters can flourish. Incidentally, recognition of the importance of such meetings is underlined by the stress the American National Park Service lays on the campfire, now obsolete for all practical purposes.

## Siting

The two jackpot questions in siting of camps are: the old problem of the integration of the camp into its surrounding landscape; and stemming from this, but of ever-increasing importance as more and more people want to camp, the distance of the camp from the place to be enjoyed. If the character of coastline, mountain or river valley derives largely from its loneliness or solitude it is impossible both to retain this character and to absorb a camp site. It is a clear case of not being able to have our cake and eat it.

In America, with her vast open space and belief in individual freedom, similar conclusions have been reached. It would be a pity if we, here in the U.K., in an effort to 'catch up' with what is happening abroad, hooked on to the thinking of the 1950s rather than of today.

In the U.S.A. discussion is long and strong as to how the clause in the National Park Enabling Act concerning conservation for future generations should be balanced against the need for public access now. Heart-searching on a nation-wide scale goes on over the fate of places like the Yosemite Valley, the visitation of which by car-borne campers is turning it from a National Park into what has been termed a national slum. The long-term answer here may be to close the valley to private vehicles, and even to ban camping on the valley floor.

In American National Parks a clear distinction is now being drawn between camping for its own sake as a means of recreation and camping in order to have a base from which to enjoy a particular area. 'Perhaps in certain parks of the System (NPS) it would be advantageous if camping were eliminated altogether and handled by private enterprise on less spectacular or non-historic lands adjacent to those which we administer. But so long as we provide camping in national park areas we must limit the space and the time for this activity in order that we observe our mandate "to conserve the scenery and the natural and historic objects and the wildlife therein and to provide for the enjoyment of the same in such manner and by such means as will leave them unimpaired for the enjoyment of future generations".'[1]

Camp sites, and particularly caravan sites, are among the most difficult things to integrate into the landscape, even when obvious hazards like skyline siting are avoided. Vans tend to dot a field restlessly, too small and spread out to contribute to the general pattern of the landscape; too large to be integrated as incidental to it. Scale is usually basically wrong. And, unfortunately, British caravans, unlike many on the Continent and in the U.S.A., are often sloppily designed in terms of form, and are unsatisfactory to look at in their own right. In the context of their surroundings their colour and texture are often out of key.

Like everything else new to a stretch of countryside, camp sites need to be considered both from the point of view of the user and the onlooker. Luckily in this case the two

---

[1] Lykes, Ira B., in a memorandum on camp site development in American National Parks, 1967.

outstanding requirements of each are complementary rather than conflicting, so some hard thinking on the ground, and not in two dimensions only over a plan, may produce a solution that satisfies both.

From the point of view of the camper some shelter from the elements is essential; from outside, the site must be anchored to the landscape by something visually more important than itself, which is in scale with the general landscape pattern. This may be some natural topographical feature such as a small valley or fold in the ground, or a man-made feature like a disused quarry, an old orchard, walled garden or an abandoned hamlet. Abandoned railway stations have possibilities with their available hard-standings, buildings, services and drainage. Scrubby light woodland (of little value as timber), trees, hedgerows, earth embankment or terracing—any or all of these can be helpful, and those who have to find sites in windswept coastal areas may feel with some justification that wooded areas produce few problems. Trees can absorb most wonderfully by providing degrees of shelter and broken cover: an open glade is one of the most attractive of all sites from everyone's point of view.

However, treeless areas are often less treeless than is supposed. Consider the salt-bitten sycamore clump, cut triangular in section by the prevailing south-westerlies, which is typical of so many Welsh coastal farms. There could be no more effective way of integrating a foreign element, be it a camp site or a factory, into this kind of scenery than by giving it the protection which anchors the traditional farmstead. If sycamore (or whatever may be common to the district) is given a start by planting in the lee of a field bank, results will be both quicker and more akin to the landscape pattern. Sea buckthorn has been planted with great success both to stop dune erosion and to give shelter (its use is limited in some districts because of the difficulty of getting rid of rabbits). This book deals mainly with the 'hard landscape' but it would be absurd to discuss the design of camp sites without stressing in passing the importance of planting and of planning ahead so that planting has time to make headway.[1] However obvious it may seem, we seldom do it enough, particularly within a site, and not merely round its edges. Earth banks, grassed and allowed to harbour the local wildflowers as did the hedgerows not so long ago, have also been used most effectively both to integrate a camp into its surroundings and to give privacy and shelter. (See Plate 79.) Co-operation with a neighbouring project which has surplus soil (e.g. from road works) can make such designs relatively cheap.

It must be remembered that most special camp sites (as against farm sites) are fenced off and therefore will not merge with the surrounding country. This fencing has been found necessary both by the developers who do not want non-campers who are not paying for the camp's facilities to wander in and use them, and also by the campers who like to feel their possessions have some degree of protection when they are not on the site.

[1] Black Italian poplar, for instance, can grow three to five feet in a year but may itself be an intrusion.

III

## Future expansion and economic viability

It is important to plan for success. It is difficult to make well-equipped small seasonal camp sites in remote areas viable in economic terms so it may be very helpful to be able to expand a site when its popularity is proved. If this is not considered at the initial planning stage it might be found to be impossible practically (no suitable ground, insufficient access) or inadvisable aesthetically (e.g. no possible screening).

Such sites might survive economically if allowed a small quota of static vans which would pay rent the whole year round. From the landscape point of view the conditions of wholly static sites apply. But the character of sites which have *no* permanent buildings (e.g. even lavatories) could be quite altered by static vans and it is likely that they should be strongly resisted on any site which might otherwise be cleared each winter.

## Soil

Light gravelly and sandy soils are naturally best suited to camp sites. Chalk drains well but can be very slippery if it becomes bald. It is vital to check that a site is not subject to occasional flooding. Damp sites can be drained to ditches with 4 in. [10 cm.] clay field tiles; a local expert or a firm of agricultural drainage contractors should be consulted. Heavy vehicles are likely to crack unprotected drains so the expert will want to see the proposed plan of the camp.

Traditional tents with wooden pegs must be pitched on ground into which the pegs can be driven. But many of the small modern air tents (domestic scale) and framed tents are fixed with a few metal skewer type pegs. They mostly have floors so the weight of things within the tent is useful in preventing them being blown away.

## Slope of site

Tents and dormobiles need fairly level pitches because they cannot accommodate a fall as does a jacked caravan. Some fall is acceptable if people can sleep with heads uphill. Falls of 1 in 15 are fairly common. Steep sites, properly terraced and planted, can be particularly attractive to campers since one line of pitches can look over the top of the next. Planting must be in scale with the bold form of terracing and in keeping with the landscape as a whole. A rock garden attitude is unlikely to answer.

## Car parking on camp sites

Few British campers want to be separated from their car. It is invaluable as an extension of the tent or caravan; a giant lockable pocket. But there are occasions when a separate car park and a trolley service from it to the camp pitch can greatly enhance the quality of the camp, either from the landscape angle or from the campers' point of view.

In *tented camps*, sites can be developed in much greater sympathy with the existing topography if they are not cut by roads. This may also mean greater privacy for the individual camper, e.g. tented pitches in woodland glades can be linked to a cark park by small paths; gradients and contours do not have to be levelled as they might for car access. In dunes where erosion from car wheels would make a camp site impracticable, foot and trolley access may be quite acceptable. Tents can lose themselves in folds of the ground which could never be reached by a motor vehicle.

On certain *caravan sites*, particularly those where children are likely to spend a considerable amount of their time playing around the pitches, life can be much more peaceful if cars are parked separately.

Where the principle of separation between pitches and cars is adopted the camp should be planned with direct footpath access to service buildings, car parks and main gate, and with a one-way ring road system feeding the various camping areas. This is simply a form of Radburn planning as now adopted in many housing schemes.

## Separation of tents and caravans

The system whereby many sites will only take either tents or caravans is still fairly common in the U.K., but was not found overseas. It probably derives from the two separate Acts of Parliament under which sites are administered: tents, Public Health Act, 1936; caravans, the Caravan Sites and Control of Development Act, 1960. (Siting of both is of course governed by the Town and Country Planning Act.) It is an artificial distinction which can cause considerable inconvenience to campers, especially to dormobile owners who do not belong to either category, particularly if they carry a tent (even worse off are the enterprising do-it-yourself converters of non-standard vehicles). Provided the would-be camper is adequately equipped with chemical closet, etc., on those sites where no facilities are provided, and club members have priority, it is difficult to see the advantages of this system. Separation can be equally inconvenient to planners since it could mean that two separate sites are necessary where one might be adequate.

The condition of the ground and type of terrain may be an important consideration in the allocation of pitches. Some sites or parts of a site may be unsuited to vehicles (including cars). Conversely, the grass of pitches which have taken tents may need a rest from tent floors or groundsheets; after a week 'fallow', grass might take a van rather than another tent.

But it is usually much more important from both the campers' and warden's point of view to group like people with like. Thus a site which is initially planned to allow for a certain amount of grouping is likely to be more successful both socially and visually. Campers feel they belong to their part of the site and enjoy it and look after it accordingly. Planting can make a cohesive pattern of a medley of separate units. Some of the best Dutch and Danish sites are subdivided by planting. Family camps and girls are grouped together; other sections are for youths or for group camps (e.g. a canoeing club). This means that families with small children are not disturbed by those returning from hilarious

H                                                            113

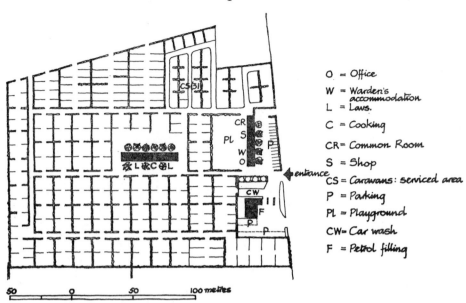

The Sundbyvester Camping Site, opened 1966—Architect: J. Hansen. Site: flat land in the suburbs of Copenhagen, lately an allotment site. A well designed, efficient camp ground. Allotment hedges have been retained to give both privacy to campers and visual cohesion to the camp.

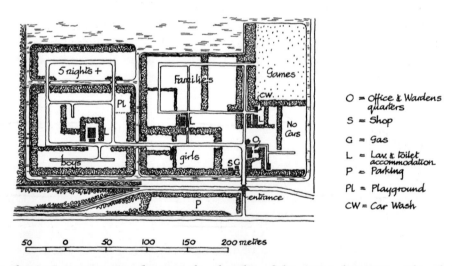

Amsterdamse Camp Site. Site: flat ground at the edge of the Amsterdamse Bos. This pleasantly designed site is inward looking, subdivided by generous hedging and planting. Both this and the Sundbyvester Site make no attempt to be unnaturally 'natural'.

parties; nor are youths bothered by parents demanding that their transistors should be turned down unreasonable early.

In other camps (both high density transit camps and low density recreational camps) there may be no attempt at division. The warden leaves it to the camper to find his own pitch. He then returns to register at the office.

## Internal planning

An opportunity for sociability is an important ingredient of many camping holidays. Since many 'high-class' sites seem to be planned primarily to keep campers away from each other it may be worth looking at them from the opposite point of view.

Chance meetings are as likely to flourish in the first instance in the vicinity of the service buildings (i.e. no man's land) as in the camping area itself. This is probably because the territorial instincts of campers generally (and not just the British) are fairly highly developed. The office and shop are both focal points of camp life where people naturally congregate. But they are usually small buildings, and those inside are chiefly occupied with business, so casual conversations tend to start outside rather than in the building. Too often they are fraught with wind and rain. Here a generous sheltered area, porch or verandah, protected from the prevailing wind, can immeasurably improve the comfort and quality of camp life and, incidentally, the performance of the building by sheltering the entrance. Oddly enough, in the British climate where deep porches or covered space would be most appreciated they are rarely considered to be necessary. Yet they are relatively cheap and campers who will anyway be wearing outdoor clothes and usually have plenty of time, are ideally equipped to enjoy them. But shelter and some sun are essential if people are to pause.

A bench or two set in the angle between, say, the camp office and shop, preferably under a projecting roof, can provide quite cheaply a place to foregather while waiting for the office to open, or for the rest of the party, or for the milk or mail to arrive. The camp office will be near the main gate and so a sitting space outside can become a vantage point where the comings and goings of camp life can be idly watched; a sort of village green of the community. On a French camp a broad flight of steps outside a camp shop became a focal point in camp life.

Too often, in fact, the only place likely to provide shelter is either the dustbin compound (screened for aesthetic reasons) or the lavatory block. The hub of a community was once the village well and there seems to be every indication that the fresh water points on a camp could, often at little additional expense, be given their traditional status. Again they should be sited with some shelter from the wind, and if a low wall has to be provided to protect the standpoint, it can be made the right height for sitting on (15 in.–18 in. [35–45 cm.]). Failing this, the simplest perch, a plank on two stumps or a fallen log, sited right, can change dull chores into sociable ones. People often have to wait their turn at water points so it is as well if they can do so in comfort. If this idea is adopted, bins should not be incorporated into the same 'service' units. A play area for small children with a few very simple bits of equipment could be sited near one of these gathering points (not the main gate). Or in big camps it can form a social nucleus in itself.

## Types of camp site

Camps fall into five main categories:

(1) Transit camps: length of stay one to two nights.
(2) Recreational camps.
(3) Group camps for organizations (e.g. Guides or Scouts).
(4) Individual camps for solitary minded campers.
(5) Static sites for recreational use.

There is often overlap of use but it seems easiest to discuss the types separately, and to group the camp buildings and services which are common to most types at the end of the section.

## (1) Transit camps

The real function of this type of camp (typical stay one to two nights) is not always taken into account. Too often they are considered simply as ordinary camps for overnight stops, but they have much more in common with an eastern caravanserai. The true transit camp has an urban character whether it is sited in lonely country or on the outskirts of a town. It hums with activity and the coming and going of travellers into the unknown. To be bound for the Cornish Coast, or the Western Isles, particularly, if you are aged ten and it is the first time, is exciting. It is part of the function of a transit camp both to provide efficient servicing for such journeys and to sharpen the excitement by allowing such camps to be different from others.

*Siting.* It could be enormously helpful if transit camps were set up as stage halts to the main holiday areas: the West Country, Wales and Scotland. This is not the place to discuss the overall strategy, but a few general points about siting are worth consideration:

A transit camp may generate between seven and fourteen times as much traffic as the recreational camp. If they are run to meet the demand of travelling at off-peak hours, this traffic will be on the move at any time throughout the day or night. It is, therefore, essential that transit camps should be sited close enough to the main route which they are intended to serve, otherwise country lanes and by-roads which act as feeders from the trunk road will be congested, both by the quantity and the weight of the traffic, and those living in farms and villages on these roads will be disturbed. From the point of view of the camper, proximity to a trunk route need not cause a noise problem. In Germany, camps have been sited round the sandpits from which autobahns were constructed. Relatively thin screens of conifers combined with a change of level (the surrounding ground being below the roadway) are enough to reduce the traffic roar to a light hum at only a couple of hundred yards' distance.

## Camp sites

*Plan.* Campers using transit stages will usually be tired. First and foremost, they need an efficiently designed camp-ground where they can find what they need with the minimum fuss, relax after a long drive, sleep and move on.

Lay-by sites. Fear has been expressed that trunk road lay-bys where public lavatories are provided may turn into overnight halts. Instead of being dismayed we should grasp this almost ready made solution by encouraging individual operators or local authorities to step in and provide an overnight parking service at these sites. A full time warden (living on the site, perhaps in a caravan) would be responsible for the running and cleanliness of the site and collect parking fees; he might also run a filling station.

When choosing new sites for public lavatories on lay-bys, provision for this type of service might be borne in mind. The only extra requirement is adequate parking space for vans and pitching space for tents. Technically this might be described as an overnight (or day, for those who prefer to travel at night) parking ground. This might absolve it from the low density requirements of the Caravan Sites and Control of Development Act, 1960, provided escape in case of fire is properly considered. There seems to be no reason why vans need be more than 5–10 ft. [1·5–3 m.] apart for such brief stays. Tents simply need enough space for their guy ropes.

A more elaborate transit halt would include the following services:

(1) A *petrol pump* and, if possible, a *service station* probably let to a concessionnaire and sited immediately outside the camp gate.

(2) The *camp office* will be busier in proportion to the size of the camp than in a long-stay camp. It should, therefore, be proportionally bigger: 6 ft.–8 ft. [2–2·5 m.] minimum of counter space, rather than a guichet, may be needed.

(3) In a transit camp, the *warden's quarters* must be immediately adjacent to his office.

(4) *Lavatories and washrooms:* see pages 135–149. Lavatories for camp pitches may be central or dispersed according to the size of the camp.

(5) A *camp shop.* A particularly attractive concession since campers beginning a holiday or making for the wilds will stock up here if prices are competitive. Many continental camps have small supermarkets.

(6) A *cafeteria,* possibly an extension to the shop, can be exceptionally popular in transit camps, where tired travellers may not want to cook.

(7) *Play space* sited near the shop is particularly valuable since children will have been cramped in cars all day.

(8) *Hot showers, a launderette and a drying room.* All these can make a transit camp sited at a route junction a very popular port of call between more rugged spells of camping. (Cf. the Stage house, Inverewe.)

(9) *Lean-to shelters* to individual pitches can be particularly useful on transit sites. Gear can be quickly dumped under cover for the night. (See page 167.)

(10) *Chemical closet emptying point* sited apart from the rest of the service area. See page 149.

Shade is important to campers in many parts of the U.S.A. so camps tend to be merged in woodland, often at fairly low densities, but where pitches are not defined, density may be very high on nationally famous sites at peak holiday periods; solitude, or the illusion of it, is not sought by many American campers.

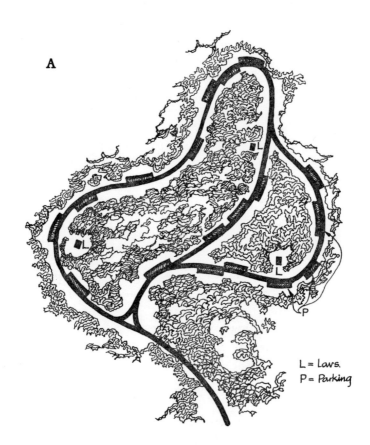

**A**

L = Laws.
P = Parking

(A) Camp site with cars parked in groups (not in one big car park) and tents pitched freely in gladed woodland.

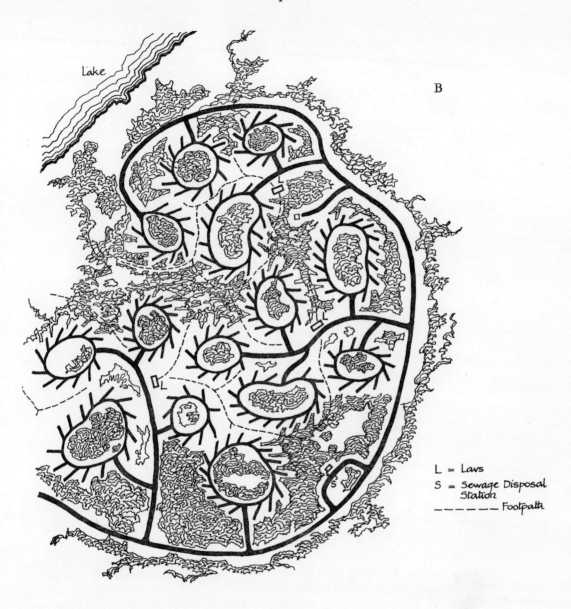

Lake

B

L = Laws
S = Sewage Disposal
Station
_ _ _ _ _ _ Footpath

(B) Layout for campers (often with trailers) in which each car is parked by its own pitch.

119

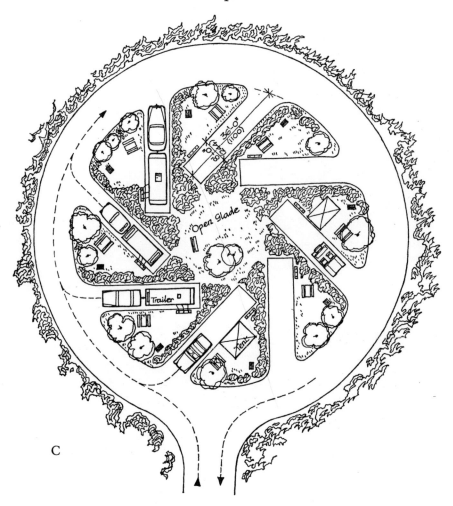

C

(C) This plan, based on a recent NPS design by Ira B. Lykes, aims to increase density and cater for the growing number of touring campers who spend one or two nights only in one place. Large caravans, like the typical suburban house, make poor use of a site because they have windows all round: a view or outlook on all sides is unnecessary. Here the outlook of the van is limited to two directions, i.e. on to its own private camp area which is screened from the next van by planting (initially helped by hurdles). The centre of the circle (which contained a lavatory block in the NPS design) could become a small glade with a play area for children (safe from traffic) and a sitting space where campers can foregather. The overall diameter of the site has been reduced since the typical British car plus caravan does not need the 50′ 0″ required by the Americans.

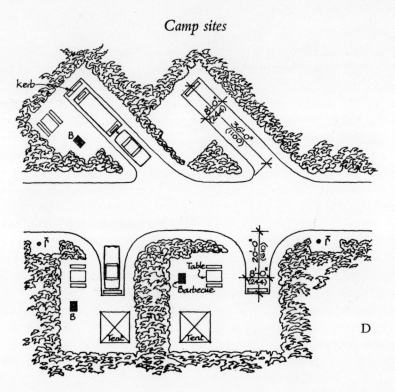

(D) NPS camp parking details, scaled down to sizes of British cars and caravans.

*Pitches.* Unless natural features lend themselves to an informal layout of vans and tents it seems sense to plan a transit camp in a regular pattern, getting in as many pitches as the regulations will allow. A higher density, perhaps 30–40 to the acre, could be acceptable on transit sites. Depending on overall size and topography the camp can be divided up into sections of say 10 to 20 pitches with high hedges or other screening between to break down the disturbance caused by late arrivals and early departures. Cars will always park on pitches rather than in a separate car park, and it is useful if vans and cars can park in line. The camp will be quieter if the reversing of vans can be avoided.

## (2) Recreational touring sites

There are as many types of recreational site as there are types of holiday, but both the much greater mobility and the degree of self-containment of today's camper have blurred the distinction between many transit and recreational camps. An example in an American National Park illustrates this shift of emphasis. Trailer campers preferred to camp on a macadam car park (near a river) rather than on the adjacent traditional camp site where, in 'natural surroundings', they had far more privacy, individual fire places, picnic tables, etc. Campers achieved their objective by arriving at the site as late as possible; if the camp was full, overnight camping on the car park was permitted. The Superintendent who was discussing this problem pointed out that campers are now completely self-sufficient and that for the great majority camping is touring. Most of the holiday is spent on the road. Whether or not this makes for a good holiday is not the question here. But this situation underlines the importance of analysing the function of a site from the camper's point of view. Within one recreational site there may well be need for differing types of pitch and layout at different densities: rental might be charged at different rates. Diversity is needed.

There are certainly many sites where low density is an asset (e.g. in gladed woodland where each pitch has the illusion of being by itself) but there are others where low density is no virtue in itself. If the *raison d'être* of the camp is other than camping for camping's sake, densities can usually be satisfactorily raised. The territorial instincts of most campers are highly developed so there is little concern about privacy or trespass.

Acceptable densities of vans on a recreational site will also depend on the surroundings of the site. On many continental sites, and on those American sites where the individual pitches are not defined, the density of twenty-five vans to the acre laid down by the Model Standards is repeatedly exceeded to the evident satisfaction of all concerned. It seems unreasonable to assume that the British are less civilized campers than other nationalities.

Campers on city sites (Paris, Cologne, etc.) who are there to see the city, are well content with high densities for the convenience of being close to the centre of things. It has been pointed out (by a camping couple with over forty years' enjoyment of solitary sites) that the closeness of pitches in the Bois de Boulogne is perfectly acceptable provided your van is equipped with venetian blinds. In one of the best German sites (open only to members of a distinguished motoring organization) pitches were scarcely bigger than the tent or van which occupied them at the height of the season (see Plate 85). A sense of openness prevailed since the site sloped down to a big lake. This lake was also its *raison d'être* since most campers owned sailing dinghies or canoes.

On the other hand, those sites which have no important outside attraction, where campers may spend a considerable part of their holiday in the camp itself, need a lower density. On some Dutch camps, for instance, families bring bicycles as well as their car and young children spend hours whizzing round within the site. The grassy areas around the pitches as well as the games area are used for shuttlecock, deck quoits, etc.

Noise and regulation of use of transistors is integral with density. Members of an organization are likely to respect each other's feelings because they are similar to their own. Some wardens delight in exercising their acumen in separating the various kinds within a camp and this can help in roughly dividing, say, those who thrive on continuous background sound from those who happily survive relative silence.

The traditional camper seeking solitude can enjoy some woodland recreational sites where judicious clearing and a density sometimes as low as two caravans per acre have created a sense of backwoods.

*Requirements.* Self-contained campers on a recreational site may not need or want anything more than the minimum essential for hygienic camping:

1. Water point.
2. Chemical closet emptying point.
3. Refuse disposal system.
4. Camp office in neighbouring farm.

Facilities kept to the minimum help to maintain the illusion of camping alone.

At the other end of the scale, the camp which functions as a small holiday colony may provide any of the following:

1. Office.
2. Warden's quarters.
3. Fresh water points.
4. Lavatories and wash-rooms.
5. Vegetable sinks and pan wash-up.
6. Drying room.
7. Laundry.
8. Refuse disposal.
9. Chemical closet emptying point and/or trailer sewage disposal station.
10. Shop(s).
11. Cafeteria.
12. Play area(s).
13. Recreation room.
14. Swimming pool.
15. Boating, tennis etc.
16. Car wash.
17. Petrol pumps and service station probably outside main entrance.
18. Water, electricity and sewage disposal may be laid on to individual pitches in a section of the camp.

## (3) Group camps on permanent sites

Group camps for organizations such as the Scouts or Guides lend themselves to design and siting sympathetic to their surroundings. They usually consist of a few h.q. buildings and recreational provisions, e.g. swimming pools, with decentralized camp sites for the separate groups who may be using the camp independently of each other. They can therefore easily adapt themselves to the terrain. The general notes on camp buildings apply equally to this section. Each organization will have its own brief. Cooking may be centralized but many organizations prefer that each group be self-sufficient. Some organizations have a few disabled children and adults within a group who also want to camp. This must be borne in mind at the planning stage: e.g. ramps should supplement steps; at least one low w.c. can be useful for handicapped children; a handrail should be provided to help disabled people in and out of the swimming pool. A camp specifically designed for the handicapped has, of course, its own brief.

## (4) Individual camps

This section includes those sites where a few tents or vans may be taken without a licence under Schedule 1 of the Caravan Sites and Control of Development Act, 1960. These are for the self-sufficient, solitary-minded camper who wants no facilities or neighbours other than perhaps an equally solitary-minded pair of green sandpipers. Nothing need be said about them except that vans should be sited as inconspicuously as possible. Tents, both for visual and psychological reasons, are usually more acceptable in the landscape but the general siting notes in this book will also apply to them.

## (5) Static caravans

*Living in a caravan*, a Consumer Council study, gives a detailed account of living conditions on residential sites. The notes here concentrate on the design of sites for recreational use. The static van has the great merit of relieving the road of a tedious burden of traffic by providing holiday accommodation which does not have to be towed from a home site.

*Types of static recreational site:*
   1. *Week-end parks.* Vans act as a logical substitute for the country cottage. Owners usually want the illusion of country surroundings but will opt for well designed arcadia since isolation is obviously impracticable. Vans can easily be integrated into the landscape, usually in light woodland; or a garden (house may have been demolished). Character: informal; bosky; vans lost in landscape.
   2. *Holiday parks.* Vans may be individually owned but are often let by the week or fortnight to holiday-makers. A much more sophisticated atmosphere and layout is likely to be acceptable, particularly on sites near towns. Character: spic and span; flag poles; white paint and trim lawns.
   Recreational provisions depend on those of locality: tennis courts; bathing and boating pools; dance halls and restaurants are often provided if there are none in the vicinity.
   These types lie at each extreme of the range; between, countless permutations are to be found. Visually the danger lies where character is undecided: a sophisticated site trying to be artfully natural, or an informal site needlessly urbanized.

*Sites for static vans.* The first question to consider when weighing pros and cons of a static site is its true function: residential housing estate; cottage/chalet colony; site for individual bungalow or holiday house? A static site has far more in common with this type of development than with that of a touring site and the merits of its siting should be judged on these grounds.

Both the badly designed, ill-sited individual van and the static van slum have given the whole breed a particularly bad name. But the existence of the garish bungalow has not ruled out the possibility of other single storey development; nor has slum housing precluded good new housing schemes. Static vans, like tourers, can be hideous and their hideousness is made the more intolerable by their continued presence; there is no relief. The lone static van, sticking out like a sore thumb, on the fringe of a group of farm buildings, is particularly irksome visually. At the same time it seems most reasonable that a farmer should have the right to put a van (often for a farm worker) on his own land. Much can be done in these cases both by *detailed* attention to siting (e.g. in orchards) and the design of the individual van.

Blanket criticism of static sites is not justified. A well planned site, absorbed in light woodland or parkland, can have several visual advantages over the equivalent accommodation in a housing estate of detached or semi-detached. It can be integrated much more easily into the landscape. Usually the ground is owned by one landlord. It need not be broken up into plots by fences. Young trees can be grown close to vans without fear of damaging foundations. A certain amount of gardening tends to go on in the immediate vicinity of the van, but by and large the whole site can merge into its surroundings.

A static site also has an important visual advantage over those where vans must be moved at the beginning and end of each season, since the site itself need not be churned up by this upheaval (in spring the ground is at its wettest). Planting and trees can also be more closely integrated among the vans themselves, if they are not to be moved.

Some so-called mobile homes (often 10 ft. 0 in. wide × 40 ft. 0 in.–50 ft. 0 in. long [3 m. × 12–15 m.]) are of higher standards of design than either typical housing or touring vans. These, even on open sites where identical vans are parked in orderly rows, are usually no worse and at times may be a great deal better than many a housing estate, provided they are sited sensibly in the overall planning scheme. If every effort is made to knit them into the landscape by contours and planting they can be a positive asset.

*Site details.* Static sites are controlled by the Caravan Sites and Control of Development Act, 1960, Model Standards, which covers:

1. Density. A maximum gross density is allowed of 20 vans to the acre (25 to the acre on sites not used in winter). Vans in separate occupation shall not be less than 20 ft. [6·10 m.] apart and not less than 10 ft. [3·05 m.] or more than 150 ft. [45·7 m.] from a carriageway. Such high densities are possible on formal sites, but good informally planned sites are usually at very much lower densities.

2. Roads and footpaths.
3. Hardstandings to vans. (Gravel or hoggin are generally preferable to concrete on visual and practical grounds. Where mains services and drainage are supplied, concrete is expensive to dig up and therefore planning is inflexible. It also reflects heat and cold.)
4. Fire fighting appliances.
5. Water supply.
6. Drainage, sanitation and washing facilities.
7. Laundry.
8. Chemical closet disposal.
9. Surface water drainage.
10. Refuse disposal (1 bin per van on static sites).
11. Storage space (minimum 30 sq. ft. per van).
12. Car parking (N.B. 1960 figures of a minimum of 1 car to 3 vans, with additional space to be set aside for future parking, no longer seem relevant. Badly parked cars can wreck a site visually. 1:1 or 2:1 are now more likely proportions.)
13. Recreational space.

## Buildings and services

Whole books have been written on most of the building types which may be needed in a modern camp: office, warden's accommodation, lavatories, shop, recreation room, etc. In the following pages only those points particularly relevant to camp design and layout are discussed. For *general notes* on buildings see pages 163–170. For notes on *camp lavatories and washrooms* see pages 135–150, where they are included with public lavatories. For *litter* disposal see pages 201–208.

## Camp offices

Camp management and choice of warden obviously depend both on the size and function of the camp itself. It might be expected that the immense variation of camp types would immediately be reflected in the types of office from which they are run but this does not necessarily follow. Perhaps the difference is not fully recognized when the brief for the office is worked out. Size of office is proportional to turn-over as well as size of camp. So long as the daily routine of the warden is accurately visualized a clear brief must follow. This can only be worked out by each organization or individual for himself, but the three examples here are given for guidance as to what should be considered. An efficiently designed office goes a long way to oil machinery of a warden's daily routine (which is itself only a small part of his role in the camp).

## Offices: transit and large recreational camps

On big sites, particularly those which are used both for transit and as holiday bases near big cities (e.g. Copenhagen, Amsterdam) the office has several functions. In addition to being headquarters of camp management it will serve as a travel agency (which ferry, when?) and an information centre (which gallery, where?). The warden, incredibly dedicated, spirited and well informed, deals with passports, electric irons, culture and faulty plumbing in half a dozen languages at top speed. While in the camp he can never be truly off duty.

To stand this tempo most wardens are young and usually married (wives not only do much of the work but are indispensable in case of illness among the campers). It is likely that they have several small children. These factors must be taken into consideration in siting the office in relationship to the warden's quarters.

Since wardens have so little time off it is best to plan for their convenience while on duty by siting living quarters immediately adjacent to the camp office. Often a door from the flat to the office is provided.

The office will be sited so that it overlooks the main gate. If the floor can be raised 2 ft. 0 in.–3 ft. 0 in. [60–90 cm.] above ground level, overall view and supervision can be much easier. Incidentally, a flight of broad steps on the way up to the office makes an excellent gathering/gossipping point for campers. Some offices have remote control over the operation of the gate.

The area adjacent to the office will have hard standing for temporary parking for at least half a dozen vehicles in its immediate vicinity and for ten to twenty nearby. This must include sufficient length for trailers, which should be able to pull through without reversing.

*Office requirements*

1. Counter space for (a) registration (b) general information (c) use of campers while completing forms, etc. (this need not necessarily be adjacent to the registration counter).

2. Wall space: plenty of uninterrupted wall space behind the counter will be necessary for the registration system, camping carnets, etc., unless an 'island type' of registration system is used. Poste restante or message pigeon-holes may be needed. First Aid Box should be obvious and easily accessible.

3. Map space: on a wall away from the counter in the general milling area. A duplicate map on the counter itself is useful.

4. Window space: for overseeing the main gate and with good general views of the camp. The office is in a sense the control tower of the camp.

5. Sales space: unlikely in this type of office except perhaps for the sale of maps and guide books.

6. Store: for stationery, literature, etc.

7. Brewing-up facilities: sink and power point should be provided (probably in a cupboard) so that the warden's wife need not be disturbed.

8. Large porch or verandah: this may be the same size as the office itself.

9. Public telephone booth(s) will be provided in or near the camp office.

## Offices for country recreational sites

The amount of office business naturally depends to some extent on the average length of stay. A country site averaging around a hundred pitches with stays limited to a week is fairly typical, and is often run by a retired couple. Their requirements are at the opposite pole to those of the transit camp but they need an equally efficient office tailored to their demands.

*Siting*

The office should be near the main gate but control-tower type supervision is not essential. It may be a disadvantage (undue disturbance, etc.) to site the office and warden's quarters together. The warden may prefer to live off the site. Parking for half a dozen vehicles on hard standing near the office is useful, but on well-drained sites it may be sufficient to allow for pulling-off on the grass.

*Office requirements:*

1. A short counter or a guichet at which two enquirers can be served simultaneously. Counter top for campers taking notes and looking at maps.

2. Wall space: uninterrupted wall space behind the counter for the registration system, and poste restante or message system.

3. Map space.

4. Window space: it is useful for the warden to be able to see the main gate from his desk.

5. First Aid Box.

6. Storage space for stationery, literature.

7. Brewing-up facilities.

8. Shop: in this size of camp the warden may also run a shop. If so, he should have access to it direct from his desk (e.g. the village post office/store set-up). Or the warden may sell a few pieces of camping equipment in the office: allow for storage and limited display space.

9. Large porch or verandah: may be considerably bigger than the office area itself.

10. A public telephone, provided in the porch, allow for its use when the office is shut.

*Offices and farm houses*

For many campers the most congenial offices are those in the corners of farm kitchens. Even so it is much easier for everyone concerned if some form of 'office unit' is used. This

# Camp sites

**Notice board**

**SECTION**

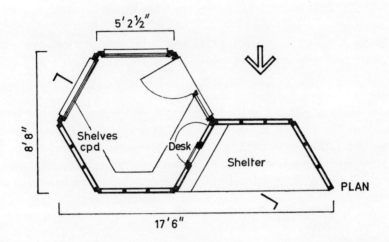

5' 2½"

8' 8"

Shelves
cpd

Desk

Shelter

**PLAN**

17' 6"

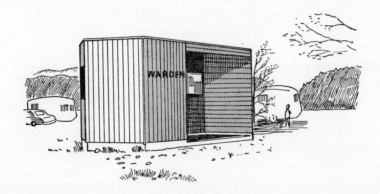

Warden's paybox office: Glenmore Forest Park (Moira & Moira). A small, trim building which allows shelter for campers waiting to register and views of the camp site for the warden.

may have been knocked up in the yard or be a more finished workshop job. It simply provides a work-top for writing, storage space for documents and wall space for registration. It helps to prevent camping documents from being lost among the milk returns and subsidy application forms or simply being submerged in the general welter of daily life.

## Warden's quarters

The siting of the *warden's quarters* depends on the type of camp. In a transit camp or big recreational camp his quarters are usually immediately adjacent to the camp office. It is also important that his family should have privacy. This seeming contradiction need not be difficult to resolve since the office will face the main gate and the flat in the opposite direction. It should be possible to plan a terrace which catches the sun but is screened from the camp.

On smaller caravan sites the warden often lives in his own van or he may prefer to be off the site in a nearby cottage.

### Accommodation

Wardens in transit camps are likely to be young and married, with several children. These are seldom allowed for in allocation of living quarters. A basic unit of living room/kitchen and bathroom to which other rooms could be added might provide an answer for camping organizations. Young children and parents must sleep under one roof, so it is useless to hope that additional camping accommodation can be used as an overflow from a warden's flat.

## Recreation rooms

Rooms for use both as common rooms and for indoor games are provided in some commercial camps. In a Dutch national park it was considered to be more economical to erect a special building and to pay the salary of play-leaders to look after groups of children than to stand the cost of making good the damage that might be done if the children were left to their own devices.

Camp recreation rooms are usually more satisfactory if they are rugged in character, without being folksy. Natural timber is helpful; artistic carving is not.

## Outdoor play areas

It is important to provide simple equipment for small children who would otherwise be running around tents, bored, while their parents sleep in or get ready for the day's expedition. This can be of the simplest kind: old tree trunks; climbing structures made from logs and scantlings are especially suitable to forest sites; swings made of rubber tyres (safer

*Camp sites*

An old *tree trunk*, left where it was felled, or dragged by tractor to a sunnier more sheltered position, can give enormous pleasure with little trouble. Equally important, it is a piece of 'play-equipment' which is likely to be in scale and character with its surroundings and one which will require minimum maintenance. It will probably be necessary to put down some gravel where the ground gets most wear, although from the users' point of view, puddling may be considered an advantage. On some camps, tree trunks are put in big sandpits.

without supervision); sandpits (perhaps a large sand area containing the play equipment).

Camps are often on the edge of dunes if not actually on them. If an anti-erosion scheme is in hand it is vital to put the idea across in the camp both in the office and by the play area. Dunes to the British child are for climbing up and galumphing down, not for the painstaking planting of marram grass. One or two slopes might be left unplanted for this purpose (as in some Dutch schemes).

Table-tennis was very popular on a German site (hard standings behind the table are essential). Hard play areas for use after wet weather are provided in some camps.

A drinking water point will be much used near a play area.

The play area can be at a focal gathering point in the camp where there will automatically be intermittent supervision. Provide a few benches where mothers can gossip.

## Swimming pools

See pages 195–200.

## Car washing

A well-drained hard standing, 20 ft. 0 in. × 8 ft. 0 in. [6 × 2·5 m.] with 3 ft. 0 in. [1 m.] of gravel bordering it, supplied with a water stand point and hose is usually popular.

## Drying rooms

The first amenity for any camp site in the north or west of the U.K. should be a *drying room*. It is specially important where campers are out of doors regardless of rain (climbing,

131

sailing, etc.) and have only small tents, but anyone is glad of it. (Failing a drying room proper, a covered drying yard is useful). It should be sited near the laundry and not far from the camp office, since some supervision will be necessary.

Size depends on both size and use of camp and regional weather. Permanent ventilation plus hot air from electric fan heaters is probably the most efficient system but any constant source of heat with natural ventilation can be effective. Pegs and racks for wet clothes are essential. Wet clothes are usually left on trust. It is possible to run the drying room upon an exchange disc system, like a cloakroom in a museum or at a hotel, but this will be too complicated for most camps.

## Shop

The brief is similar to that of other shops of the same type. Many camps have self-service stores. Storage space may need to be more generous since delivery to out-of-the-way camps may be infrequent. Collection of packaging by the local authority's refuse truck may also be infrequent and storage space should be allowed for this. An incinerator can be very useful for disposing of cardboard and paper, but it must be down wind from the camp. In most camps the shop is best sited near the main gate.

## Cafeteria

Where no cafeteria is provided, benches and picnic tables outside the shop can become an unofficial outdoor café for shop products. In big camps a simple cafeteria, often let to the same concessionaire as the shop, may pay. Design details are as for other cafeterias except that a larger proportion of the eating space can be out of doors and in covered areas. Tough picnic tables and benches may be more useful than the typical lightweight cafeteria furniture. Wherever disposable cups etc. are used, plenty of litter containers must be provided.

Slot machines for drinks: the paving here should fall to a surface water drain otherwise one dropped cup means murky puddling. Generous litter receptacles are also necessary.

## Fire points

Provision for fire-fighting appliances is laid down in the Caravan Act, Model Standards. (See paragraph 5.) Fire points are required on the scale of one point for every two acres (or part of two acres). Like water points, these should be central and easily accessible. It would therefore seem sensible to combine the two services wherever possible. (See Plate 83.)

## Camp service kerbs

Many caravans are now equipped to take mains services. Fully-serviced areas are often set aside on camp grounds to provide for these vans. Mains water, electricity (a power and light point) and a sewage connection (less common) are fixed in line either on a raised kerb (rather cumbersome) or at ground level, protected by a kerb. This protection is necessary as the points could easily be damaged by the wheels of heavy vehicles.

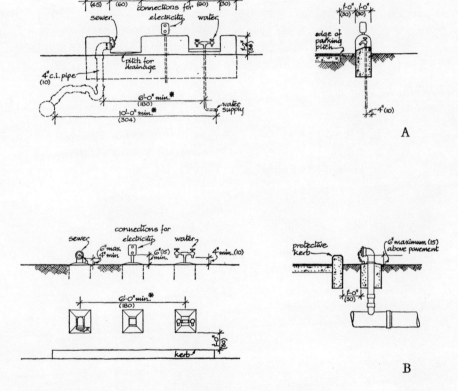

(A) Camp service kerbs and (B) utility collars (based on designs by the American National Park Service). The concrete could look hideous if it is not well detailed. An exposed aggregate finish could greatly improve its appearance.

133

## Mains lighting

On some camps which do not rise to the provision of service kerbs, power for lighting can be taken from the camp ground lighting system for a small charge. Three or four terminals are provided at each light point and caravanners run cables from them. Voltage is either at mains level or is stepped down to 12 volts. (See Plate 88.)

Lights within the vicinity of the camp buildings can be bracketed from the buildings themselves rather than be fixed to separate posts. Lighting of roadways leading to pitches should be by low lights, say 3 ft. 0 in. above ground level. Ordinary street lighting looks out of place and over lights the pitches where people may be trying to sleep.

## Touring vans: typical sizes

The maximum permitted width of a touring van in the U.K. is under 7 ft. 6 in. [2·28 m.]. It is very rare. 6 ft. 6 in. [2 m.] wide vans, 12 ft. 0 in.–16 ft. 0 in. [3·65–4·85 m.] long are the most popular. Therefore a total length of car plus coupling plus van will not often exceed 36 ft. 0 in. [11 m.] and will commonly be around 32 ft. 0 in. [9·75 m.].

Typical widths and lengths are:

| WIDTH | LENGTH |
|---|---|
| 6 ft. 0 in.–6 ft. 6 in. | 10 ft. 0 in.–16 ft. 0 in. |
| 7 ft. 0 in. | 16 ft. 0 in. and 18 ft. 0 in. |
| 7 ft. $5\frac{7}{8}$ in. (very rare) | 22 ft. $11\frac{1}{2}$ in. |

# 9

# Public lavatories and camp wash units

The notes in this section apply generally to lavatories on lay-bys, picnic sites, camps and those provided at ancient monuments, etc. Please see relevant section for particular details and Chapter 10 for general building notes.

## Names

We seem to have indulged in euphemism ever since the Middle Ages and probably before. Garde-robes were followed by Necessaries. Lavatories really describe washplaces and the word sounds almost as refined as Toilets with which, thanks to the Worboys traffic signs and foreign travel, it seems we are saddled. 'Toy-let' is now understood internationally. Comfort Station is too long. Loo, though far from being generally used, has much to commend it for brevity.

## Numbers

It is almost impossible to estimate numbers of w.c.'s, urinals, and basins which would be required in lavatories on lay-bys, car parks, etc. because if lavatories are well designed and clean they are likely to attract more users, particularly on trunk roads. But standards can only remain high if design is accurate and cleaning is budgeted for. It is a good rule (but seldom financially practicable) to design for maximum numbers with minimum maintenance and no continuous supervision. When estimating proportions of facilities, men: women, it should be noted that lavatories used mainly by families (e.g. those on picnic sites or camp sites) need a larger provision on the women's side than the men's. Women have the children to look after; small boys as well as girls are taken to women's lavatories. Numbers are therefore greater and turn-over much slower. (Most publications ignore this fact.) A 50–50 distribution is therefore wasteful. 60–40 is probably nearer the mark.

Most countries recommend basic facilities which, like the minimum recommendations given below from the Council of Europe Report, *Camping Hygiene* (1961), are exceeded in most of the better camps. The Report stresses the variety found and the difficulties of making recommendations for numbers of wash basins as so much depends on other provisions such as showers and footbaths.

10 tap points with basins or conduits (5 for men, 5 for women) per 100 campers.

3 showers per 100 campers.

1 w.c. for 20 women.

1 w.c. for 30 men if urinals are also provided.

It is usually assumed that for the purpose of calculations the average number of campers per pitch is 2·5 (Camping Club of Great Britain).

## Siting

(See also page 151.) Public lavatories like bus shelters and other small buildings too often make irritating interruptions in the landscape, not only on account of their dismal design but because their siting seems accidental and unrelated to their surroundings. Nor are they important enough in size or form to make a contribution to the scene in their own right.

Often when a lavatory could form part of another building it is a separate entity simply because it is the responsibility of some other department. It would be in everyone's interest, both aesthetic and financial, to clear away the administrative obstacles which cause this sort of planning.

But where the building must be sited by itself it can be welded into the landscape by use of the lie of the land, planting, walls, etc; all these can overcome the uneasy sense that the building has been dropped at random.

Lavatories are usually best sited near a car park, but where a country house is on view existing buildings (e.g. stables) may be suitable for conversion themselves or provide a convenient but not too obstrusive site. Occasionally an existing building in a prominent position can be usefully converted. This may be more successful if there are a pair of buildings (e.g. garden pavilions) framing a view rather than a single building on an axis.

On camp sites ideally no pitch should be further than about 100 yards from a lavatory unit with w.c.'s and basins. This will decide whether all services are centralized or whether small units should serve different parts of the camp. This rule of thumb will not of course apply where vans are self-contained with their own chemical closets, but fresh-water points and drains for the disposal of washing water will still be needed in the vicinity of the pitches. Showers, laundry, etc. are usually centralized.

## Building notes

See also pages 153–157. A good public lavatory should be very light and well ventilated: it should feel dry and be easily cleaned. Really robust ironmongery (the British are usually mean about this) and the walling off of all pipes and cisterns in ducts will also discourage vandalism. But, however well designed, the building will fail if it is not kept spotlessly clean. A good guide to design, therefore, is to put oneself in the shoes of the cleaner. The clearer the floor the easier it is to keep clean. *All* fittings and furniture should be bracketed from the walls without support from the floor. This includes basins, benches, litter receptacles and, wherever the budget allows it, w.c.'s.

There is much to be said for providing lavatories in *mobile factory made units* (e.g. Rolla-long) which can be quickly assembled and dismantled. They can be taken back to the factory to be overhauled and refitted each winter. This caters for seasonal needs, eliminates danger of vandalism when they are unused and avoids the inevitable weathering of a building during the winter months.

## Access

Public lavatories consisting of w.c.'s plus a wash and brush-up space can usually be planned to give adequate privacy without a separate lobby or screen at the entrance. Immediately opposite doors may need separation in the porch. Some shelter may be needed, particularly on bleak moorlands. Doors should be on the sheltered sides of the building away from the prevailing winds. A projecting roof or wide porch can be very useful where crowds may have to wait for their turn, e.g. coach parties. Two doors giving 'in' and 'out' circulation save time on busy sites. The best small lavatories seen were those on Danish lay-bys, some of which are planned with no entrance lobby.

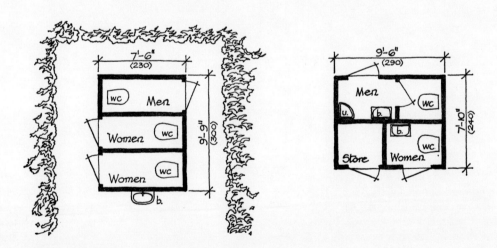

Lavatories on Danish lay-bys, sited so that planting screens entrances.

137

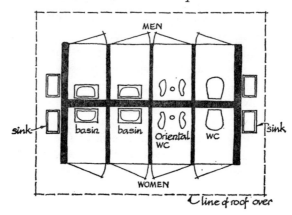

Simple **lavatory** block on a Dutch camp. Units to this plan are dispersed throughout **the** site. Showers are centralised.

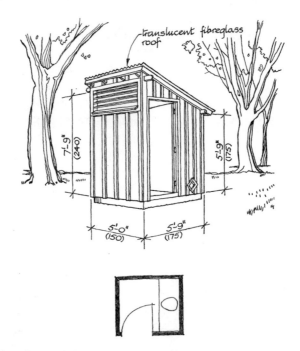

Modern timber shelter for a pit latrine which could be used for a chemical closet. Its special points are: the translucent fibre-glass roof concentrates the light which reflects from the white enamel painted walls; the interior is therefore very bright and easily maintained; permanent ventilation by louvres; no windows to break or need cleaning; the door is normally kept shut by a heavy spring; the whole structure is light enough to be moved around as necessary. (Designed by State Highway Commission and State Parks Dept., Oregon, U.S.A.)

## Natural lighting

A really light building is usually kept much cleaner than one with normal day-lighting. Roof lighting gives far stronger general light than a window. It also solves the problem of window breakages, poor ventilation via windows, and grubby sills and glass which often need cleaning. It is usually cheaper. Roof lighting can be by prefabricated dome lights or by clear or translucent PVC or polystyrene sheeting. Sheeting is manufactured to the same sections as standard roof sheeting and can therefore be cheaply installed. Among the best looking roadside lavatories are the Danish timber ones referred to above, roof lit, without windows.

## Artificial lighting

Most lavatories must be open all night and must be really well lit if they are to remain clean. Some of those on trunk roads have an outside arc lamp to light the whole area; this lights the interior through roof lights. This system is unsuited to other situations, e.g. camps, where a brilliant general light would prevent campers from sleeping. Here a light at each door and bulkhead fittings against the roof or ceiling should be arranged so that purlins do not produce shadows. Lights over mirrors should light the face and not the mirror; strip lights often do the opposite.

## Ventilation

The expense of adjustable ventilation may not be worthwhile unless there is an attendant to vary it. Fixed wooden louvres, with a fly screen protection, give free circulation of air in w.c. compartments. Shutters may be needed if the lavatory is used in winter. Where corrugated roof sheeting is used, good permanent ventilation can be arranged by the omission of the eaves-filler piece. Again the gaps should be screened to keep out birds and insects. Permanent ventilation can be arranged at the roof ridge by leaving an open end (not facing the prevailing wind) to asbestos cement ridges. Wind lift must be watched.

## Floors and skirtings

Floors and skirtings must be of an impervious material, usually granolithic or quarry tiling. All angles should be coved. Floors should be designed so that they can be scrubbed and swilled down like a ship's deck. To this end all fittings should be built in and supported on brackets clear of the floor. Allow adequate falls (say 1 in. in 10 ft. 0 in. [2·5 cm. in 3 m.]) to drains set in the floor, and points for hoses which should be fixed high enough to fill a bucket.

**Walls**

Wall finishes must be impervious, discourage graffiti, and be easy to clean. Either a glossy surface or a *coarse* rendered finish (e.g. one of those applied by a spray gun) are frustrating to most doodlers; but pentel goes on smooth surfaces with exquisite ease; fortunately it wipes off. Rough rendering is cheaper but is difficult to clean. But it has proved useful on many 'quiet' sites: a tile splash back skirting should be fixed above wash basins.
Smooth finishes include:
*Glazed tiling*, both the conventional $\frac{3}{8}$ in. thick wall tile, and the thinner varieties designed to stick to rigid panels in framed buildings, give a trim finish.
*Laminated plastic sheeting* also looks good provided the edges are well detailed. Partitions may be damaged by impact in vandal-prone areas.
*Spray paints* on hard plaster are cheaper and give a durable finish. The colours must be watched since the process usually consists of two applications of different colours; a background and a fleck finish. White seems the most attractive background with a light fleck (e.g. straw).

Traditional *gloss oil paint* or an *emulsion paint* can be a useful answer particularly where old buildings are to be converted.

In many situations (e.g. washrooms in small camps) it is enough to carry the impervious surface to a height of, say, 5 ft. 0 in. [150 cm.] above floor level. Above this creosoted boarding is cheap and gives a warmer, less clinical, character.

**Ceilings**

For summer use, unlined roofs are usually adequate and can be whitewashed. Where insulation is needed a strawboard, distempered white, looks attractive and has the added advantage of absorbing sound.

**Partitions**

In the U.S.A. w.c. partitions are usually carried at least 12 in. [30 cm.] clear of the floor. This makes for easy cleaning and obviates corners harbouring rubbish. A typical top height is 5 ft. 6 in. [168 cm.]; in some cases even lower. The usual British practice of taking the partition up to or close to the ceiling makes both ventilation and lighting more difficult. A 5 ft. 0 in. [150 cm.] partition fixed 9 in. [20 cm.] clear of the floor, giving an overall height of 5 ft. 9 in. [170 cm.] seems a useful compromise.

**W.C.'s**

*Cubicles* are seldom wide enough for a mother who has to deal with small children. At least one-third of the cubicles in women's lavatories should give 3 ft. 6 in. [105 cm.] clear width inside (as against the more typical 2 ft. 6 in. [75 cm.]); this should then be indicated on the door. But it would be better if all cubicles were squarer in plan (as in some Danish examples) instead of long and narrow. Each cubicle would require no greater floor area but the overall plan may be less economic. With shorter cubicles it is necessary for the doors to open out (as is usual in the U.S.A.). Once people are accustomed to the idea of outward opening doors collisions do not seem to occur. Doors should have at least one hook for bags, cameras, etc. In some countries a collapsible shelf is provided; it is fixed in a position where it blocks the door opening, so that parcels, etc. are not forgotten.

*For disabled people:* At least one w.c. cubicle should be provided with hand-grips or bars fixed 3 ft. 0 in. [90 cm.] above floor level on each side partition. This inexpensive provision can make an enormous difference to disabled or arthritic people who may otherwise be unable to tour. Provision should be noted on the w.c. door.

*Admission costs:* It is generally recognized that coin operated locks are uncivilized; they also provide scope for vandalism. A voluntary box for pennies has been successfully provided in some privately owned public lavatories.

*Paper:* Apparently less is pinched from rolls than boxes, though the decorative possibilities of unfurled rolls prove irresistible to some people. Holders like the Dreadnought which prevent the cardboard core spinning freely dampen such enthusiasm. A holder for spare rolls should be provided in each cubicle. In continental camps, campers often have to provide their own paper.

*Flushing:* Foot operated flushes are best for cleanliness provided there is adequate supervision. But they are more expensive, there are moving parts to go wrong, and people tend to kick them angrily if the flush does not work.

*Flushing valves:* In the U.S.A. and several continental countries a flushing valve often replaces the cistern which the British so optimistically and quaintly call a 'waste-water preventer'. Abroad, the valve can be held down to allow the necessary amount of water to flush the pan, instead of taking the standard two gallons which is used up each time a British cistern is flushed. Enlightened Water Authorities in the U.K. also allow this valve but here it is usually required to discharge a two gallon flush, whether or not this is necessary. The advantages of the flushing valve over the cistern could be:

1. A real saving of water since only the amount needed would be flushed.
2. The cistern (cumbersome) and its works (which can go wrong) would not be needed.
3. No time-lag occurs while a cistern refills (annoying for queues).
4. Disposal of purified sewage effluent can be a serious problem. In public lavatories (as against houses where waste bathwater, sink water, etc. forms a high proportion of sewage), effluent could be much reduced.

Water boards are concerned that if a valve should develop a constant leak, wastage is unlikely to be detected. Concern has also been expressed about the risk of siphonage between the fresh water supply and the w.c. This risk does not seem to affect American systems.

It must be noted that there are cisterns on the market which have two capacities of flush according to the way the lever is manipulated, the idea being that 2 gallons are not automatically needed each time the lavatory is flushed. The difficulty in public lavatories is that the public may not understand these subtleties and that the necessarily more complex mechanism has more moving parts which could go wrong. *Cisterns,* if used, must be designed to fill quickly. This depends on local water pressure and the size of the supply pipe. *A flushing trough* (long on plan) instead of individual cisterns allows for flushing at frequent intervals (say 30 seconds) and this cuts down on queueing. Fibreglass troughs are now on the market.

*W.C. pans: type of flush:* Siphonic flushing, which has the advantage of being non-splash, is not recommended in public lavatories. The small bore of the flush may be blocked and is very difficult to unblock. An ordinary wash-down flush is much cheaper.

*Women's W.C.'s:* In a recent survey[1] it was shown that 97 per cent of women prefer not to use the seat in public w.c.'s. Seatless w.c.'s, called women's urinals, are now installed in the lavatories attached to Italian autostrada service stations/rest places in Italy, where they are very popular. They are also being introduced by the National Park Service in the U.S.A. They are manufactured in Britain but are evidently not well known. In factories they are not always popular, having the disadvantage that they do not provide a place for a comfortable read and a smoke. These w.c.'s keep cleaner, are easy to clean and easier for mothers taking infants. (See Plate 92.)

Dispensers for paper bags for sanitary towel disposal should be fixed to partitions. Incinerators should be provided in camps and elsewhere where there is some supervision. Otherwise disposable sacks, approximately 15 in. × 9 in. [38 cm. × 23 cm.] should be provided in each cubicle. These should be held by purpose-made brackets with lids, bolted to the partition (a smaller version of the typical litter sack). Bins standing on the floor are inconvenient and difficult to clean.

*Urinals:* In the type of public lavatory described in this book, in order to allow maximum use, urinals are best designed as a continuous wall undivided rather than by separate stalls or bowls. A fibreglass slab is cleaner than a fireclay having far fewer joints. Flushing spreaders fed from an auto-flushing system itself in a duct are recommended: an exposed pipe system is a vandal's delight.

The floor should fall towards the trough for hosing down when cleaning. A step in front of the stall can be dangerous.

*Oriental closets* are not popular in Europe possibly largely because of unfamiliarity. In theory they are far more hygienic than ours. They are easier to clean and, having no parts projecting above floor level, are nearly vandal proof. But really efficient water-closets (as against earth closets) are rare. Even in Holland where they have been installed on some of the Staatsbosbeheer camps they have a faint but unmistakable smell evocative of the

[1] By Mrs. R. McBretney, Dipl. Arch., A.R.I.B.A., in association with Bedford County Council and Messrs. Adamsez Ltd.

Middle East (this is no worse than that of many European w.c.'s, but different). Any firm who could market a really well designed model would deserve success.

## Washrooms

*Wash-basins:* Most public lavatories whether on camps or for day use provide rows of wash-basins reminiscent of those in camp ablution blocks which linger among the less cherished memories of World War II in the U.K. It is doubtful if such basins are preferable to the old enamel bowl which was tipped into an open gulley. These bowls were easily cleaned, having no waste outlet to be clogged by someone else's hair and old soap.

Looking at the problem from the warden's, the user's and the owner's point of view, it is questionable if the typical wash-basin layout provides the best answer. Long rows of basins are quite expensive and take space (itself expensive) which might be put to better use. They are not easily kept clean.

Even if a basin is clean, in public lavatories people usually prefer to wash under running water. This is recognized in the fittings now provided in public cloakrooms by most forward-looking authorities: a small basin, usually without a plug, which catches the water from a spray mixer tap.

Generally speaking campers want either a hot shower or a minimum wash; a row of basins in a cool room with other campers and children milling round is not conducive to more, anyway for women. This suggests that the domestic wash-basin with two taps and a plug is not fulfilling its purpose; it is either a wasted luxury when all that is wanted is a jet of water from the tap, or a doleful inadequacy if the real need is for a proper shower. Its only justification would seem to be when it is in a separate cubicle (as provided in some Dutch camps).

From these observations it seems that the most useful provisions for washing fall into three categories: washing in a public washroom under running water; in a basin in a hired cubicle; under a shower.

*Taps where people can wash under running water* (Plates 89–91).

The basin whose function is simply to take the water to the waste-pipe can be a *small individual basin* (say 12 in. × 9 in. [30 × 20 cm.]), or a *large circular bowl* (say 7 ft. 0 in. [215 cm.] diameter) with taps on a central column. These work well but tend to be expensive because the parts are not mass produced. (A circular bowl, say 7 ft. 0 in. diameter, with 8 taps might cost over £200; 8 individual basins planned in a circle with similar water points, under £100.) Basins grouped in a circle instead of standing against a wall score on several points over the conventional plan:

1. More economical use of floor area.
2. Use is usually quicker and therefore turnover greater.

3. There can be something dismal about long rows of basins (this applies particularly to large camps). They seem more inviting when free-standing.
4. Soap dispensers can be fed from a central tank.
5. Plumbing and services are concentrated.

**Disadvantages**

1. Unsuited to camp wash-basins for men because of the difficulty of fixing shaving mirrors.
2. Give minimum privacy so only suitable where adequate showers or wash cubicles are also available.

Probably the answer is to provide some basins against the wall and some free-standing. This too should plan out economically.

*Long channels* where the waste water has to run from end to end, are not recommended. Soap suds have to swill past downstream washers before reaching the drain.

*Taps* should be wall mounted. They are then easier to wash under and it is also easier to keep the basin clean if it is clear of all projections. A mixer valve with a spray is best for washing under and economical where hot water is provided. The hot and cold water must be at the same pressure therefore the cold supply must be off a storage tank.

*Plugs* should not be provided if washing is under running water. Plugs and chains trap murk.

*Soap dispensers* must be robust and firmly screwed to the wall. They may need frequent refilling. A central tank (possible where basins are grouped) saves time for the cleaner, and frustration for the washer, who may find the individual container empty.

*Shelves* should be provided over basins for bags, cameras, etc; hooks are also useful. Space for tooth-mugs and sponge bags must also be included where circular groups of basins are planned in camps.

*Towels:* Hot air driers work well if there is a certain amount of intermittent supervision, but they cause queueing. Automatic roller towels are particularly susceptible to vandalism and therefore unlikely to be useful in the lavatories discussed here. Paper towels are a better answer but must be in proper containers plugged to the wall. A large litter sack without a lid should be bracketed from the wall adjacent to the paper dispenser (but not underneath it: people get in each other's way).

*Litter:* All washrooms should have at least one litter sack (for old tissues and toothpaste tubes) whether or not paper towels are provided.

*Mirrors:* should be made of metal to prevent breakage. They must be positioned where the light is good. Except when they are to be used by men for shaving, they should not be over wash-basins. Those washing and those doing their hair or making up get in each other's way and hair gets into the basin.

A 9 in. [25 cm.] shelf should be bracketed 6 in. [15 cm.] below the mirror for bags etc.

Heights of mirror: the average British woman is said to be 5 ft. 3 in. [160 cm.] tall; many are 5 ft. 0 in. [152 cm.] or 5 ft. 9 in. [175 cm.]. An 18 in. [45 cm.] high mirror with its top 6 ft. 0 in. [180 cm.] and bottom 4 ft. 6 in. [140 cm.] above the floor will therefore suit most people. In men's lavatories add 5 in. [12 cm.] to these dimensions. Where several mirrors are provided, one should be fixed low for children.

Mirrors in men's lavatories on camp sites will be over wash-basins with light points for razors at each basin. Adaptors can be fixed by a small chain.

A long mirror is welcome on camp sites in women's wash-rooms. It should be positioned near the door.

*Coat hooks:* Enough hooks are seldom provided in camp lavatories. Even an ordinary cup hook can make a great difference to a camper's comfort. Everything taken into a wash-house has to be put down or hung up and most things will hang (towel, sponge bag, clothes). Hooks should be at a variety of levels to suit both small children and tall men. *Shelves* are needed for tooth-mugs, sponge bags and shaving kit.

*Benches,* sixteen inches above the floor, are useful but not essential.

## Wash-basins (with plugs) in cubicles

These have an advantage over showers in camps where only cold water is supplied since campers can bring their own hot water. A bowl built into a worktop is convenient to use but not easy to clean at junction with worktop. The dressing table/wash-basin units on the market may not be sufficiently robust. Provide also shelf, mirror, 2 to 3 hooks, points for electric shaver. Overall size of cubicle: 3 ft. 6 in. × 3 ft. 6 in. [105 × 105 cm.] provided the door opens outward.

Cubicles can be used for short periods (10–15 minutes) or could be hired for the whole length of a camper's stay. A family or pitch would take over the key and be responsible for cleaning. To make such a system feasible in terms of capital expenditure, the cubicles could be operated on a hiring system at off-peak seasons only; they would be open to the public whenever numbers in the camp reached a certain figure.

## Showers

The best showers have hot water; they are usually coin operated. Several wardens have suggested that it might be an improvement if the cold water was also only available by coin as children naturally delight in playing in them and cause a good deal of mess when adults are not around. This might not be a sufficient deterrent to someone with 6d initially destined for ice cream, unless the meter were out of reach.

*Shower compartments* consist of a dry and wet area.
wet area: 3 ft. 0 in. × 3 ft. 0 in. [95 × 95 cm.].
The floor of the wet area can be Oroglas, Perspex or fibreglass tray with a non-slip surface (Perspex and Oroglas are trade names for acrilic.)

The shower compartment needs a recessed shelf for soap and sponges. Shoulder spray

K                                                   145

showers are more popular than the old ceiling sprays. Fixing at a height below 6 ft. 0 in. [180 cm.] will allow it to be directed clear of the head.

Taps: two taps with an anti-scald mixing valve set so that the mix can be really hot but not dangerously so have been recommended.

Dry area: minimum size 3 ft. 0 in. × 3 ft. 0 in. [90 × 90cm.]. More space welcome. Provide: (a) drain in floor (b) slatted bench supported clear of floor by bearers on partition (c) hook for clothes (d) hook for towel within reach of shower (e) slatted duckboard mat.

A mirror should not be provided since it slows turnover. Fix one to wall outside. Most dry areas are protected from the shower by a plastic curtain. Inevitably this gets torn and dejected and where possible is better dispensed with. If the shower is fixed so that it cannot be directed into the dry area, and the bench and hooks are fixed on the same side wall as the shower this may be feasible. A 12 in. [30 cm.] nib partition partially separating the dry and wet can make a considerable difference.

## Sinks for washing clothes

Many campers bring small babies to camp sites. One or two sinks for nappies and smalls have proved popular. Where there is no laundry these go in the women's washroom. Adequate shelving (depth 12 in. [30 cm.]) should be fixed near sinks.

## Coin-operated hot water supply

A coin-operated geyser allowing, say, a bucket of water for 2d, to be taken to pitches, adds greatly to a camper's comfort. It can also be used at basins or sinks where only cold water is laid on (plugs are then necessary).

## Tables for bathing babies

In some camps (e.g. in France) mothers bath their babies in the washroom. Where this practice is encouraged solid tables must be provided both for the baby's portable bath (when it is not bathed in the sink) and for drying the baby.

## Vegetable sinks

*Sinks* for vegetable preparation and pan washing are provided in a covered area outside the lavatories (because of water supply and drainage already existent) on many big camps. Sinks will be subject to heavy wear. Porcelain enamelled cast iron though expensive is probably worth the capital outlay. It is unlikely that vitreous enamelled steel will be sufficiently durable. Fireclay sinks are the most commonly provided; they will stand fairly heavy treatment and are much cheaper than iron. Taps should be fixed from the wall, not the sink. Worktops and draining boards will be used for chopping as well as draining. Laminated plastics could hardly be expected to withstand the onslaught. Teak, or some similar very hard wood will be worth the outlay. Worktops should be fixed with a generous fall for washing down. There should be a coved skirting or impervious material between worktop and wall or a 2 in. [5 cm.] gap which can be properly cleaned.

## Laundry

Where there are several camp sites in an area a launderette may be best run independently by a concessionnaire outside the camp premises, but it will probably be difficult to find anyone willing to do this for a limited season.

*Launderettes* are now common in most big camps and in a few enterprising small ones. Provisions vary from a basic minimum of two washing machines to a full scale launderette with a dozen machines and three or four spin-driers. In wet regions a spin-drier should be considered as essential from the start.

An *ironing room,* separate or semi-separated from the laundry, is useful whether or not other laundry equipment is provided. Shelves and hooks for clothes to be ironed are essential. Irons are usually hired from the camp office and since occasional supervision both in the ironing room and laundry will be necessary, it is an advantage if these are sited near the office.

For *Drying Rooms,* see page 131.

*Hair Drying:* in bad weather it may be impossible to dry your hair on a camping holiday. Hand hair driers might be hired as are electric irons. Sockets, if in washrooms, should be positioned so that driers are out of reach of basins. In big camps a space at the end of the ironing room would be convenient. Where driers cannot be provided, sockets for campers' own driers would be very useful.

## Drinking water points

Drinking water points are in relatively little demand in the U.K. The usual dampness of the atmosphere may be the cause. They are useful on picnic sites and picnic lay-bys and can be fixed to the outside wall of lavatories or in the porch if it is large enough. Water Boards usually demand a self-closing tap to prevent possible waste of water. This tap must be adjusted so that it is not too stiff for children to operate. A hooded downward jet, or a jet from which it is easier to drink on the down curve, is considered more hygienic and is the only type allowed by some authorities.

The mounting of a free standing water point presents unexpected problems. It must be at a convenient height for drinking (a step can be provided for small children) and waste water must run away without making much mess. Indoors this is usually solved by a small fireclay basin. Out of doors the water point needs a sound housing for the pipe and some form of bowl to catch the water. The result often tends to look over-important for the job and is expensive. Wherever possible they should be incorporated in an existing wall or building. Unexpectedly successful solutions have been provided by the re-use of old kegs and nineteenth-century cast-iron street standpipe housings (see Plates 77–78).

Brass taps and fittings, even when thoroughly tarnished, look much better in the countryside and out of doors than chromium plated (glittering but streaky). Since almost all fittings are made of brass and are then given a chrome finish it is only necessary to ask the manufacturer to omit the final process.

In Britain, water to drink on the spot is often less in demand than a point at which to fill kettles or jerry cans. Here an ordinary self-closing tap is all that is needed, with a drainage gulley or self-draining gravel under it. Since the operator will have to hold the self-closing tap with one hand it is important on picnic sites that the kettle should be able to stand under the jet without being held: it may be too heavy for a child to manage one handed. This is of greater importance on camp sites where 2 gallon jerry cans are filled. A step or level ground should be provided, about 18 in. [45 cm.] below the outlet (Jerry cans are typically $14\frac{1}{2}$ in. [36 cm.] high). Ground surrounding water points should be well drained (hardcore fill under a gravel finish) or be paved to fall away from the point.

### Frost damage

All cisterns and pipes should be thoroughly insulated but this will be of no avail in a hard frost unless the building is heated or low voltage electric wiring is wrapped round pipes and tanks. Central ducts are easy to warm. Polythene pipes which can expand slightly without bursting should be used for all cold runs. Traps are less subject to freezing since they are warmed by sewer gas.

### Service duct

A 2 ft. 6 in. [75 cm.] wide service duct containing all cisterns and as much of the piping as possible can separate the men's and women's lavatories. This can also be planned as a maintenance room for the cleaner. If hot water is provided, immersion heated tanks or gas water heaters should be in this duct. Access should be outside the lavatories.

### Sewage disposal

The Water Resources Act 1963 Part VII 72 forbids the discharge of untreated effluent into underground strata where water gathering grounds may be affected. It is unlikely that main drainage will always be available. The other three most common systems of sewage disposal are:

1. *A septic tank* is the most usual and generally satisfactory answer. But a septic tank, relying as it does on bacteria for purification, can be rendered ineffective by the use of modern detergents. This must be explained to the maintenance staff. Unless the tank is large enough for peak usage and sub-soil conditions are favourable for the draining away of pure effluent, the system can become what is virtually an overflowing cess-pit.

2. *Sealed cess-pits.* This method relies on the efficiency of the emptying service. In times of high usage it may be impossible to maintain this.

3. *Continuous chemical process.*[1] Where none of the above systems is practical or where water supply is critical this method should be considered. It should not be confused with chemical buckets. It relies on the sewage deposited within the system being sterilized by chemical and mechanical means. It then overflows either direct to a soak away or through overflow tanks. Non-flush stainless steel lavatory pans of special design are fixed above the purification tank. The equipment is fitted with mechanical agitating devices manually operated by the raising and lowering of the pan lid. Since a lay-by lavatory with conventional cisterns and w.c.'s may use 30 or 40 thousand gallons of water in 24 hours this method has great advantages in economy both of water supply and sewage disposal.

The American system, *Destroilet*, using a car battery and gas cylinder, is said to reduce waste to ashes. So far as is known it has only been developed for individual chemical closets in camp trailers.

## Chemical closet emptying points

Chemical closets can be emptied via a trapped gulley (as in a slop sink) into a mains sewer. The ordinary 2 gallon flushing system (as used with w.c.'s) has not been found satisfactory as it will not clear the trap. A short length of hose from a water point with which to swill out both the chemical closet and the trapped gulley seems the most practical answer.

The bacteria in a septic tank may be killed by chemical closet waste. Emptying points are therefore direct to a soakaway or Otway pit (check that the Water Resources Act, 1963, is not contravened). An untrapped gulley is connected direct to the Soakaway. A hardwood cill on which to rest the pail is fixed to the front apron wall about 15 in. [40 cm.] above ground level. A short length of hose connected to a cold water point is provided for swilling out pails.

## Trailer sewage disposal stations

On American sites sanitary stations are often provided for emptying the sewage tanks of trailers. (See page 150[2].) A foot-operated cover seals the drain. One end of the drain hose

[1] Information by Elsan Ltd.
[2] Design by Mobile Homes Manufacturers Ass. U.S.A.

is connected to the holding tank of the van and the other to the drain. A hose is provided to swill down the concrete apron in which the drain is set. A timber kerb protects the drain from the wheels of a van.

In the U.S.A. one station is recommended for every 100 parking spaces, or fraction thereof, but in the U.K. where only a small proportion of vans so far have self-contained drainage, this figure might prove over-generous.

Initially, a short notice explaining the use of the station will be necessary.

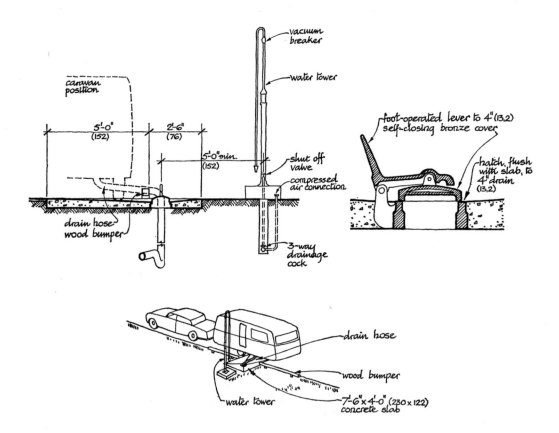

Caravan sewage disposal station.

# 10

# Buildings in the landscape

## Siting and character

Certain general principles apply to the design and siting of most buildings relevant to this book, whatever their function. In order to avoid repetition these points are collected here. Particular details are covered in each section.

First it must be recognized that in terms of landscape the countryside would be 'better', i.e. more itself, without the majority of these buildings. Many of them are destined for areas whose intrinsic character *as countryside* is what the tourist seeks: the very places which were planned to be free of all new development. This is an entirely different problem from that of an acknowledged change of character through a change of primary use, such as the creation of a new resort: a ski centre for instance. Once the desirability of a change has been allowed the problem is relatively straightforward. Much can be done by channelling car-borne tourists into certain areas planned for their reception, and elsewhere *not* catering for them but allowing the countryside to get on with its own work (as at Beaulieu in the New Forest). But to build for the servicing of tourists in open country (e.g. the Peak District or on the Pembrokeshire coast) is a quite different problem.

All buildings have a psychological as well as a purely visual effect in the landscape. A lone croft can, by contrast with its surroundings, make the lonely moorland seem lonelier. On the other hand a single bungalow can suburbanize a rural valley. A lighthouse as an outpost of humanity can underline the splendour of the coastline. The chimney of a power station has a different effect. A luxury hotel yet another. It is probably those buildings which reinforce the original character and use of the landscape which are the most acceptable. In our minds the croft is directly related to the shepherding even if in fact it is now a holiday cottage and the shepherd arrives by Jaguar from a distant village. The lighthouse reinforces our awareness of the dangers of the coast. The bungalow, on the other hand, probably belongs to the commuter. One instinctively likes it better if it houses some real character like the local schoolmistress or postman. These factors are strictly non-visual. A new building, however good in itself and in its siting, may be detrimental only because there are so many other new buildings and artefacts to be integrated in a limited countryside. Each of these must to some extent dilute the existing rural character by its very presence.

In this connection there seem to be three major difficulties to be overcome:

1. Much of the English and Welsh countryside (and quite a lot of Scotland) is small in scale and easily disrupted. It already has as many buildings as it can take if it is to retain its character.

2. In well wooded country intelligent siting makes absorption easier but many of the new buildings, camps, etc. are needed in coastal or hill country where tree cover is hard to find.

3. Functional requirements, the need for shelter, water, water power, etc. once confined most buildings to the valleys where, automatically, they were inconspicuously absorbed into the landscape. These conditions no longer apply. We now find ourselves reimposing them artificially for reasons which are not even primarily aesthetic: because we feel that considering a region *as a whole*, it cannot take any more intrusive buildings if its character is not to be basically altered. The resulting need in visual terms to play down new development can be irksome both to designers and developers. It produces a situation which highlights the attraction of building in, say, Newfoundland or Siberia where, it might be imagined, anything new is still felt to be a stake for humanity in the wilderness, and to merge with the landscape would be absurd. But it is a situation, however frustrating, which must be faced in the U.K. It is one that can only be resolved by an exceptionally mature approach. It will seldom be answered by aping vernacular design but rather by a thorough understanding of the essential ingredients of that design and their translation into contemporary terms. True integration of a building with its surroundings can only be achieved by skilled siting, sympathetic overall form and scale and suitable materials and colour. It is a subtle problem demanding the simplest answer.

Everything considered in this book might be looked upon as a service building (or artefact) whose function is simply to provide for the basic needs of those going into the country for informal recreation. The visitor wants to find the country as country uncluttered by things put there for his benefit. The traditional counterpart of these service buildings might be said to be farm buildings, saw-mills, water-mills and agricultural cottages: background buildings whose architectural quality is unostentatious. They complement the follies, mansion houses, windmills or parish churches whose visual function, in addition to giving satisfaction at close range has been to punctuate the countryside with the *occasional* landmark. It is essential that the new service buildings are not confused with this latter category.

A characteristic of this type of building and its surroundings is *compactness* and economy of land use. Farm buildings are in direct contact with fields. There is no 'amenity landscape' although the resulting visual amenity is top grade. Too often the type of building that goes into the country for leisure has an unwanted no-man's land around it, such as grass which needs to be mown, which divorces it from its surroundings. If this land is really unwanted it should be part of the field or open moor. It cannot be beyond our skill to design so that sheep and cows can harmlessly rub against the walls of the buildings; or to sort out the legal implications involved.

Another failure in siting, brought about largely through administrative difficulties, is our tendency to scatter small buildings which might logically adjoin each other or which might even be under one roof, or be integrated with some larger building. Public lavatories, bus shelters, custodians' huts, and countless others remain separate entities standing apart and aloof from their neighbours usually to the detriment of the landscape itself.

## Architectural character

The design of buildings for leisure in the countryside can be approached in many different ways but the most successful answers to the problem often result from two opposite extremes. The building may seem to be hewn out of its background; it is almost part of the landscape itself. Many traditional stone and brick buildings belong to this category. At the other extreme is the structure which seems to have alighted like a bird or a bubble (and which may be as temporary). A Danish bus shelter on a country road, remote from any building, constructed of translucent polystyrene sheeting, is a nice example of this type (Plate 100). It makes little obstruction in the landscape since the light comes through it; sky, trees and hedgerows are scarcely interrupted.

Many timber framed buildings which are raised a few feet above the ground (usually for practical reasons such as flooding) also allow the scenery to flow on unimpeded.

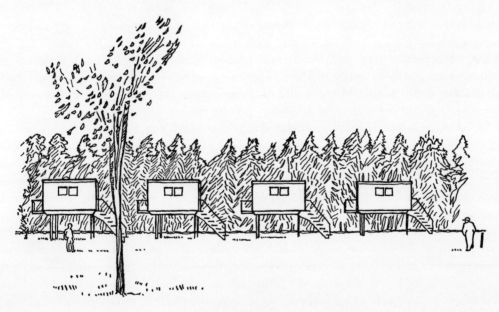

Buildings on stilts may be better integrated with their surroundings than ordinary single storey buildings since the landscape can be seen through them. There is no break at ground level.

153

The provision of large enough windows is often aesthetically awkward in buildings with load-bearing walls. These traditionally have window and door openings which could be easily spanned by a stone lintel or a flat brick arch: the wall area is large in proportion to the glass area. This usually worked well enough for the traditional house or cottage. In many of the buildings needed for leisure a far greater glass area is thought to be desirable. Large windows are often very much more difficult to handle successfully in aesthetic terms in a masonry building than in a framed building. Compare a typical Georgian façade with that of a timber framed building and note the disastrous results which often follow when new windows are cut in a traditional masonry façade. This can be a major difficulty when buildings are converted for leisure purposes.

## Materials

Unsatisfactory design is now often attributed to economies in *materials* introduced to cut out costs. Like other generalizations this contains a good deal less than the whole truth. Mies van der Rohe's maxim that it isn't the materials but how they are used might be more applicable. It is certainly enormously satisfying to build in, say, stone or slate, but it is absurd to imagine that nothing good can be achieved outside the materials traditional to a district. A bad building may perhaps be less of an eyesore if the use of local materials helps to merge it with its surroundings, but that is all. Not all buildings in stone are marvellous: some very depressing examples spring to mind. Nor are, say, corrugated iron buildings necessarily shoddy. A good Dutch barn, for instance, particularly if painted black, can be very satisfying indeed. Some of the best camp buildings, lay-by lavatories, etc., which have been built in recent years have been in sawn timber, unpainted but treated with preservative, with corrugated asbestos roofs (Denmark). Such buildings are infinitely preferable to many of their expensive counterparts in British National Parks (slate roofs and rendered block walls). If there can be any broad generalization about materials it might be: whenever in doubt consider timber.

In the U.K., materials tend to be divided into 'sheep and goat' categories with inevitably inhibiting results. This is probably because many of the early buildings erected in the new cheaper materials were of the shack-bungalow variety and were badly detailed. Deterioration or disfigurement due to bad weathering was inevitable and these materials undeservedly got a bad name. At the same time, any new material was very naturally resented when seen alongside splendid traditional masonry. Where natural stone was too expensive artificial stone was often introduced as a compromise. Few things look worse than reconstructed stone or concrete block aping the real thing. It is particularly disastrous visually where it is most often used—in immediate juxtaposition to a genuine stone wall. Comparisons are inevitable: it is like eating steam-oven bread after a home-baked loaf. But where reconstructed blocks are accepted as such, satisfactory results can follow. It is imitation of the genuine material, rather than the intrinsic characteristics of the blocks (texture, colour, etc.) which spells disaster.

There is also widespread faith in *variety* of material: it is supposed that variety will be in keeping with the rural landscape because 'nature is not standardized'. But nothing makes more surely for monotony in the countryside than a wide variety of materials and colours of materials. The character of the place is diluted; the eye distracted.

In our most prized regional landscapes there is a high degree of uniformity in both walling and roofing particularly among the humbler buildings. Farms, cottages and medium-sized houses are of the same materials and therefore have the same general colour. We are not bored by the stone of the Peak or Lake District any more than by the brick and tile of Herefordshire. There are villages, particularly in the south of England, where slate, tile, and thatch are all used but that is about the limit of the variety which a village can comfortably absorb. Churches, chapels and country seats provide contrast, often by form, scale and size rather than by materials or colour.

Manufacturers are ever increasing the range of roofing materials, wall blocks and external plaster finishes to satisfy every taste. It is up to us consumers to choose the 'right' type; obviously our opinions differ. The country suffers accordingly.

Some planning authorities give firm guidance on the selection of materials and colour. This may inhibit a few very good designs and it can never produce good design in itself; but it can prevent the countryside from the disfiguring rash of too much variety. Individually each may be acceptable but the variety undermines the fundamental character of the countryside.

## Industrialized building systems

These three words are enough to halt all logical discussion in otherwise rational committees. It is often not realized that these are systems of *construction*. The end product may be clad in, say, timber or tiling and be indistinguishable to the layman from a traditional building. Incidentally such systems can have the advantage of reimposing a degree of restraint on the variety of materials used which has been lost since the industrial revolution. Then limitations disappeared with the new ease of transporting materials; now they might be reimposed by factory techniques.

One drawback to the use of industrialized systems may lie in the small quantities needed in the type of building considered here. But a basic building module can be used in a variety of ways to suit different sites and conditions. The Ministry of Public Building and Works now uses industrialized system for custodian huts and lavatories of different shapes and sizes on several of its Ancient Monument sites. See Plate 107. Intelligent use of a system can bring about surprising economies even over direct labour. Unfortunately the erection of units may produce difficulties. It is not always easy to find a manufacturer who will erect his own units, or a contractor who will undertake to do so. Site procedure is therefore the first thing which should be checked when industrialized systems are under consideration.

## Roofs

Arguments in favour of *pitched or flat roofs* tend to be more emotional than logical. Obviously each has advantages as well as snags both in landscape and functional terms. The following points may be useful:

1. Exact *degree of pitch,* whether it be to reflect a local tradition or to be in sympathy with a fall in the land, is very important.

2. A pitched roof on a single storey building inevitably increases its *overall height.* The building may therefore be less easily absorbed into the landscape than if it had a flat roof. Where two storeys are needed it is often both economical and architecturally more interesting to devise a first floor room within the roof space. Where this is achieved the overall height of the building will obviously be lower.

3. The *finish of flat roofs* is particularly important in hill country where they will be seen from above. From this viewpoint they are rarely as satisfactory as pitched roofs which have a more interesting texture (derived from the lap of the slates or tiles, or the corrugation of the roofing sheets). A flat roofed building will automatically be double the scale of a conventional two-way pitch because it is not divided by the ridge.

4. *One way pitches* of around 10°–20° are often useful in the type of service building considered in this book.

5. The importance of *eaves and verge details* is seldom sufficiently stressed. Nothing affects the character of a building more. Too often, where local materials have been expensively used to harmonize with the vernacular, the effect is nullified by a non-traditional eaves detail, e.g. a 7 in. projection where an eaves with a 2 in. overhang is typical of the locality.

In windswept coastal and hill districts 'clipped eaves', that is with a minimum overhang, are traditional. In Regency times when low pitches with deep projecting eaves came into fashion they were foreign to the vernacular, although very attractive in their own right. Over the last century there has been an enormous variety of detail, the 7 in. compromise being as common as it is visually unsatisfactory. It seems that the trim clipped eaves of the last ten years has come to stay; it is very much in character in the types of buildings described here.

## Walls

Most satisfactory buildings, particularly small buildings, have one, or at the most two, *wall facing materials.* But there are plenty of post 1945 houses which would do service as samplers for a builder's yard; brick, tile, rendering, laminated plastic, reconstructed or natural stone; all are crowded in. Aesthetic success seems to be in inverse proportion with the variety achieved.

No building material can be selected out of context but the following notes are of general application:

1. *Timber* seems particularly suited both to the service buildings and to the rather casual and often lighthearted character of the leisure buildings considered here. Either horizontal or vertical boarding (according to the structural system) looks shipshape provided waney edges are avoided. For camouflage, vertical boarding is more easily absorbed in woodland than horizontal. Timber may be the best alternative to natural stone in stonewall country since it does not provoke comparison with the genuine article.

2. *Reconstructed stone and concrete blocks.* The natural aggregate can be exposed by splitting the block or by hammering or spraying. Blocks thus treated have a quality of their own when laid to a workmanlike bond which does not mimic natural stone.

3. *Grey brickwork* is a useful material where natural stone is too expensive in stonewall country. The colour of all brickwork should be settled when bricks are damp rather than bone dry.

4. *Concrete breeze blocks* painted white have been used successfully either as boundary walls, or internally or externally in buildings.

5. *Joints.* Wherever the colour of masonry is under consideration the colour and type of joint (flush, recessed, etc. effect shadows) need as much attention as the block itself. The colour of the mortar will be radically affected by the type of sand used. Sample panels of masonry should always be set up and allowed to weather.

6. *External rendering.* All forms of rendering have to be carefully specified and detailed to prevent cracking and staining. See *External Rendering* (Cement and Concrete Association Publication).

True white is seldom available in a self-coloured rendering with the result that 'white' rendered buildings look dingy when seen beside traditional lime-wash. To look white these renderings must be painted.

7. *Plinth details.* A tarred plinth with a good projecting drip above it is necessary where the wall will stain through contact with the earth. For perfection the soil adjacent to the building can be dug away and replaced by pebbles. See Plate 103.

# 11

# Colour and texture in the context
# of the countryside

## B.S. 2660

The reference numbers given in this section are those of British Standard 2660:1955 (amended 1958 and 1966). These are now used by most leading paint manufacturers and those concerned professionally and in the trade. The B.S. provides an invaluable means of communication about colour and of preventing confusion (e.g. olive green may mean that of an olive on a cocktail stick or the silvery grey-green of an olive grove). It is not intended to help in the subtleties of colour decision itself. Colours should be selected from a fair sized sample, say 2 in. × 3 in. minimum of the same texture, e.g. gloss or matt, as that finally intended.

*Munsell system:* See end of chapter.

## Colour decisions

Everything which goes into the countryside involves a colour decision. This to some extent has always been true but when local materials, stone and brick, slate and tile, were in common use the problem largely looked after itself. Broad decisions of colour policy within a region may (or may not) be successfully controlled by a planning department. In the long run the result naturally depends on individual judgment of the most subjective kind. Who knows what the other man sees?

This is not the place to discuss colour theory: plenty has been written on this subject. But since the smallest custodian hut or public lavatory involves colour it seems useful here to analyse the effect of colour in the context of the countryside: why some schemes are successful and others are not. The alternative for many of us is to jog along hopefully from one inspiration to the next. Anyone who is interested in the effect of colour in the landscape is conscious that some of the most likeable examples break the usual 'rules' (a warning against improving other people's colour schemes?). But the success of these heartlifting rule-breakers usually has logical grounds.

A few general points immediately emerge:

1. No colour can be judged to be good or bad in isolation from its *surroundings*. What counts is how it complements other colours or contrasts with them.

2. Colour can only reinforce or play down an existing situation. Form and siting are more important. Colour cannot do much for a really bad building but it can detract from a good one; it can be very useful on a mediocre design.

3. Colour cannot be considered in isolation from the *texture* of the material of which it is part, which will affect its light absorption and reflection. This is particularly true of colours in the countryside where, with the exception of water, every natural surface is textured, and is therefore broken up by thousands of minute shadows which deepen its tone. Conversely a smooth surface, particularly with a gloss paint (e.g. a caravan) reflects light and the surface appears to be lighter.

4. *Position* of material will affect its light reflection and therefore its apparent colour. The same colour may seem lighter when used on a roof than when it is used on a wall. (In some regions self-coloured grey asbestos sheets are required where the traditional roof colour is a stone slate.)

5. It has been argued that the light colours of *caravans* cannot be logically criticized when the whitewashed cottage is found to be acceptable in the same landscape. Feelings are all too easily roused. It is too seldom realized that many critics of caravan colours are not against caravans as such (only against the none too rare shoddily designed ones). But by their enormous numbers, vans not only inevitably alter the basic character of any land-scape which they dominate, but they introduce too large an area of contrast in terms of colour. A deeper tone value could help to mitigate this effect. The lone cottage on the other hand is a foil to its background, providing a single element in terms of contrast and increasing the sense of wilderness by its very solitariness. (See also pages 151–153.) Larger groups of farm buildings are acceptable for complex reasons which include scale, form, size and relationship with the existing landscape pattern.

6. When confronted with any problem of 'blending with the countryside' most Britons (and many Europeans and Americans) reach for the green paint pot: preferably, it seems 'municipal' green (similar to 6–074). Faith in green seems as strong a bastion of our national life as habeas corpus or toast and marmalade. A recent reaffirmation occurs among the Worboys traffic signs. The one certain thing that can be said about green is that it will rarely match a natural background since the 'green' of the countryside not only contains infinite variety but is constantly changing both with the seasons and with the light. Grass is an attractive dun colour much of the year. Discords are therefore inevitable. Almost every example of green paint against a natural background is inevitably a solecism. On the other hand, green paint in a town, such as grey-green stucco, with white trim, can look both attractive and smart.

7. Stone, timber, earth and brick consist of a multitude of varying colours and paint samples should be tried beside the actual material.

8. Colours sympathetic to the countryside are usually in the *earth range*: yellow ochres (rather than chrome yellow), terracotta red, browns (including greenish brown and warm greys). These colours can either be used to blend or stand out by choice both of hue and

tone value. Yellow ochres (e.g. 4–057) are very useful for drawing attention to objects in rural surroundings without seeming garish. For example, litter bins in a Dutch forest park painted a drab greenish-brown were almost invisible until a 2 in. [5 cm.] diameter yellow spot was painted on them. This seemed to give exactly the right degree of conspicuousness. Black and white are excellent colours wherever contrast is needed in the country, and are more sympathetic than most greens. See also pages 53–54 where blue and red on signs are discussed.

9. *Tents.* White, orange, blue and even green tents can enhance the landscape in a way seemingly impossible for a caravan. The reasons are only partly psychological: admittedly tents are truly temporary in a way vans are not, and this, combined with the gaiety of their colours, puts people in the mood to enjoy them. They are also on the whole a better shape than many vans and they are usually lower since floor level is ground level. Above all the texture of the canvas or nylon (matt) and tone of their colours is sympathetic to the tones and textures of the countryside.

10. The plea that *caravans* must be finished in pale gloss paint for insulation purposes seems hardly justifiable since the introduction of so many new cheap insulation materials which give a far greater degree of protection.

11. *Timber preservatives,* in an understatement kind of way, can be particularly sympathetic to natural surroundings. Chemical preservatives (e.g. Tanolith or Celcure) which give wood an uneven appearance usually weather to a good background colour. Creosote is particularly suited both aesthetically and practically to many of the types of buildings used on camp and picnic sites. It is cheap, but needs to be renewed annually.

By the sea untreated hardwood and western red cedar soon bleach like drift wood and are particularly suited to these surroundings.

12. *Trim* on buildings. White window frames in natural stone and brick buildings nearly always improve the looks of the building. A caravan painted to merge with its surroundings may look dismal at close range. A little white trim (e.g. at door and windows) would do much to mitigate this effect without making the van stand out from any distance.

13. *Gutters and downpipes* are now available in plastic which does not need to be painted: a great saving in terms of maintenance. The colours now available include some warm greys which are usually much more sympathetic to stone and brick than the steely bluish greys. Black (also available) can look very smart.

14. *Roofs.* The variety of colour available in new roofing materials, particularly concrete tiles, is causing havoc in some parts of the countryside. The difficulty lies in the enormous range of colour that can now be used in any region. Great variety dilutes character and quickly makes for monotony, particularly when the buildings concerned are relatively small (e.g. private houses and bungalows and most of the building types mentioned in this book). Most districts would be immeasurably improved if new buildings with tiled or slated roofs had to stick to one or at the most two colours. Green concrete tiles should be confined to urban areas.

15. *Contrast.* Some man-made structures add greatly to the landscape if painted to stand out from their surroundings: e.g. bridges, particularly foot suspension bridges. This is most effectively done by using light greys or whites rather than strong colours. But, for the reasons already given (pages 151–153) it seems unlikely that many of the buildings or artefacts discussed in this book will fall into this category.

16. The Institute of Landscape Architects, while stressing that it is essential that colours are chosen *for a particular site,* has issued a list of colours taken from B.S. 2660. These 'are considered suitable for the painted surfaces of buildings, caravans, bridges and other engineering installations, fences and railings and similar detail'. Green–green is notably absent.

| | |
|---|---|
| From the Yellow-red Group | 3–036 |
| | 3–037 |
| | 3–038 |
| From the Yellow Group | 4–047 |
| | 4–048 |
| | 4–049 |
| | 4–050 |
| | 4–051 |
| From the Green-yellow Group | 5–059 |
| | 5–060 |
| From the Blue-green Group | 7–078 |
| From the Grey Group | 9–095 |
| | 9–099 |
| | 9–100 |
| | 9–101 |
| | 9–103 |

17. *Signs.* For colours of signs see pages 52–55.

18. *Camouflage:* Colour has obvious potential in this respect but camouflage is an enormous subject. It is worth pointing out in passing that for little or no extra expense, intrusive objects can be made much less so, by sympathetic choice of colour. Tone matters as much as colour. For example, the posts of overhead cables can be made less conspicuous where they run through valleys if insulators are brown where chiefly seen against a hill, instead of translucent or white: the latter are best when seen against the sky. Plastic coated mesh fencing in greenish brown can be very inconspicuous. The typical 'grass green' so often chosen has little in common with the greens of the countryside.

19. *Camouflage of mud:* Buildings close to roads and car parks (e.g. ticket collectors' huts) can look very smart in fine weather if painted white or black but the mud thrown up by the wheels of vehicles often wrecks this effect. White trim (e.g. window frames) with colours which effectively camouflage mud spattering, such as olive brown paint or creosoted wood, can make these potentially drab colours spic and span.

## Munsell system

The Munsell system of colour reference is used internationally. B.S. references also give Munsell references, as do many British paint manufacturers.

DEFINITIONS:

*Hue* refers to the part of the spectrum to which the colour belongs (e.g. red-purple, yellow-green). Munsell divides the spectrum into 10.

*Value* refers to its lightness or darkness. Low value colours are dark; high value colours are light. (0 = black; 10 = white) maximum reflection. Thus colours of the same number have similar reflectance.

*Chroma* is colour strength or pigmentation. 0 is neutral grey; 16 maximum strength.

> *Example* pale pink = 7·5 R 9/2
> 7·5 R is on the yellow side of *red*.
> Value 9 is a very light colour
> Chroma 2 is a low colour strength.

# 12

# Shelters, cabins and hides

**Porches**

*Porches, verandahs and covered areas* are invaluable extensions to most of the buildings considered in this book. Not only do they protect the building but they form that link between outdoors and in which is so much needed in our climate. Too often campers must dash from office to caravan, visitors from Information Centre to car, to avoid a downpour. Even drizzle is to be avoided when the drying of clothes is a problem. Yet it is the essence of a holiday to be able to linger unhurried, chat to acquaintances, or pore over maps or guidebooks. A deep covered porch or verandah can enormously increase the value of a building in terms of quality of use. It must be of generous proportions; perhaps as large again as the room it adjoins. It should be sheltered from the prevailing wind and wherever possible catch some sun. A porch can be particularly useful in winter since the low sun will reach far into it.

Porches need not be expensive. They can be constructed as extensions of the main roof or as separate lean-to's. Translucent and transparent polystyrene and PVC sheeting make a very effective roofing, which has the great advantage of allowing light into both the porch and the building which it serves. It is cheap and needs only a light structure to support it.

**Shelters**

Simple *shelters* can add greatly to the visitors' enjoyment and comfort both as places to pause to admire a view or as refuges in a sudden storm: many people leisure bent in the countryside are optimistically clad. Shelters are exceptionally useful at picnic places, at the furthest point from base on paths or trails, and in gardens.

A simple lean-to shelter, with open sides (depending on site conditions) and a one-way pitched roof, can be cheaply constructed with local timber and direct labour. If not exposed to the prevailing wind, it need not be more than 6 ft. 0 in. [1·83 m.] back to front, with a bench along the back wall. Long low shelters usually fit unobtrusively into the surroundings if sited against planting, rising ground or a rocky outcrop, or if an existing wall is used as part of the structure.

If a shelter is needed on open ground, a round or octagonal building may be easier to site than a rectangular structure. It must be in scale with the space around it.

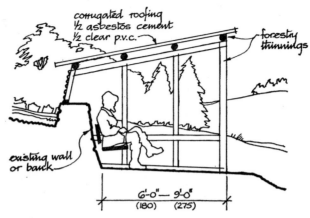

Shelters can often be more closely integrated with their surroundings if they are designed as simple lean-to's, from existing walls or field banks. Extra height can be gained by building up off the wall and the space filled with clear sheeting or timber boarding if protection is needed against draughts. Sides can also be filled where protection is needed. Precautions must be taken against wind lift.

*Gazebos* will usually be most satisfactory if they are treated as a sophisticated intrusion and not played down.

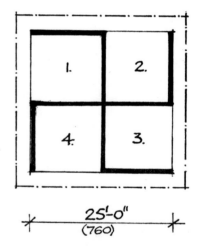

Hikers' overnight shelter for tour parties.

### Hikers' shelters

Very simple hikers' shelters on a swastika plan (above) have recently been devised by the American NPS. These provide welcome shelter for long-distance walkers. Orientation cannot be ideal for everyone if all compartments of the shelter are in occupation, but the protection given would certainly be cosier than the open air.

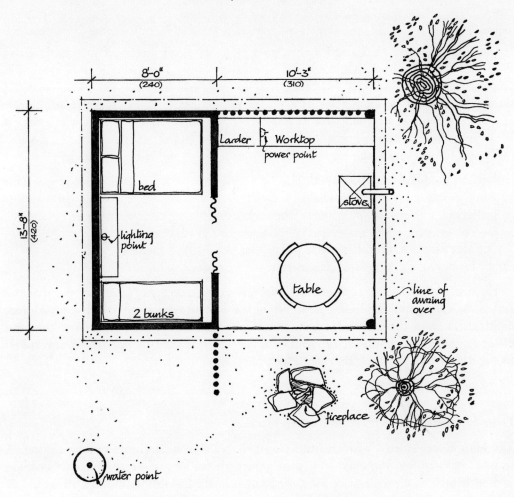

Camping shelter (a Housekeeping Unit) in Yosemite National Park.

## Camping shelters

The provision of camping shelters has proved to be a highly successful experiment in the Yosemite Valley, California, one of the most famous and popular of all American National Parks. It was made by the concessionnaire responsible for tourist accommodation in the Valley: hotel, châlet, and dormitory. These shelters are the most sought-after accommodation on offer. Although the idea would not work as it stands in the British climate, its enormous success makes it worth recording here for possible adaptation (see also Plate 109).

165

The shelters are grouped under the redwoods which form a giant canopy and which knit the whole camp together visually.

Each unit consists of a lean-to shelter, 13 ft. 8 in. [4·1 m.] wide × 8 ft. 0 in. [2·4 m.] deep. This is roofed by canvas sheet and a canvas flysheet which extends as an awning in front of the shelter forming a generous porch across its whole width, 10 ft. 3 in. [3·05 m.] deep. The walls of the shelter are of 4 in. [10 cm.] concrete block; the 6 ft. 0 in. door [1·83 m.] opening is screened by a canvas curtain. The floor slab over the whole area is concrete. A hurdle screens one side of the porch.

The equipment and fittings consist of:

Porch: full-length work-top with electric point, meat safe type larder, wood stove for cooking, round table and four chairs.

Shelter: double bed, 2 single bunks, shelf unit for dressing table mirror.

Annexe tents for additional sleeping space are also available.

Outside: fireplace, drinking-water point (shared by 2 or 3 shelters).

Public lavatories, showers and a launderette are provided.

The concessionnaire, who describes these units as Housekeeping Units, stresses that one reason for their popularity is the flexibility of the scale of equipment which can be hired. This ranges from the basic necessities listed above through bedding, and cooking and eating equipment down to the last teaspoon. Hire of the basic equipment (summer 1967): $8 per day or $44 per week for one to four persons.


## Lean-to shelters for individual camp pitches

The Islamic caravanserai provided individual shelter as well as communal protection. A series of bays around the open courtyard gave each family a place to unroll its bedding and brew up a meal, with space for goods and animals. Camp sites in the U.K. could be made very much more comfortable by the provision of simple lean-to shelters which would not only break the prevailing wind but could help visually by screening a site. This has been done at the Stage House, Inverewe (National Trust for Scotland) with an encouraging measure of success. Here bays, typically 10 ft. 0 in. [3·04 m.] across × 9 ft. 0 in. [2·75 m.] deep have been formed against the concrete block screen wall (painted white). These are covered with asbestos cement sheeting. Where tents are pitched to open on to the shelter, campers can use them for cooking, storage etc. In some cases people choose to pitch inflatable tents actually under the shelter itself. It is important that the lean-to roof should slope away from the opening, that the concrete floor of the shelter should fall towards the outside (say 1 in 100) and that the ground immediately outside the shelter should not drain into it. Ground should be suitable for pitching tents/parking vans close to the opening of the lean-to.

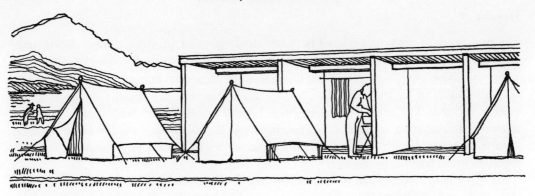

Simple shelters give protection to campers and also screen the site (National Trust for Scotland).

## Timber screens to camp pitches

Timber screens of sawn timbers, 7 ft. 6 in. [2·28 m.] high have also been erected on the Stage House site. They are useful practically and visually. They must be sturdily constructed to resist wind pressure. 7 in. [18 cm.] diameter poles are erected in pairs at 7 ft. 6 in. [2·28 m.] from centre to centre; they are connected at the top with $\frac{1}{2}$ in. [1·25 cm.] diameter bolts. Between these posts 3 in.–4 in. [7–10 cm.] horizontal poles, resting on the ends of those of the adjacent panel, form the screen.

Timber screens erected to protect caravan from gales and the landscape from caravans (National Trust for Scotland).

167

## Domes

The two types of dome considered here are air domes and geodesic domes. Both, until recently, were thought of mainly in terms of military or outer space programmes. Various designs are now available which have characteristics particularly suited to the provision of outdoor shelter for leisure activities. They are light, compact, can be easily transported and quickly erected. The price per square foot is very competitive[1] wherever a large uninterrupted floor space is needed. So far, in the U.K., their chief use has been for bulk storage, but they have a great potential for indoor sport and for any event for which a marquee is the traditional answer.

*Site Conditions*: Domes can be erected on any level reasonably well drained field. They are usually secured by a cable round the base, which is itself anchored to the ground by steel bars. Anchorage is complicated on paved surfaces into which anchor bars cannot be driven, but this problem is being solved by weighting with sand or water bags. There are presumably sites, such as those between high buildings, where extraordinary local air conditions could make special anchorage necessary. The dead load of the dome (itself remarkably light) is evenly distributed: ground which would not carry even a lightly constructed conventional building might offer quite enough bearing for a dome. Although it is easier if the truck delivering the components can drive right on to the site, this is not essential. Therefore where access is restricted dome construction has advantages over traditional structures.

*Air Domes* fall into three categories:

(a) Single-skin domes. These are like puffed-up marquees; the air pressure inside replaces the poles and guys. The whole tent is inflated and there must therefore be some sort of air lock at the entrance. For social functions revolving doors are commonly used; for sports and storage a simple two doored air lock is effective, if a little gusty. The disadvantage of this type of air dome is the inevitable isolation between the interior of the tent and its surroundings. Casual circulation between indoors and outdoors is restricted to the use of the air lock; the tent cannot be thrown open to the garden. Incidentally, the clear soft light inside the dome and the pattern of the seams of the material can be astonishingly beautiful.

(b) Double-skin domes. The space between the two skins is inflated so the air pressure inside the dome is the same as that outside it and no air lock is necessary. Openings can therefore be made anywhere in the dome to suit its exact function. There is therefore no restriction of circulation: people can wander in and out casually.

(c) Ribbed domes. A single-skin tent is supported by inflated ribs. This construction has been used for family scale tents.

*Geodesic domes* were invented by the American designer Buckminster Fuller. In America they have been used both for large exhibition buildings several hundred feet in diameter

---

[1] Around 10 shillings per sq. ft. was the approximate figure given by several manufacturers in 1967.

and for quite small structures (the American National Park Service has used 40 ft. 0 in. [12·2 m.] diameter domes for temporary visitor centres). The domes consist of a series of triangles framed up to form polygons. These are assembled like a giant construction toy. A small dome can be assembled by one man in a few hours (see Plate 95). In-filling panels can be clear or opaque. Spaces at ground level can be left open.

## Holiday cabins

No simple prefabricated holiday cabins seem to be on the market in the U.K. One firm of manufacturers of prefabricated buildings of high repute has withdrawn its only chalet because it did not comply with interpretations of the new (1965) Building Regulations. The alterations necessary, though not extensive, would have put the building out of a popular price range and it was therefore not worth continuing its production. The same regulations govern conventionally built cabins and have a similar inhibiting effect.

In a holiday cabin, insistence on standards now applicable in an all-the-year-round dwelling may cut down a very useful amenity. It would seem logical to regard a cabin as a substitute for a tent. It should be soundly constructed, water-tight and hygienic but other qualities could be left to the discretion of the owner. It is worth analysing the structure and finish of various huts in which you may have lived comfortably for a matter of days or months, here or abroad, to see if they could be allowed by enlightened interpretation of the present building regulations. Heat insulation, for instance, however desirable, is not *essential* to the well-being of a camper.

Simple timber weatherboarding or shiplap boarding must, under the Regulations, be lined both for insulation and, unless it is specially treated, to prevent possible surface flame-spread. This new regulation (E.14) is interpreted differently by local authorities. Some still allow untreated matched boarding which is now so popular as an internal wall finish, and which seems particularly suited to a holiday cabin.

The basic characteristics of a successful holiday cabin are:

1. *Robustness,* which must include a sense of warmth and relaxation; a feeling that walls and partitions will survive the odd knock; that foot marks will not show up on the floor. Internal timber finishes are usually much more satisfactory than plaster. Whatever the actual total insulation value of a wall, a timber surface has the great advantage of *feeling warm* to the touch and rapidly warming when the room is heated.

2. *Lightness:* the cabin will usually be inhabited by townspeople who for a week or two of the year want to feel they are out of doors, even when they are inside.

3. *View:* a long view is not essential. A short interesting view (e.g. into a glade) is admirable.

4. *Simple, tough, generously proportioned furniture* designed to reduce housework to a minimum. As much furniture as possible should be built in. Nothing should have legs which could be bracketed or cantilevered from the wall. Plenty of shelving and hooks.

169

*Plan:* The amount of privacy wanted by those who rent holiday cabins varies surprisingly. Some new motels in the U.S.A. are designed for five to a room (two double and one single beds). This plan apparently suits the typical American touring family: parents with three or more children. Motel management generally closes its eyes to the precise number of children parents choose to stow in a typical motel room. Probably bunks are not popular for this reason: only one child can sleep in each; accommodation is more flexible where double beds are provided since several can sleep across a bed.

Some separation is more likely to be popular in the U.K., particularly in cabins not specifically designed for touring. But conventional holiday house plans are usually extravagant in their use of space. The brief for a family cabin may include the following but it is likely to be scaled up or down according to need.

1. A generous living-room/kitchen, reminiscent of a farm kitchen, is the heart of a cabin. It may include some built-in bed or bunk space. The food store should open off the kitchen space.

2. A deep porch can lead off the living room; it should also have benches and a table for eating. It must be sheltered from the prevailing wind and trap the sun.

3. Small sleeping compartments (say 6 ft. 6 in. × 7 ft. 0 in.) can lead off the porch or the living room. Provision for locking these must be made when the cabin is shut, if they lead off the porch. Each should have bunks (2 or 3 decker); shelving for clothes, dressing table and wash basin (bowl on shelf); hooks; individual lighting for bunks.

Dunlopillo mattresses have made the design of bunks cheaper and easier (all that is needed is a shelf to take the mattress). Fitted sheets have speeded bunk-making. Sleeping bags are still far simpler.

4. A slightly larger bedroom can be provided for parents, who may want a retreat from open-plan holidays.

5. A drying room.

6. A w.c. or chemical closet preferably approachable under cover.

7. A shower is the first luxury to be contemplated if piped water is available.

## Hides

Hides can immensely extend the human enjoyment of places where birds or animals habitually feed. This is not only for the obvious reason that they can be watched undisturbed but because a hide allows for watching in comparative comfort whatever the weather. Thus those whose watching is limited to weekends and annual holidays have greatly increased scope; it is in really hard weather conditions that some of the most spectacular gatherings (of both watchers and fauna) can be seen.

*Light* is the most important general consideration when siting a hide. During the most important watching hours, the sun should be behind the hide.

The *approach* to the hide should be naturally screened wherever possible. This is particularly important where a considerable turnover of watchers is expected. Earth banks provide the best cover. Gaps and gateways in the natural screen must be covered with brushwood, furze, timber, or hessian on post and rail frame work. Overhead netting can be used to camouflage an approach where flying birds coming in to feed could see people moving up to a hide.

The detailed design of a hide is most important to its success. That given in the drawing on this page and the notes in this section are based on long experience of the Wildfowl Trust, Slimbridge.

*Size:* It has been found that hides 5 ft. 6 in. [1·68 m.] wide × multiples of 6 ft. 0 in. [1·83 m.] in length (internal dimensions) are the most satisfactory and economical. Space in the hide must be allowed for the required number of people (possibly with bulky clothing and hung around with instruments) to get in and out of position silently, without undue jostling or scraping the walls.

*Requirements:*

(a) An *observation opening* 7 in. [18 cm.] deep in which a 6¼ in. [15 cm.] shutter is placed, allowing a ¾ in. [2 cm.] preliminary viewing slit at the top. The shutter, hinged at the

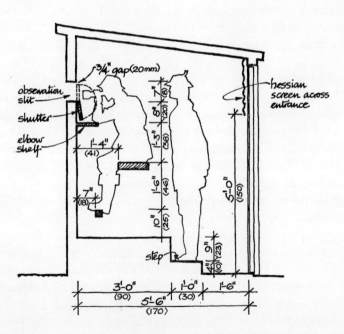

Section through hide (information supplied by the Wildfowl Trust). The observation slit is continuous. The step allows for people of different height to watch between those seated.

171

bottom, must be capable of opening right down, and is secured by a turn button at the top, and provided with a 14 in. [36 cm.] chain and hook to allow it to be held in any position.

(b) An *elbow rest,* placed 8 in. [20 cm.] below the bottom of the opening, projecting 8 in. [20 cm.] from the wall face (take measurements at foot level if wall is not vertical).

(c) *Seats* 1 ft. 11 in. [58 cm.] below the bottom of the opening, and 1 ft. 4 in. [41 cm.] from the wall face at foot level.

(d) A *foot rail* or foot step 18 in. [46 cm.] below seat level, 7 in. [18 cm.] from the wall face.

(e) For people standing behind those who are seated it is best to provide two levels by means of a step (as shown in drawing); the main walkway, 5 ft. 4 in. [162 cm.] below the bottom of the observation slit, for tall people; and a continuous step 5 ft. 0 in. [152 cm.] below, for shorter people.

(f) It may also be useful to fix a *bar* on which these people can rest their elbows while using their binoculars. A height of 4 ft. 9 in. [145 cm.] above his particular floor level is comfortable for someone 5 ft. 9 in. [175 cm.] tall; others can adjust their arms positions quite comfortably.

(g) *Entrance:* It has been found advisable to hang a loose flap of hessian from the top of the doorway into the hide, reaching to the level of the bottom of the observation opening, to prevent birds noticing movement against the sky behind.

(h) *Notices* warning against noise may be required.

(i) *Photography* from the hide. Small openings below shelf level and clear of seats are useful if cameras are to be used on tripods standing on the ground. If the hide has block walls they should be splayed like arrow slits.

*Construction.* Normal methods of construction may be too expensive for hides whose function is simply to shelter people (in outdoor clothes). They must be robustly constructed, resistant to the wind, have a watertight roof and a solid floor which will keep dry and not puddle. But ventilation will automatically be of a high standard so walls will dry out in a way impossible in an enclosed shed or room. The Wildfowl Trust offer the following notes on construction for hides built at ground level.

*Materials.* A wide range of materials and designs are possible depending on position, degree of performance, usage and cost.

*Walls.* 4 in. [10 cm.] concrete blocks or 4½ in. [11 cm.] brickwork for wet sites, permanence, building into banks, etc. (In very long hides half partitions can be used internally to buttress the walls at, say, 18 ft. 0 in. [5·5 m.] centres.) Walls can be camouflaged if required with weather boarding nailed outside, or with paint, or can be hidden by creepers or bushes. A hide built into a bank is largely disguised by the bank itself. Timber framing clad in weather boarding: 3 in. × 3 in. [8 × 8 cm.] posts at 3 ft. 0 in. [1 m.] from centre to centre are taken 2 ft. 0 in. [60 cm.] below ground level, and set in concrete. All timber is first treated with preservative. Where earth may be heaped against the sides of the hide, blocks or brickwork should be used instead of weather boarding. Framing can be clad in corrugated asbestos sheeting (will not stand rough usage).

*Roofs.* Felt on 1 in. [2·5 cm.] close boarding on 2 in. × 3 in. [5 × 7·5 cm.] rafters. Corrugated asbestos on 2 in. × 3 in. [5 × 7·5 cm.] rafters and 2 in. × 2 in. [5 × 5 cm.] battens. Weather boarding on 2 in. × 3 in. [5 × 7·5 cm.] rafters (pitch should not be less than 40°). Traditional roofs of slate, tile, thatch or wood shingle are expensive but may be appropriate in exceptional circumstances.

Roofs of hides in exposed positions will need special fixing to resist wind. Galvanized strap ties can be used to fix the plate to the studs at, say, 6 ft. 0 in. [2 m.] centres. Lean-to roofs can often be of lower overall height than 2-way pitched roofs. With such a small internal span (5 ft. 6 in. [1·68 m.]) little economy in timber will be derived from use of a 2-way pitch.

*Floors:* Necessary wearing quality will depend on traffic. If subsoil is suitable and well drained (light gravelly soils are easier than clay) it may wear well enough with a $\frac{3}{8}$ in. [1 cm.] gravel finish *thoroughly compacted* (gravel must not kick loose or scrunch). A paving slab should be laid in the doorway to take heavy wear.

Alternatively floors may be of thoroughly consolidated hoggin on subsoil, or of 3 in. [8 cm.] concrete slab.

*Costs.* Even an approximate total cost of erecting hides as described is impossible to give in view of the unknown expense of labour, but the Wildfowl Trust gives the following costs of materials only for 12 ft. 0 in. [3·66 m.] hides. These costs are based on retail prices after the November 1967 devaluation, and include a small amount for cutting and waste.

Cost of gravel, sand, cement, blocks, timber, roofing felt, ironmongery and nails.

1. Hide with concrete block walls and felted boarded roof with 2-way pitch: £33 per 12 ft. 0 in. run.
2. Timber framed hide with weather boarded walls and same roof: £47 per 12 ft. 0 in. run.

## Forestry Commission Observation Towers and Hides (Plates 104–106)

The Forestry Commission has constructed observation towers (for, say, a dozen photographers or naturalists), safari hides (4 people) and individual high seats (for stalkers), which have proved to be very popular. The pioneer tower in Grizedale, erected by a local builder, is 25 ft. 0 in. [7·6 m.] above ground level; floor area, 8 ft. 0 in. × 10 ft. 0 in. [say 2·5 × 3·0 m.]. Cost of material £59, cost of labour £78. Safari hides cost £20–£30 (1966). Towers have now been constructed in other parts of the country. These are mostly on fire tower bases and are slightly larger so costs are not comparable, but at a rough estimate the costs are around five times that of the original tower. It is extremely difficult to detail a structure in such a way that prices can be kept down. Once away from the

'Let-Bill-get-on-with-it' method of design and construction it is inevitable that prices soar.

Safari hides are the cheapest form of observation tower. Comfort apart, the viewer must be shielded from the light if slight movement is not to disturb animals. A roof is therefore essential. For functional reasons a hide will be generally erected in a sheltered position in forests where it is unlikely to have to withstand gales. It will anyway not be used in such circumstances. Hides are guyed to trees and may use a convenient tree for partial support.

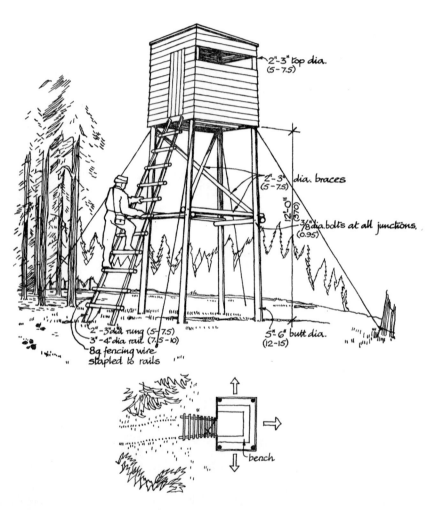

Forestry Commission safari hide.

174

## Viewing platforms

Everyone enjoys watching other people work. Watching can enormously enhance leisure both on account of an intelligent interest in what is happening and for the simple satisfaction of seeing others hard at it.

This pursuit has been admirably catered for by many of the large building firms who operate on city sites. Their viewing platforms are crowded at every lunch break. The same idea could well be extended to the country. A platform may not be necessary; some barrier which clearly defines the limit beyond which the public is not welcome may be all that is needed. A large explanatory drawing (see *Signs*, page 59) describing the operation and what it aims to do is most helpful. This can be moved from site to site.

It may also be advisable to erect one of those depressing signs explaining that the public is watching at its own risk and the management accept no responsibility. . . .

Where possible the viewing platform should be sheltered from the prevailing wind, sited so that spectators do not look into the sun, and provided with a bench or two, and a bar for elbow propping when watching through binoculars.

*Possible places:* The works to be viewed will mostly be temporary; forestry operations such as timber extraction; dam building; netting for fish; quarrying. Others like sawmilling and stone-cutting have permanent sites. When choosing operations for watching it should be borne in mind that a great many people going into the country take binoculars.

# 13

# Pools and small lakes

During the eighteenth and nineteenth centuries a practical knowledge of the construction of small lakes was part of the equipment of most countrymen. Many of the holes they dug and the dams they built still hold water and are now often regarded as 'natural'. They are of immeasurable value in the landscape.

Today, with modern techniques at our disposal, we seem loath to take on anything less than a reservoir or formal reinforced concrete pool, both the province of the civil engineer. The small 'natural' lake of perhaps less than an acre (up to, say, 2–3 acres or 1 hectare) is not their province; it is difficult to discover whose it is.

Safety is obviously of utmost importance. The *Safety Provisions of Reservoirs Act,* 1930, lays down that when five million gallons are to be stored above natural ground level the reservoir must be designed by a qualified civil engineer.

To visualize this quantity of water it may be helpful to know that one acre, flooded to a depth of 44 in., represents one million gallons. It will be seen that many amenity pools are unaffected by this act, and are too small fry for the civil engineer unless by happy chance he is already engaged in some larger part of the project.

In searching for people experienced in the techniques of such humble construction one landscape architect was found; others included an ornithologist, foresters and farmers (who construct reservoirs for fire-fighting and irrigation), and a reluctant architect determined on a lake but unable to find anyone more capable than himself.

Undoubtedly the most experienced smaller-scale pool constructors are those officers of the Ministry of Agriculture, Fisheries and Food who advise on the construction of farm reservoirs. Advice based on such experience would be invaluable, but it might be difficult for an official to find time for a non-irrigation project. *Water for Irrigation*[1] is an indispensable handbook on pool construction for anyone new to the field. Its object, underlined by the title, must be borne in mind; landscape design is not in its terms of reference. However, a civil engineer's advice may also be necessary, particularly with regard to impounding dams and flowing streams; it is anyway always welcome whether or not it is legally obligatory.

[1] Ministry of Agriculture, Food and Fisheries Bulletin No. 202. HMSO.

176

The *Water Resources Act,* 1963, is administered by the River Authorities. Under this Act both impounding and abstraction licences must be obtained before pools are formed. Abstraction is unlikely from an amenity pool, but whether or not impounding is envisaged, the appropriate River Authority should be approached at an early stage (for addresses see *Water for Irrigation* Appendix 1).

Neighbouring landowners and local natural history societies should also be informed, since a new pool can have a marked ecological effect on its neighbourhood; both may give helpful practical advice. It should be noted that where a pool is formed by an impervious sheet and is fed from some distance the surrounding land is likely to remain unaffected by the pool and therefore its natural plant life may seem 'unnatural' to the water side. See page 198 (notes on small swimming pools).

## Types of pool

There are three main types of pool:

1. *Seepage holes* make use of *a high natural water table.* Where the water table is only a foot or so below the ground level, the earth is simply dug away to expose it. The excellent pools dug out of sand, constructed by the Netherlands Staatsbosbeheer, are a good example (see also page 98 and Plate 114). Wet gravel pits have a great potential.

2. *Off-stream pools.* A reservoir is fed by a channel from a stream. Intake can be controlled by small weirs and a flood gate so that in times of flood all the water is taken by the main stream. This is obviously a great economy both in dam and spillway construction. But in terms of design (as against irrigation), small on-stream reservoirs may be more easily integrated into the landscape than off-stream pools.

3. *On-stream pools.* A dam is constructed across a stream. It must therefore be designed to take the whole flow of a catchment area (i.e. usually not more than about 10 acres [4 hectares] for pools considered here). This means that the project is likely to be more expensive than off-stream storage. But conditions certainly exist where the arm of a small valley might be a very suitable site and expert advice should be sought.

## Siting in relation to landscape

See also page 35. Water inevitably becomes a focal point in the landscape: a pool can transform an otherwise uncoordinated design; nor should its attraction to people be underestimated. New pools should therefore be sited where people are wanted and not only where a stretch of water will enhance the landscape. From the landscape point of view a new pool is likely to look its best where water naturally lies after rainy weather. The existing trees and shrubs will then be moisture tolerant and the new pool will be quickly integrated into the landscape. Unfortunately trees should not be planted on the dam itself

M                                                              177 since their roots will grow towards the water and form channels of seepage. Shrubs which might otherwise do no damage may look out of place unless they are of a species which already grows in the vicinity of the pool. Most ornamental shrubs would divorce the pool from its surroundings; heather or gorse on the other hand might be planted together with grass in moorland country.

In Germany and Holland a contract to dig for sand or gravel often contains clauses which cover the reinstatement of the working to an agreed landscape plan. (This practice is becoming more common in the U.K.) It includes the grading and the plan of a new pool, as well as the phasing of the operation so that a part of the pit may be put to recreational use while the rest is still being worked. Planting plans may also be included in this contract.

*Borrow pits* are the quaintly named holes from which the earth is dug to form a dam. Since this soil is removed for ever not to be returned, the siting and shaping of such pits is important in the landscape scheme, and should not be left to chance.

## Pool construction

Trial holes are essential and need not be expensive. A light excavator can usually work down to a depth of 11 ft. [3·35 m.]; some to 14 ft. [4·26 m.]. Essentially all pools have the following requirements:

1. A *source of water*. The pool will lose by evaporation whether or not it loses by seepage, although in the wet west it may gain more from rainfall. In the case of seepage pools the source is that of the *water table* itself.

2. *Means of retaining the water*. Earth dams are commonly used for the type of pool considered here. Seepage pools lie in their own natural saucers.

3. A *spillway* for flood water. It is essential to guard against the danger of flood water overtopping the earth dam. An overflow pipe or trickle tube connected to a drainpipe can fix the normal water level a few inches below the spillway. This reduces erosion in the spillway (assuming it is not a walled channel) and, in fish ponds, reduces the loss of small fish when the pond is stocked.

4. Means of *emptying* for cleaning: by means of a *valve* at bottom level; or the water can be pumped out of the lake into a convenient stream or drain.

5. On pools fed by streams, a small *catchment pool* may be formed to collect sediment between the supply and the lake. This can be more easily cleaned than the lake itself.

All these points and many others are covered in *Water for Irrigation*.[1] They will only be touched on here in order to give an idea of factors involved in the siting of the pool, the types of soil suitable for an earth dam, how much space it is likely to take, and such things as edge details which are of much greater importance in amenity pools than in irrigation reservoirs.

[1] ibid.

# Earth dams

The *stability* of low dams depends on:

1. Soil used in their construction.
2. Soil on which they rest.
3. Section of the dam (i.e. width and slopes).
4. Prevention of internal erosion.

1. *The soil of the foundations.* The whole dam could slide if the horizontal thrust of the water was too great. The dam should therefore be on a horizontal bed. Rock foundations should be avoided since it is very difficult to get a bond between the rock and the earth of the dam; this junction could form a seepage path.

2. *The soil used for building the dam* should contain 20–30 per cent clay, with well-graded sand and gravel. If there is too much clay it means the dam will shrink and expand. With too little, it will leak.

3. The *detailed cross section* of the dam depends to some extent on both the preceding points, but an idea of the profile is given by the following table (allowing at least 10 per cent for settlement):

SHAPE AND SLOPES OF EMBANKMENT AND EXCAVATIONS[1]

Using suitable soils on suitable foundations, stable embankments *not exceeding 15 ft. in height* may be constructed if the following conditions are adopted:

1. The wet or upstream slope must not be steeper than $2\frac{1}{2}$ horizontal to 1 vertical.[2]
2. The dry or downstream slope must not be steeper than 2 horizontal to 1 vertical.
3. The minimum top width of the embankment must be as follows:

| Maximum height of embankment | Minimum top width |
|---|---|
| 6 feet | 8 feet |
| 9 feet | 9 feet |
| 12 feet | 10 feet |
| 15 feet | 11 feet |

Where there is any danger of the embankment leaking a vertical diaphragm of impermeable soil (i.e. soil treated with bentonite[3] or with a higher proportion of clay) cuts the dam and is keyed into the foundation. Similarly an impervious core can be carried down into an impermeable layer where the dam sits on permeable soil.

4. The prevention of internal erosion depends on a variety of factors including the provision of collars on any pipes cutting the dam since they form lines of seepage.

[1] ibid.

[2] Some authorities give 3 rather than $2\frac{1}{2}$.

[3] A natural clay, usually supplied as powder. The grains swell on contact with water and increase the water tightness of the soil with which they are mixed. Extensively used in the U.S.A. Not much tried in the U.K.

## Depth

All aquatic plants tend to cease at a depth of about 6 ft. 0 in. [1·83 m.]. 4 ft. 0 in. [1·22 m.] seems to be deep enough in some circumstances. Bathing pools in the Dutch sandpits are usually 1 metre deep. Where bathing or paddling is to be discouraged weeds and water plants are a far more effective and attractive looking deterrent than a forbidding notice. This method is adopted in German recreational pools. Any large area of water is likely to be improved visually if certain parts carry water plants; here the depth should be reduced to 6 in.–18 in. [15–45 cm.].

## Edges

Water is a fascinating design material since it never weathers: the surface is the same on the day the pool is filled as it will be a hundred years later. Edges are a different matter: they have an enormous visual as well as practical effect on any pool. See pages 182–183. Where there is to be no access to the water from the bank, edge design is a relatively straightforward problem of linking the pool with the natural terrain.

An amenity pool is unlikely to be subject to large variation in water level, the bugbear of much reservoir design. Where variation occurs the gradient of the shore will decide how much is exposed at low water; gradient will depend on angle of repose of the soil. Local shingle with small boulders can make an enormous difference to the edges of pools which would otherwise have a low water of mud. The banks of the pool can also be seeded with grasses which will stand a mobile water level.

## Wave fret

Stone pitching (rip-rap) may be necessary on a bank to prevent wave erosion. The extent of the wave action will depend on the exposure of the pool and its length. The height of waves can be calculated from the formula[1] $h = 0.025\sqrt{L}$ where

$h$ = height of waves in feet,
$L$ = greatest length of water surface

The dam must have enough free board to ensure there is no danger of its being topped.

## Bathing beaches

In sand pools intended for bathing, beach cleaning is simplified if the area of sandy beach surrounding the pool is limited to a relatively narrow strip of sand (say 10–20 ft.) which can be renewed at intervals. See also page 98 for note on litter clearance. Gradient: up to 1 in 10.

[1] Technical Bulletin B-205, Wright-Rain Irrigation Service.

## Edge erosion caused by waterfowl

Wherever birds feature on water there is an erosion problem along the banks where they get in and out. Ducks, with their big flat webbed feet, are particularly destructive; unless precautions are taken the pool will get bigger and shallower as the bank slithers into the water. Unfortunately it is usually particularly important that these bird pools should seem to be natural, so ingenious edge detailing is necessary.

## Concrete edges

Concrete edges have been used with particular success at the Wildfowl Trust, Slimbridge, where few visitors realize that the pools have not 'natural' gravel edges. This concrete is taken 3 or 4 ft. inland beyond the water line where the bank is to survive heavy duck traffic. Angle of bank: 30°. It is important (and extremely difficult) to achieve the necessary rough finish to the concrete, which most good concretors would consider to be poor workmanship. Unless this is achieved, the sand and gravel which is scattered on the green concrete will soon slide off and the bare concrete that may be exposed will look smooth and urban. It will be pointed out that the uneven concrete will harbour water in its crevices and that this will expand and cause cracking in frosty weather. Small cracks will not matter much (this is a concrete edging, not a reinforced concrete pool). In fact the rough concrete, being less prone to surface shrinkage, may have fewer cracks than a standard job.

## Timber edges (Plates 112–113)

Steep banks can be retained by small timber piles. The Dutch follow this practice but these banks cannot be negotiated by waterfowl without a ladder. A neat compromise allows ducks to swim over under-water piling which retains the bank proper and then to land and waddle up a shallow bank. 2 in. or 3 in. [5–7·5 cm.] of water over the piles is enough to float a duck (see drawing page 183). European larch thinnings provide suitable timber.

## Methods of waterproofing

The traditional method, still useful where soil conditions are not conducive to seepage (e.g. in clay soils and loamy clays), is to apply a layer of *puddled clay* where there is a potential danger of seepage. This is only now economical where clay can be dug on the site and where very little puddling is necessary. More recently, methods such as *asphalt* or *bitumen* waterproofing, *concreting*, or the use of *rubber sheeting* have been used. For the type of pool considered here *polythene liners* have a great many advantages including cheapness and, it would seem, durability. They are also non-toxic to plants and fish.

Edge details of a lake lined with polythene sheet. The sheet is anchored in the soil; this also protects it from sunlight which can cause rapid deterioration. The resulting lake can look like a natural pool.

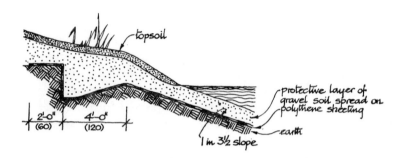

A

(A) As at Wyddrington Lake, Birmingham (architects Casson and Conder, in association with British Visqueen Ltd.). See Plates 110–113.

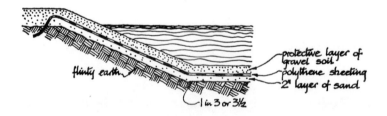

B

(B) The simplified basic detail now developed by British Visqueen. Topsoil would also be necessary for a natural looking edge.

# EDGE DETAILS TO PREVENT EROSION BY WILDFOWL

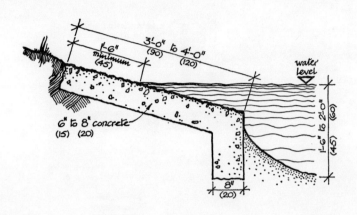

A

(A) Concrete edging with a rough surface which appears 'natural'. (Severn Wildfowl Trust.)

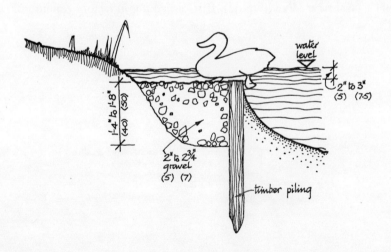

B

(B) Bank retained by timber piling below water level. This will take less heavy wear than the concrete edging above.

183

## JOINT DETAILS FOR POLYTHENE LININGS

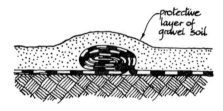

A

(A) Heat sealing (as used at Wyddrington). Best carried out in factory conditions.

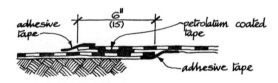

B

(B) Pressure sensitive adhesive tape with mastic bead seal is generally used on site. The petrolatum coated tape (up to 2″ [5 cm.] wide) is protected by adhesive tape on the upper surface; it may be thought worthwhile to seal the lower surface too (as illustrated). N.B. This method uses up much less polythene on the joint than that above.

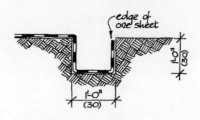

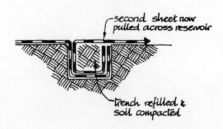

C

(C) Edge burying is used in U.S.A. but has not yet been tried in Britain. It is extravagant in sheeting material on the joint, but has the advantage of needing neither tape nor heat sealing.

## Polythene lined pools[1]

Polythene lined pools have been used successfully for some years; their long-term durability cannot be accurately forecast but it is known that the material is weakened by direct exposure to the sun's ultra-violet rays. Black polythene might survive ten years; natural or coloured, two or three. But if the sheet is properly protected from the light at the edges near the waterline it should have a long life since under water, where the light rays are broken up, they will do little damage to the polythene. If the whole sheet is covered by 6 in.–8 in. earth, deterioration seems most unlikely.

*Joints:* Welding or seaming tends to weaken the polythene, therefore sheets should be made up in the factory in large sizes, e.g. 60 × 24 yards [55 × 22 metres]; these can be joined on the site to form a complete membrane (see opposite and above). In a large lake, such as the 4½ acre [1·82 hectare] lake at Birmingham University, Plates 110–111, any small seepage through the welds is said to be negligible in comparison to the volume of water.

*Gauge of polythene:* the manufacturers' advice should be consulted about gauge. 500 is usual for duck ponds and garden swimming pools; 1,000 for small lakes.

[1] Information supplied by British Visqueen Ltd.

SIZES OF SHEET:

| gauge | colour | widths in feet | | | widths in metres | | |
|---|---|---|---|---|---|---|---|
| 500 | natural or black | 12, | 24, | 36 | 3·65 | 7·31 | 10·97 |
| 500 | blue | 12 | | | 3·65 | | |
| 1000 | natural or black | 12 or 24 | | | 3·65 | 7·31 | |

*Colours:* Black may be three times as durable as natural; blue comes between. In visual terms black will look much more natural than blue. Clear turquoise pools are harshly discordant in the English landscape.

*Laying the sheet:* It is vital to protect the sheet from tearing or puncturing. After excavation all sharp projections and roots must be removed, and the soil tamped to as smooth a surface as possible. A 1 in.–2 in. [2·5–5 cm.] layer of moist sifted earth or sand makes a good bed for the sheet on rocky or flinty soil. The sheet can be shaped at the corners by folding on the site or it may be shaped in the factory. Sharp corners should be avoided; it is easier to fit the sheeting to gentler curves.

*Edges:* Firm anchorage and adequate protection from sunlight and impact are important at the edges. The profile of the sheet is shown in the section on page 182. A side slope not steeper than 1 in 3 prevents the earth cover from sliding. Where the whole sheet is not to be covered with earth the pool should be gradually filled with water before the sheet is fixed by backfilling with earth in the side trenches. This allows for the sheet to take up any irregularities in the profile without being unduly stretched.

*Bathing* in polythene lined 'natural' pools, as against swimming pools, could cause damage at the edges since the earth protecting the polythene might be dislodged by bathers wading in and out. Jetties should overcome this problem. No experience seems to be available of the effect of children paddling on the soil covered bottom of a polythene lined pool.

*Springs:* Underwater springs, often helpful in maintaining the water level in pools, can displace the polythene sheet which may appear above water level in ominous bulges.

# 14

# Marinas and boat harbours: siting problems

## The demand

Just when the need has vanished for any Briton ever again to set foot on a boat, even in order to emigrate, the urge to do so has caused a demand for moorings which is completely outstripping the supply. This, naturally, is at its most acute within weekend reach of the large centres of population, particularly in the south and south-east of England, but there is every likelihood that it will spread. The natural deep water moorings are nearly all taken up. It is now no longer enough to own a yacht; it may remain high and dry without a berth. To meet this demand planning applications for both new marinas and harbour extensions have come in to every county planning office whose area includes English Channel coastline, besides others on the East coast, Wales and Scotland. Most of these proposals are having a sticky passage, and many have sunk without trace. The object here is to ventilate some of the problems that are automatically raised by such development, since many new projects are likely to come up for consideration in rural as well as urban areas.

In some quarters there is opposition to the very word *marina* and, without a clear picture of what it describes, serious confusion is likely.

## Marina: definition

Like so many words it has different meanings on each side of the Atlantic. In America, where the word was coined back in 1928, it was defined as 'the modern waterfront facility for recreational boats'. In the U.S.A. today this can mean anything from the vast yacht parks of Long Beach to the humble shack advertising BAIT, TACKLE AND RAMP: the staple requirements of any boat-trailing fisherman. In Britain *marina* is translated in the former sense as an artificial yacht harbour which is planned so that the owner can walk aboard at any state of the tide without using a dinghy and which provides all the services he is likely to need (see page 193). Some developers wish to include other schemes in order to offset the high cost of the marina itself.

If 'Marina' is thought to be synonymous with the traditional 'Yacht Harbour', considerable confusion can arise. They can have a very different impact on their surroundings.

187

To many of us a yacht harbour conjures up a picture of sailing boats riding at their moorings, swinging freely with the tide; each boat is doubled by its reflection; masts and rigging mix with the clouds below them. They are protected by a steep rocky headland and an immense stone breakwater, as permanent as the rocks. Since its buildings crowd round the quays, the harbour provided the original *raison d'être* for the town. There is no quicker way of getting into the heart of a town than to sail into it. Inevitably such harbours have a sense of enclosure and shelter even stronger than that given by many a formally planned piazza. The simple forms of old warehouses, boat-sheds, houses and pubs, walling in the water, make not only a marvellous back-cloth to the fine lines of the yachts, they also absorb the odd untidy shack, rubbish dump or rusting hulk in such a way that they do not stick out like a sore thumb.

A marina is not like this: it differs in almost every way. In siting since it may be on the edge of open country or on a featureless site (Plate 120). In planning because the idea demands that a maximum number of boats be moored in a given space; the boats are therefore closely packed but on the land there may be an amount of 'spare' ground unfamiliar to the usual economy of land use connected with traditional harbours. Much of this land will be needed for car parking: essential but not attractive. At least two car spaces are needed per boat. In *use* because, although it is greatly to be hoped that the few marinas which are planned in old established sailing centres are for sailing boats only, there is little doubt that elsewhere power will dominate.

In addition to these differences, British marinas may be designed to meet the needs of a different type of customer from the man popularly associated with harbours. Forget that description from *The Wind in the Willows* which has been quoted with so much affection and so often in books on sailing and cruising. Marinas are not necessarily for those who want to mess about in boats. On the contrary they are primarily for the man who feels that pressure of work, lack of time and an adequate income call for a service whereby one telephone call will arrange that his yacht will be serviced and ready for sea at any specified time throughout the twenty four hours, *regardless of tide*. An efficient service is what he needs and he must be willing to pay for it. Many yachtsmen are.

This brief comparison of the ideas behind a modern marina and a traditional harbour is only intended to dispel any notion that because a marina is concerned with boats and harbours, it is automatically an attractive project. Like any other it must first be properly sited and well designed. It then has immense possibilities, both in itself as useful, shipshape and good to look at, and also as the greatest asset to its surroundings. (Plates 118 and 119.)

## Types of marina

Marinas fall into four main types. Conditions outside the harbour (sheltered or exposed), range of tide, soil and hydrographic conditions, effect choice of type and size.

## Marinas and boat harbours: siting problems

(a) *The Locked Basin*. Most locked harbours have one (sometimes two) single gates which allow boats to enter for a certain time on each side of high water depending on the height of the sill of the lock and the dredging of the channel outside. The disadvantage is that the time of entry to the harbour is limited and boats might have to wait outside in rough weather for the tide; nor can they leave at will. The advantage is that once a lock is formed, the harbour has a tide range limited by its design; piles to which the pontoons are secured can therefore be much shorter (and cheaper), and such problems as those of connecting the pontoons to the shore are greatly simplified.

(b) *The Tidal Basin* with pontoons, moored to piles, floating the full tidal range. Piles are usually also used to moor boats at the non-pontoon end. Used where tidal range is small or the building of a locked harbour is impracticable. With big tides the long piles necessary will have to be braced for stability. They cannot be braced below water level (fouling of pontoons) therefore an additional 7 ft. 0 in. [2 m.], say, will be added to their length in order to take bracing which allows headroom on the pontoon at high tide. Such piles are not only expensive (although in many cases the best answer) but they can give the harbour visually an entirely different character from that of a tideless basin. It may be a character scarcely realized by the designer himself at the earliest stages of the design. It can be exciting: a forest of piles, rising thirty or so feet above your head at low tide, dwarfing the yachts, contrasts strongly with the uninterrupted fingers of jetties lying quietly on the water, the subject of so many perspective sketches. It is essentially urban in character and in keeping with the dolphins, cranes and other giant furnishings of a port. It could alter the scene in some lazy backwater more radically than any new building.

(c) *The Haul-out Marina*. The Americans regard this type as a true marina and it is now popular for sizeable boats as well as dinghies and small power craft (a vertical marina has been developed where boats are stacked three deep). If sailing is to continue to expand, particularly among the less well-to-do, we should consider the particular problems of the haul-out marina right away. It is much cheaper to construct (little or no dredging, piling or pontoons are necessary). Visually the boat parks, often behind security netting, deserve careful design, otherwise the place may look like a Ministry of Defence dump. Dinghy parks will save the trailing of boats at weekends (it would be interesting to know in this connection how many do-it-yourself kits are sold to home boat-builders each year).

Haul-out marinas would seem to have great possibilities in Britain, in spite of the problem that many boats deteriorate from not being kept in water. However, modern glues and the use of materials like fibre-glass may eliminate this problem. A haul-out service is included in some of the conventional designs. A factory on Southampton Water has developed a system whereby boats of up to 31 ft. 0 in. [9·5 m.] o.a.l. can be put in the water in a matter of two or three minutes from specially designed trailers. (Plate 116.)

(d) *Marinas on Non Tidal Waters* (rivers, lakes and gravel pits). These are obviously much cheaper and only have some of the problems considered in this section.

## Siting

The problem of siting has to be tackled both from the yachtsman's and developer's angle and from that of the marina's effect on the area as a whole. This includes appropriate land use (e.g. is a marina an asset on a lonely estuary?), harbour traffic, land traffic, other users (e.g. the shell-fishing industry) and so on. One thing is clear: to find an ideal site which satisfied all conditions might mean no marinas. But at least a site must satisfy the majority of conditions. *From the yachtsman's point of view* it must both be accessible from his work and be somewhere where he wants to sail. This is so obvious that it seems to be forgotten by many would-be developers. There must be reasonably sheltered water and other harbours within reach (preferably within this shelter) *to sail to* (hence the popularity of the Solent). *Power boats* are less dependent on shelter. Newhaven, where one of the few new marinas proper has been built, might, by comparison, seem bleak outside the harbour. But here power-craft owners are in the majority. It is well situated to run across to France, and if a chain of marinas was constructed at about 40 mile intervals along the south coast, the very real problem of where to go would be solved.

## Tidal range

The range of the tide is a prime consideration for the developer. This makes an area like Poole Harbour with its 7 ft. [2·13 m.] tides or parts of the Solent with their double high tides particularly attractive. However, developers at Newhaven were undeterred by their 25 ft. [7·60 m.] tide.

## Harbour traffic

Most sheltered waters in the south of the U.K. already carry tremendous traffic. The idea of a marina can naturally cause a harbour master grave concern. Visions of small craft drifting under the bows of big merchant ships are, however, not realistic since marina yachts are powered and much more manoeuvrable than most merchant shipping. The Dutch, incidentally, apparently manage these matters well in a confined space at Rotterdam.

*Dinghies.* Some marinas plan dinghy parks in addition to their deep water berths; their shallow draught should make it possible in theory to regulate the traffic: at low water let each craft sail in the shallowest water in which it can float.

As a council of perfection new marinas should be near the mouth of a river in order to prevent congestion in upper reaches, but this is not necessarily a major consideration.

## Landward traffic

The ever growing landward traffic problem has also to be remembered. A conservative estimate put the number of car-parking spaces per boat at 1·5 to 1 (1965); 2 or 3 to 1 may soon prove nearer the mark. A marina on the outskirts of Washington, D.C. has a car park used by sailors at weekends and by office commuters, who leave their cars and use public transport to reach their offices, during the week. Small country lanes, or small country towns, could be quickly jammed by a weekend rush of traffic to a new marina added to an already groaning road system. If they can be sited near main roads (or airports or rail-heads) so much the better.

## Effect on adjacent land

American experience suggests that the effect of a marina on the adjacent land values is not to be ignored. It can also be a great asset visually. A well sited marina can become a focal point in an otherwise depressed area, particularly an area of unused derelict land, which would otherwise be difficult to make positively attractive. For this reason marinas are quite often part of a much broader redevelopment scheme which contains housing development as well as its own basic necessities.

On the other hand a marina at times appears to be designed to provide a *raison d'être* for housing development (holiday or otherwise). The first question to ask is whether this is the right place for *new housing?* If it is, well and good. If not, whatever the merits of the individual design, it should be resisted.

## Misuse

The planning officer also has the potential problem of a floating gin palace whose owner seldom intends to put to sea. The marina may seem very tempting to anyone searching for a 'weekend' cottage'. For the rent of a berth, say, £200 per annum, and the cost of his boat, his problem is solved, but he and his like will turn the marina into a water-borne caravan park, which was not the planners' intention.

## Power-craft

If the increase in boats is anything like the forecast, marinas will have to be built in the non-traditional sailing areas. Those with a high proportion of power-craft (i.e. the great majority) should not be planned in a relatively quiet sailing estuary. The thrill of a fast motor boat must be counterbalanced by the noise, wash and smell it can create. It is exhilarating to watch high speed turns from, say, the Thames embankment where no sound can be heard above the din of the traffic, and the river lies empty under a winter sun, but the same manœuvres would have a very different effect on a quiet green estuary, in the height of the summer. Modern power-craft are so simple to drive that on such waters little skill is necessary: press the self-starter and off you go. The peace for several miles radius is shattered. Zoning is essential. Since a marina is essentially inward looking, focusing on its harbour, suburban and urban sites should be used before we encroach further on what is left of unbuilt-on coastline and estuary. A well designed and properly sited marina can then be a positive asset to down at heel surroundings. It cannot but 'urbanize' untouched country.

## Cost

Cost of Harbour Works. The developer for his part must find a site where the cost of what is inevitably an expensive undertaking will not be prohibitive, and where he can get a lease of the foreshore and river bottom in question. The depth of water immediately off shore and the condition of the bottom are extremely important. Very shallow water for a long way out means expensive dredging and is anyway unconducive to sailing. Alternatively a steeply shelving shore, like much of the Clyde, some of which drops into 12 fathoms [22 m.], makes marina construction extremely expensive. Expert advice has to be sought as to whether the proposed harbour is likely to scour or silt, whether the bottom is suitable for dredging and whether the dredged material is suitable for dumping on land to be made up. A dig and fill procedure is the obvious economy, and if land now unsuitable for buildings can be made useful, it may be to everyone's advantage. Problems of piling for mooring the pontoons, and types of harbour wall, must be considered.

Test bore-holes must therefore be made: an expensive procedure. This, together with the possibility of a marina being the subject of a public enquiry before planning approval is granted, means that the gamble of getting a marina under way is considerable. Around £10,000 might be spent before outline planning approval was refused.

A marina, by the very newness of such projects, is likely to be on land scheduled for other purposes. If this involves a substantial departure from the development plan, the application may be referred to the Minister. This alone, rightly enough, causes suspicion among local inhabitants. The cost of a public enquiry may then be added to the cost of test-borings and the cost of the delay. Any measures to speed things up and to create a positive attitude would be useful.

## The developers

Nearly all developers in Britain are private companies. In America things started in this way but the pattern of development in the U.S.A. has shifted. It is now not uncommon for the municipality to construct a marina and for it then to be taken by a private company. Private developers in the U.S.A. are complaining about the municipalities' interest. This gives food for thought.

## Rentals

Local yachtsmen may well oppose marinas on financial grounds. Where space now taken up by cheap moorings is converted into a harbour, the existing holders may not feel inclined to pay for the services and convenience which automatically go with marina development. Yet if all other moorings in the area are taken they may have little alternative. Some companies provide a number of mud berths, which although very much more expensive than the old moorings are about two-thirds the rent of those on the new pontoons. Figures can be misleading since a marina rental will include the care of the boat in winter and all the year round security in addition to the many services already mentioned. But whereas a yachtsman paid 30s. p.a. harbour dues as recently as 1960, £90–£100 p.a. would not be unusual for a marina berth.

When marina berth rentals are compared with car parking figures, or it is remembered that the original cost of the boat to be parked often exceeds that of a typical suburban house, these figures do not seem excessive. But for the local sailor they obviously represent a formidable outlay seemingly out of all proportion to his accustomed rental.

## Services

Yachtsmen ashore still concentrate their interest on their boat. They want the sociability of the club house and the service of the repair yard, or chandler's shop, a hot bath and a hot meal; but the meal is best eaten in a restaurant looking down on the harbour, and the service buildings must be as near the water as possible. The whole focus of interest is the harbour with its comings and goings; it is inward looking. The surroundings really matter relatively little. A good design will underline this.

*Schedule of Requirements.* A typical marina has the following basic services. In some they are more elaborate; in others extremely simple.

*In the Harbour:* Moorings on floating jetties for all boats or hard standing with haul out or other facilities for handling shore berthed craft.

Water supply and electricity to each berth. Some provide telephones.

Fuelling point (often near harbour entrance).

Fire alarm and firefighting systems.

Garbage collection system.

Sewage disposal system: this obviously varies according to the site of the harbour, and whether it is locked or open. Public lavatories ashore and the sealing of heads of boats in harbour, is one solution. Other authorities let the problem take care of itself (apparently with success according to some American experience).

*On Shore:* Harbour master's office and control room.

Club house or other facilities for yachtsmen for hot food, bar, w.c.'s, shower/baths, changing rooms.

Boat repair yard.

Sleeping accommodation: very useful if yachts are not all of a size to sleep aboard. May vary from hotel to hostel standard. Chandlery; food shops; off-licence. Many marinas have a showroom, where boats, engines etc. are displayed for sale. Self-service machines for food, milk etc.

Car parking (1·5 cars per boat minimum); petrol sales; a service station where cars can be serviced while owners are at sea.

Provision for children: seldom officially provided but bigger marinas might well make provision for care of yacht-bored children while parents are at sea. A nursery for small children; dinghy sailing, etc. for older ones; hostel accommodation for over night. It is too easily forgotten how very dull sailing with efficient parents can be. But from the parents' point of view the only alternative may be to give it up.

Landscaping: ominous ideas about lawns and flower beds in some publications are unlikely to be in character. Few plants survive near the sea. Robust use of hard surfaces in the true harbour tradition is likely to be more useful.

Other accommodation: in some places, particularly where dinghy championships are sailed, more shore accommodation will be useful. A holiday village can be a real asset on the right site.

## Summary

Some local opposition to marina projects, however they are to be used or are sited, is to be expected. Few of us welcome any change in our own surroundings, particularly if these are rural and the project in question will bring in more people: this simply underlines the importance of proper siting, but some opposition seems inevitable whatever the conditions. The Duke of Edinburgh pointed out in his presidential report to the Royal Yachting Association back in 1963: '. . . whilst some harbour authorities are tackling the problem (of new yacht harbours), there is usually strong, if perhaps rather selfish objection to individual proposals for this kind of development. I am firmly convinced that if yachting is to expand additional harbour mooring space must be found.' This is as true today.

Unless a move is made it would seem that in ten years' time the boat-builders' yards and back gardens might have their full complement of craft doomed to remain unlaunched while many a would-be yachtsman resigns himself to yet another weekend spent in mowing the lawn.

# 15

# Small swimming pools

Most camp developers are aware of the tremendous attraction of swimming baths. Even a small pool can make an enormous difference to the popularity of a camp.

## Character

From the swimming point of view most of the pools on the market make satisfactory tanks for a refreshing dip or swim. In landscape terms, however, there are too many disappointments. Perhaps one reason for failures in this respect is an incurable English romanticism about what the pool is really going to look like. The word is in itself misleading: the less attractive description 'small swimming bath' is much nearer the mark. Pools conjure up mysterious depths, plays of light and shade, sun filtered through branches, leaves drifting idly on the water, all of which are conditions which most experts strive to avoid. A swimming bath on the other hand is expected to be bright, clean and hygienic; the algae are not allowed to multiply and to this end leaves are instantly removed.

It therefore follows that the pool tends to be divorced from such hazards as trees (which are often in boundary fences) and weeping shrubs; plants are discouraged even in the joints of the surrounding paving. The dream pool is pushed out into the open and the dappled depths of our imagination become a uniformly blue intruder, often out of scale with its surroundings and nearly always discordant in colour and texture.

## Functional requirements

1. *Sunlight*. In camps (as against private gardens) the pool is likely to be used throughout the day. The sunbathing space should have some shade.

2. *Shelter* from draughts, both for the pool and the sitting out space beside it.

3. *Safety*. The pool must in some way be fenced from the rest of the camp for the safety of wandering small children. The gate latch must be child proof.

4. *Changing accommodation*. Since campers will change in their own tents, changing accommodation is generally unnecessary. Where required, 3 ft. 6 in. × 3 ft. 6 in. [1m. × 1 m.] timber cubicles with partitions 9 in. [23 cm.] clear of the floor, provided with a bench

195

seat and two hooks, is an adequate answer. Lockers should be provided for clothes storage. Mirrors inside cubicles slow turnover of use.

5. *Showers*. A shower and foot-bath should be provided even with small pools.

6. *Store* for cleaning equipment.

7. *Filtration, emptying and heating*. Technical details vary and must be obtained from the manufacturer. Most pool suppliers also supply this equipment. It consists basically of a diatomaceous earth filter, a motor, pump and piping. Filter pump and heater do not have to be immediately adjacent to the pool. They can be housed partly or completely below the ground in a space approximately 3 ft. 6 in. [1 m.] square by 2 ft. 6 in. [75 cm.] deep (this obviously varies with different models). It is worth bearing in mind that if advantage is to be taken of cheaper off-peak electricity, the motor must not be positioned where it will disturb people at night. A sound which is hardly discernible during the day against general traffic can be annoying when all else is quiet.

At the end of each summer and perhaps at other times, the pool will have to be emptied into the sewer or local river. Where there is any danger of upward pressure from water in the ground under the pool when it is emptied, a hydrostatic valve should be included in the outlet.

### Underground hazards

Drains and service runs may govern siting. Underground springs can cause considerable difficulties if not diverted. The soil structure is unlikely to present problems which cannot be solved by one type of pool or another. Where a traditional pool is envisaged, a small excavator or tractor with mechanical digger must be able to get into the site. If one of the modern fibre-glass or vinyl-lined pools which stand out of the ground is to be used, this is not essential. However, a fibre-glass pool, being all in one piece, can itself present awkward problems of access, some of which can be ingeniously overcome by skilled crane operators. The cost of a dug-in pool will be considerably reduced and the design of the surroundings often improved if the excavated material is used to bank the surrounding land.

### Shape

Rectangular pools are usually more satisfactory to look at and cheaper than the various free shapes which have been tried in an effort to achieve a more 'natural' pool. The results of such attempts often seem meaningless, perhaps because landform round the pool does not reflect its shape; water following the outline of an outcrop of rock or a grass bank will give an entirely different impression to that of the same outline on a flat lawn. Scale also plays an important part, and a shape that may give satisfaction on parkland scale can seem wilfully contrived when translated into curves of a few feet radius. Round pools on the other hand seem to give an easy link between the formality of paving and clean water and the informality of grass and trees beyond. Gang planks, plank bridges or projecting slabs, on which bathers can sunbathe or simply dangle their legs, can add greatly to the attraction of a pool, particularly to children. Some pools are made with steps running the full width of the shallow end; this is attractive both to use and look at and saves the need of a ladder.

## Depth

For diving, recommendations vary from 6 ft. [1·83 m.] for diving off the edge to 8 ft. 6 in. [2·59 m.] for low spring boards.

In small pools it is often thought better to stick to one depth, since a sloping floor may be too steep and some consider either a sloping or a stepped floor to be dangerous. If a shallow end for small children is needed a temporary platform can be put into the pool and its edge roped off. But a sloping floor does give the advantage of a deep end with considerably less excavation.

## Colour

If the walls of a pool are white, sky reflection will turn the water light blue; this colour has nothing to do with the addition of chlorine. Unfortunately this blue, although attractive enough in brown arid landscapes, and customary in swimming baths, has little to link it with the greens of an English lawn or garden. Here it will always seem what it is: unnatural. This seems argument enough in itself for linking the pool to its surrounding by screen walls and paving, rather than leaving the colours to fight it out on the lawn.

Some firms recommend that the pool should be cream rather than white in order to give a less icy blue. Fibre-glass and vinyl linings come in light colours (usually blue, making the water appear deep blue), seldom in a pure white. It would be very interesting to experiment with different background colours and their effect both on the colour of the water in relation to its surroundings and on the quality of enticement to the potential bather. Is it possible, for instance, that the peat brown of the pools of mountain streams might be the answer in some heath gardens? Dark colours which absorb the heat would make the water warmer (sheets of black polythene laid on the surface of the water can considerably raise the temperature by cutting down surface reflection).

## Hard surfacing adjacent to the pool

An 8 ft. 0 in.–4 ft. 0 in. [2·50–1·25 m.] wide paved edge or sitting-out space must not kick up small pebbles, etc. which might get into the pool. It should fall away from the pool; some form of land drainage may be necessary at its junction with grass or beds to prevent the ground becoming soggy. If the area round the pool is entirely paved, drainage should be provided in it. Asphalt, which reacts to chlorine or hot sun, should be avoided. Concrete or stone slabs and brick paving and cobbles are popular. *In situ* concrete offers scope for non-slip techniques both in the shuttering or in the exposure of the aggregate. Straight-forward subdued colouring is best for concrete. Some sort of handgrip is essential in deeper pools and is often integrated in the top course of concrete blocks, also forming a scum channel.

## Pool furniture

(a) A hand mangle for wringing bathing costumes (with drain). (b) 7 ft. o in. × 7 ft. o in. × 12 in. [2·13 × 2·13 × 0·30 m.] high, sturdily built, wooden divans are useful both for sunbathing and as casual tables, but food and drink are generally not allowed in the pool area because of the danger of broken glass etc.

## Planting

This can only be touched on in the most general terms. First the attitude of mind of the owner on priorities in the conflict between clear water and foliage must be decided. Although many experts are against neighbouring trees, one or two good specimens which do not actually overshadow the pool may be felt to be well worth the trouble of falling leaves. It is in autumn, when most swimming is over, that the majority of deciduous leaves are shed.

Pools have been designed with an adjacent pool of only a few inches depth for the growing of water plants, and certainly the most attractive-looking pools are those where trees and planting are closely integrated, but it must be borne in mind that, water gardens apart, the plants which will thrive in the well drained patio-like conditions beside a pool are probably those which will tolerate dryness and heat rather than cool damp conditions, and so a conflict in types of vegetation must be avoided. Incidentally, since the typical swimming pool is so un-pond-like in character, such patio plants may look better than green moisture-loving specimens.

## Types of pool

The range extends from the traditional pool sunk in the ground, in which the earth walls of the excavated hole are retained by *in situ* reinforced concrete or block, to the new steel or man-made fibre variety which consist essentially of a waterproof shell, or a skin supported by a framework, which may be above or below ground level or be partially buried. While the traditional types are obviously integral with the garden and its landscape, the others can (but need not) be designed on opposite principles: i.e. of the light man-made object contrasted with its surroundings. But if this approach is to succeed all must be ship shape, very well detailed and maintained. Otherwise the sordidness to which all seasonal structures that have outlived their original purpose are subject can quickly creep in. What was brave and gay with white paint and new canvas may have the forlorn look of a forgotten exhibition-stand towards the end of the season.

*Concrete block, brick, reinforced concrete and gunite construction:* walls are usually rendered and then painted annually, but some renderings contain marble chippings and are not painted. Pools of these materials are usually completely sunk. Any size is possible, but the Cement and Concrete Association recommends depths of up to 3 ft. [say, 1 m.] for do-it-yourself block pools.

*Sprayed gunite:* a very useful reinforced concrete technique much used in North America and capable of following irregular contours. After the pool is excavated a basket of reinforcement is fixed in position and the liquid concrete sprayed on. Subsequent treatment is as for other concrete pools.

*Fibre-glass:* a logical extension of the idea of a washing-up bowl. The pool arrives in one unit complete and ready for installation. Its size is therefore dependent on the capacity of the road transport and the accessibility of the site. Pools of up to 35 ft. 0 in. × 14 ft. 0 in. × 3 ft. 6 in. to 7 ft. 6 in. [10·67 m. × 4·27 m. × 1·07 m. to 2·28 m.] are included in the standard ranges.

In these and vinyl-lined pools the smoothness of the wall itself discourages algae and eases cleaning without painting. The pool is designed to withstand possible water pressure in the ground only when it is itself full, and it must therefore not be left empty. Pools can be partly or completely out of the ground provided adequate support is given. White pools are sometimes available; light colours are common.

*Vinyl-lined pools:* In the shallow, 3 ft.–4 ft. [approx. 1 m.] deep standard pools these may be considerably cheaper than other types, but it should be remembered that the expectancy of life of the vinyl liner is only five years. However, it is designed for replacement and the cost of a liner for a 25 ft. 0 in. × 9 ft. 0 in. × 8 ft. 0 in. [7·62 m. × 2·74 m. × 2·49 m.] pool might be in the region of £40. The supporting frame may resemble light timber aircraft construction, or vinyl is occasionally used to line a traditional concrete pool. Untreated vinyl may deteriorate where exposed to direct sunlight, so the section above the water line is a source of weakness; manufacturers have experimented and claim to have found methods of combating such deterioration. White vinyl is not available.

*Steel pools* are usually erected free standing on the surface of the ground. They rely on a steel wall to resist the pressure of the water and a vinyl layer to waterproof it. A walling has been devised for round pools of corrugated steel sheet supported by interlocking bridge-type steel sections. It is claimed that two men can assemble a 24 ft. 0 in. [7·3 m.] diameter pool, 4 ft. 0 in. [1·2 m.] deep in a few hours.

As in the case of other pools on the surface of the ground, very careful siting is necessary, but the fact that many steel pools are round rather than rectangular often makes them easier to integrate into the landscape. Manufacturers point out that an upstand pool on the surface of the ground is safer for small children and need not be fenced: while this usually applies in private gardens the danger on a camp ground where ladders might be inadvertently left in position should not be overlooked. The popular turquoise blue of many of these pools looks better against stone or concrete rather than the greens of grass or trees.

# 16

# Litter

## Problem

In this section the problem is confined to litter in the countryside produced by people enjoying informal leisure. That of dumping (cars, old bedsteads, etc.) is not included. Opinions vary enormously about methods, ranging from Bins-universally-to-hand to Take-your-litter-home.[1] But everyone is agreed that litter is seldom singular. One beer can or one ice-cream carton in an otherwise clear lay-by or picnic place immediately attracts others. There are no magic cures or short cuts to litter-free sites at the moment. On both sides of the Atlantic the familiar answer to questions as to why there is no litter around is 'We pick it up'. Every warden, planner or owner does this with continuous zeal; the most insignificant toffee paper cannot lie since it inevitably acts as a lure. The great difference between the U.S.A. and the U.K. is that almost every American student is working his way through college, so a vast army of potential litter collectors is released just as the holiday season is gathering momentum. (There is a difficult couple of weeks during the hiatus between Memorial Week-end which marks the beginning of the season and the start of the vacation.)

The problem needs analysis from three points of view. That of the potential litter dropper; the rubbish collector; the visual impact of litter bins and/or litter in the landscape.

To consider one or two of these points in isolation is useless. As much litter may be broadcast on a windy day by a dustman dealing with a badly designed refuse bin, as is distributed by a sunny Sunday's worth of picnickers. Ill-sited bins can be as much a blot on the scene as litter itself.

## Potential litter scatterers

This includes nearly everyone at some time or other but sociologists say that young men are the most active and middle-aged women the least likely. This is probably an aspect of

[1] Recent experience suggests that the take-your-litter-home policy works. The National Trust has successfully removed bins from some sites. Some of the tidier counties do not provide them in laybys.

the broad generalization that men are the scatterers and women the gatherers. There is an added subtlety since what some of us regard as litter others do not: throwing down a cigarette wrapping, particularly the thin silver paper which surrounds the cigarettes, is to some smokers synonymous with knocking off the ash. The idea that on simple aesthetic grounds you should not thrown down litter is so new that it would seem wildly optimistic to imagine that it should be an inborn instinct. If in some places there is spontaneously an absence of litter, someone has picked it up or not thrown it away simply because it is a valuable commodity. No old tin, newspaper, bottle or plastic bag is left lying around a village on the Anatolian plateau because such things are of great value to the inhabitants. If anything is discarded by some extravagant foreigner it is immediately harboured by a thrifty inhabitant. Litter is a product and a problem of the affluent society and one on which it is very loath to spend money. But until we can instil as much pride and affection for our open spaces as many Englishmen feel for their own gardens, it seems that we must provide litter receptacles in strategic places.

*Take-your-litter-home.* Everyone has his own ideas about the feasibility of this attitude and those with wide experience may argue differently. At least one senior local government officer regretted that the relevant committee were not to be persuaded to try such a campaign on lay-bys under his care. He felt that his committee regarded provision of bins as 'progressive' whereas his own experience suggested that too many people made only an optimistic shy in the direction of the bin and missed. If the public is to be persuaded to take its litter home (and this has been achieved in a remarkable number of instances) bins can be removed for a trial period; they will not deteriorate in dry storage. It is certainly the ideal solution, tremendously worth achieving.

## Rubbish collectors

*Who does the collecting?* There is a real distinction to be made between those places where the bins are emptied by someone who never otherwise visits the site (most garbage collectors) and those where a warden or other employee, who is employed the whole time on the site itself, collects litter as a part of his work. He is naturally more interested and probably takes considerable pride in the appearance of the site; he is anyway unable to avoid seeing it throughout the course of his working day. But judging by the state in which we, the public, so often leave things, it would be unrealistic to expect a dustman to be concerned about the paper that flies around each time a conventional bin is emptied into his truck. He would never get through his rounds if he stopped to gather it.

For these reasons receptacles designed to use disposable sacks are particularly useful where

1. an outside authority does the emptying
2. an outside authority empties infrequently and litter must be stored between collections.

There are places where an efficient system has been evolved in which staff, doing rounds on some other daily job, also collect litter. It may well be felt under these circumstances that disposable sacks are too expensive.

## Litter disposal on beaches

It was disappointing to find no short cuts either in Europe or America. In a Californian park a hand operated skimmer had been designed to clean beaches. It was believed to be successful but the lifeguards responsible for its operation admitted that it was not used since it was both easier and quicker to pick up the litter by hand. On Jones Beach, one of New York's most popular resorts for a day outing, bins are spaced at regular intervals across the shore and are emptied by a truck, under contract during the night (every night). Dutch designers limit the problem round new pools at picnic places by restricting the width of the shore.

## Mechanical devices

Little experience has been gathered for rural sites. Where bins are sufficiently concentrated a forklift truck can be used to exchange full bins for empty receptacles. In Colonial Williamsburg a vacuum cleaning system is in use but this is a more urban site. It has money to experiment so results are worth watching.

## General siting of litter containers

The *siting* of litter containers is enormously important. Broadly speaking they should be sited at the greatest potential sources of litter always provided that the receptacle is accessible for emptying. Nothing is worse than an overflowing bin. Nor is it helpful to site bins between these points 'for luck'; few things are less entertaining to meet than a superfluous litter bin. There is plenty of room for experiment. Formal sites can absorb bins in a way impossible to open country. On a new site bins can be tried in various positions before their positions are finalized.

Likely sites include:

1. Places where *ice creams and drinks* can be bought.
2. Wherever people *eat*; organized *picnic sites* and *lay-bys*.
3. At *destinations* where they gather. For example, at a view point one ice cream's worth of walking from an ice cream vendor. Inside and outside public lavatories.
4. Tickets: at the point where entry *tickets are sold*. This is tricky since most of us want to get rid of a ticket as soon as we are given it but where there is no official collection visitors may be expected to keep their tickets for checking purposes.
5. At all *car parks,* particularly those places where motor coaches halt. Site clear of danger from reversing cars.

6. *Camps:* Two schools of thought thrive:

1. Individual bins are provided throughout the site (say at every third pitch). They are put along the roadways for ease of access and collection. Visually this can be depressing but seems to be generally considered acceptable. It is convenient.
2. Bin compounds are constructed. Since campers have their own receptacles in their tents and vans this is also practicable. The camp certainly looks a lot better. The compound should be down-wind from the camp. An area should be included for stacking filled litter sacks.

## Detailed siting

There is a conflict of interest here but it can usually be resolved by careful analysis of the site. The litter receptacle must be *immediately visible and accessible* (see page 160). But a badly sited bin can be almost as irksome in the landscape as litter itself. Consider the not unusual sight of a solitary litter receptacle silhouetted against a splendid open view. The criteria governing the siting of a bin are the same as that of any garden (or for that matter indoor) furniture. It should be *grouped with some larger object* such as a tree, or small building, not dotted alone seemingly at random. The smaller and more foreign the 'furniture' the more important it is to ensure that it is integrated with its surroundings in this way. Where a litter container must stand on its own in a space quite out of scale with itself, a bigger receptacle with a horizontal emphasis will probably look much better than the typical vertical shape of a sack in its stand.

Containers look much better *fixed to something larger than themselves* than free-standing: a building, wall or fence. This immediately makes them less intrusive. Many monuments would obviously be visually cheapened by such treatment but there is usually a hut or boundary wall to which the bin can be fixed.

Before any bins are brought on to a site a lot can be learnt by observing precisely how a place is used: the route taken by people leaving a car park, where they finish eating an ice cream, pause to admire. . . . A bin is likely to be used in direct proportion to the numbers of people who automatically pass within reach of it. But it should be sited a few feet from anything that actually restricts the flow of people on a busy site (e.g. a guichet or entrance gate) otherwise it may form an obstruction and be masked from potential users.

*Frequency of collection* also affects siting and may well decide whether or not bins should be installed. No one wants to sit close to a bin which is emptied say once a week, therefore it is impracticable to incorporate a litter container in the design of most country benches or picnic tables. But at Expo '67 in Montreal the designers solved the otherwise overwhelming problem of tens of thousands of meals eaten out of doors with disposable plates, cups, knives and spoons and paper napkins by providing litter receptacles built into the seats and benches. Since these were constantly being emptied they were never stale, smelly or overflowing. But as they were so conveniently to hand, most people made use of them.

The *ground* under and immediately surrounding the bin will be liable to puddle. It should be of well compacted gravel or other hard material, marginally higher than the surrounding ground so that it can fall towards it.

## Capacity

*Capacity* must be geared as much to the frequency of emptying as to use. Sacks on wardened sites can be replaced as needed by the warden and collected from his compound by the Local Authority. It seems wise to allow for large sacks since it is easier to cut down than increase. $3\frac{1}{2}$–$4\frac{1}{2}$ cu. ft. [0·095 – 0·125 cu. m.] is used on some lay-bys. 2–3 cu. ft. [0·06–0·08 cu. m.] (grade B in B.S.) is more common in less busy positions.

## Lids

All receptacles in open country (including lay-bys) need lids: otherwise the litter is re-broadcast by birds, animals or the wind. Exception: sheltered gardens and the immediate vicinity of some buildings.

Unfortunately many of the plastic or rubberized lids on receptacles now on the market are light and have to be weighted down by stones. Some manufacturers are over opti-mistic about the ability of a lid to remain shut, e.g. on gusty moorland. One solution might be to fix a weight (e.g. a large metal washer or disc, on the inside of the lid). Galvanized metal lids are probably better on grounds of weight, but they may break off.

An alternative is to provide fixed lids, like hoods, so that the litter is 'posted' through a side opening. That shown in Plate 129 is hinged for emptying. When shut it is held in position by a lug over which the door fits. The door can be secured by a padlock so the result is nearly vandal-proof.

Receptacles without lids are often successfully used in sheltered positions where they can be emptied daily. Then it is important that rainwater drains out but litter does not fall through. One cheap method is to form the bottom of the container of 2 layers of $\frac{1}{2}$ in. [12·7 mm.] galvanized chicken wire arranged so that the meshes miss each other.

## Opening for litter

The B.S. recommends that the opening should take a 9 in. × 6 in. × 6 in. [23 cm. × 15 cm. × 15 cm.] block. An opening at 2 ft. 9 in.–3 ft. 0 in. [80–90 cm.] above ground level is convenient.

## Materials

Materials are specified in B.S. 1968. Bins in rural areas must be thoroughly robust. Those on car parks may be backed into, so should withstand impact. Any ferrous metal parts must be properly galvanized after manufacture. There is then unlikely to be need to paint them for either aesthetic or practical reasons.

## Colour

Time and money are saved if the litter container does not need paint. In rural areas drab colours fit best (e.g. brown-olive). If a litter receptacle is thought to be too unobtrusive, a 2 in. diameter yellow ochre dot is all that is needed to make it stand out. Metal liners to 'Royal Parks' type containers in olive, or dull yellow, are more successful visually than the more popular red; black is also good.

Paper sacks are buff; they fit unobtrusively into the countryside particularly in sandy areas (as on some Hampshire C.C. picnic sites, the buff paper sacks in galvanized holders nearly match the sand and silver birch of their surroundings). Plastic sacks usually come in mud green (good) and shrieking crimson (unsympathetic to any country). Concrete pipes painted white look shipshape. The green favoured by some authorities clashes stridently with most backgrounds.

## Disposable sack systems

An enormous amount of litter can be scattered each time a conventional bin is emptied. This is particularly true of windswept sites where lack of cover makes the resulting mess most noticeable. For this reason many local authorities have adopted the disposable sack system. The whole sack is thrown away so litter is not broadcast at the time of emptying. The sack should be regarded as a *liner,* not as a complete receptacle. It must be protected. On many sites an efficiently protected and screened sack of a sympathetic colour in a well designed holder, is as acceptable as any other container. See Plates 123 and 124.

The following points may be useful:

1. *Sack-holders* which, reduced to their simplest form, consist of a ring and collar to secure the mouth of the sack, should be of the type designed to be *bracketed from a wall,* not on a free standing frame. Free standing frames blow over or are knocked over so they must be guyed or staked, or bolted to a concrete block. They also gather litter round the base. Bracketed containers can be bolted to a stout timber post (say 3 in.–4 in. [7–10 cm.]), set at least 18 in. [45 cm.] into the ground. The bag should be 9 in. [23 cm.] clear of the ground.

2. All sacks should be protected the whole way round. Even where there are no birds or animals to tear the sack, damage may be caused by the wind blowing it round its support.

An unprotected bulging sack can look pretty drab even if it is not torn. Minimum protection: galvanized mesh grill. A grill with a *small* mesh can look quite trim. In the U.K. the mesh is seldom small enough to provide a screen. Alternatively timber slats can be fixed to a wireguard to mask the bag completely.

3. *Both paper and plastic sacks* are on the market. Heavy duty gauge is usual for this type of use. It is difficult to get truly comparative prices but a figure of around $4\frac{1}{2}d$–6d per medium sized sack seems likely for bulk orders. A sack can save time and therefore wages. Plastic is more likely to tear if jagged tins or broken glass are thrown in but many authorities use it with apparent success. Glowing embers could destroy either type.

## Plastic liners to conventional bins

Many camp sites, etc. already have conventional dustbins which are in good condition. There is no reason why these should not be fitted with a plastic liner. Provided the sizes can be matched (N.B. the circumference of a circle $= 2\pi r$) the liner will stretch sufficiently to grip the bin when folded back over the rim. No fittings are necessary. This practice has been adopted in several American National Parks. The circular based plastic liners made to fit chemical drums are largely handmade and therefore expensive.

## Metal bins

Various metal bins have been designed, some with very effective self-closing lids. (See Plate 132.) On the whole these are more in character with urban sites. They tend to be expensive and could be tempting to vandals.

## Concrete pipes

*Concrete sewage pipes* usually with wire mesh linings and metal lids have been developed by various local authorities. They look robust and suited to their purpose but would be more effective if a plastic liner could be found to fit inside.

## Royal Parks bin

*The Royal Parks bin* (and other similar designs) is the well-known type with a slatted wood outer container on a short metal stem which holds an inner metal bin. It is suitable to urban parks (within the limits already detailed) but has no lid. It has not been designed to take a disposable liner, but liners can be fitted into the metal bin. Various sizes are manufactured. Those chosen are usually too small and are of rather too sophisticated appearance for rural sites. They can be useful in the sheltered vicinity of stately homes or monuments. In Washington, D.C. where this design has been adopted in the city's open spaces, the scale has been considerably increased (top diameter 22 in., rarely used in Britain). This is a great improvement both functionally and visually.

207

## Wire mesh containers

*Wire mesh containers* without liners are hideous. All those still in use should be scrapped or adapted to take a liner. (See Plate 121.)

## Incinerators

The management of some big picnic sites find it necessary to arrange continuous incineration of litter by the maintenance staff but incinerators which are designed to be used by the public are rare. Authorities are worried about possible danger and there is the practical problem of removing uninflammable litter. But it has been pointed out that people enjoy lighting fires and modern packaging produces an appalling amount of rubbish to be disposed of by most campers and picnickers. A stone incinerator in the Peak District National Park is apparently successful and popular.

A Danish Forest Park has produced a wire cage litter bin which the warden ignites with the help of paraffin as he makes his rounds. This has been found to be satisfactory.

Small camp sites where refuse collection is infrequent might find an incinerator useful.

**Site Use (1 – 5)**  1. Watching the World Cup in a Natur Park, North Germany, 1966. A day in the country is often an opportunity to enjoy ourselves in pleasant surroundings rather than to enjoy a particular place.

2. For the family picnic the family saloon is an extension of home and there is little doubt that some of the most popular picnicking is that with the car as its immediate base. Families come to Clumber Park Sunday after Sunday, seldom picnicking in the same place. National Trust.

3. In wooded parkland on light, well-drained soil it is possible to absorb cars into the landscape by allowing them to be parked where picnickers choose. National Trust.

4. Some of the most popular picnic sites are small pull-offs for about half a dozen cars. Success lies in doing as little as possible. Trees are left standing in the parking area; no edges have been made; a few lorry-loads of gravel have been spread. Forestry Commission.

5. Chestnut paling erected in a zig-zag line as part of a dune fixing scheme happens to form exactly the kind of edge bays which picnickers choose: parties naturally prefer their own small bay in the fence to the open beach. East Lothian County Council.

## Information Centres (6 – 18)

The best information centres give the visitor an instant foretaste of the place he has come to see.

Wildfowl Trust Information and Research Building (Architects: Hughes and Bicknell).

6. Entrance Hall. Water brought right up to a building is particularly fascinating.

7. The opposite point of view. The building from the enclosures; first floor, research; ground floor, exhibition space, lecture hall and sales area. Note 'natural' appearance of concrete edged pools (see page 183).

8. Hopewell Village, Pennsylvania. Now a national historic site. Restored by the National Park Service to show what an early iron foundry settlement was like. After an introductory audio-visual programme at the Visitors' Center, the visitor can make his own way or go in a group; taped messages are available at strategic points. Note authenticity of such details as fencing, dirt roads, etc.

9. Culloden Information Centre (National Trust for Scotland) 1967.
Re-use of an old cottage gives a focal point to the site of the battlefield
without intrusion.

10. Wright Brothers Memorial (National Park Service). The ground over which 'man first flew' is naturally featureless: there was little that could hold the visitors' attention. The hut in which the Wrights camped has been accurately reconstructed; even the canned food is correctly period.

11. Information Office and Site Museum at New Grange, Eire. The opposite problem to that of Culloden or the Wright Brothers Memorial. Here it was essential that the building did not compete with the burial mound. It is withdrawn on low lying land among trees (Architect: Kevin Fox, for the Commissioners of Public Works).

12. Blue Ridge Parkway (National Park Service). A small visitor centre with information room at road level and lavatories below. Note the deep porch.

13. Fishbourne Roman Palace (excavated 1961–65). Shelter over north wing (280×70 ft.; 85.34×21.33 m.). Function: to protect walls and unique mosaic floors from both people and weather while allowing maximum numbers to view them in comfort. Character: unassumingly shipshape; a backcloth to the exhibit. The timber roof floats over uninterrupted floorspace. Catwalks, cantilevered from r.c. supports (planted at irregular intervals to avoid Roman work) allow as many as 800 people to see these remains at one time without over-crowding. The unprecedented popularity of the Palace underlines the importance of planning for success. (Architects: Carden, Godfrey and Macfadyen).

**Yorktown Battlefield
(National Park Service)
Visitor Center**

14. Signs on roof. Note fine wire stretched across top of board prevents birds perching and messing sign.

15. The battlefield seen from the roof of the visitor centre. Cannon (here iron) can be realistically cast in fibreglass.

16 and 17. Dual purpose notice which pivots on post at beginning of tour.

18. Stakes (concrete) reinforce embankments and incidentally help to define them visually. It seems over-optimistic to hope that a path will be followed when a gun acts as a magnet to male visitors of all ages.

19. Timber sign, bleached like driftwood or painted light grey in keeping with the sea-shore. Shape gives direction. A rather large sign is needed here as for a target; it is unaggressive since it does not interrupt the sand and grass which are seen through it. A solid sign of this sort could also produce problems of wind resistance and warping. National Park Service. Fire Island National Seashore.

20. White lettering gouged on timber stained deep brown. The separation of the boards prevents this large sign from dominating its surroundings: the forest can be seen through it. Netherlands Staatsbosbeheer.

21 (*left*). Where several signs must be fixed together they can look trim if designed as one unit with a standardized width and related colour. National Trust for Scotland.

22. Occasionally there is a good case for fixing a sign to a tree: it will look much better if carried free of the bole as in this trim example. Ulster Folk Museum: Robert McKinstry in association with Ian Campbell.

23. Worboys sign, well designed in itself, but totally out of scale both with the problem to be solved and with its surroundings (the direction of slow moving traffic leaving a small minor road). Compare its size with that of the old Ministry of Transport warning sign, and also with the width of the lane and the size of the caravan in the background.

24. Old-fashioned passing place sign: a black and white timber post. Effective; cheap; no metal parts to be damaged; low maintenance.

25. Worboys sign to be read by people walking or driving slowly to park their cars off a woodland ride. Target area of white seems excessive. This sign might be halved in height and condensed in width with the same sized lettering. It would be equally informative and sufficiently obtrusive.

26. P.B. stands for Parson's Bridge, as everyone who has started on this footpath knows from the sign at the beginning. At points of doubt along the way a minimum sign of this kind gives exactly the information needed without fuss.

27. To the left of the path the land falls steeply to a green valley of water meadows and comfortable farms; beyond roll the Denbigh moors to the mountains of Snowdonia. There is a breathtaking illusion of having the whole world at your feet. Suddenly these two identical notices stand against the sky, warning of penalties if cars are driven on the path. It is questionable if such signs are useful and whether they are not themselves as objectionable as what they intend to prevent.

28. No Comment.

*Two examples of Nature Trail numbers.* Used where no existing fence or wall can be marked.

29. Paint on stone; excellent for long-distance reading. Nature Conservancy.

30. Laminated plastic on timber; easy to change. National Trust for Scotland.

31. Temporary 'no camping' sign used when it is necessary for the grass to recover on a particular pitch. Amsterdamse Bos.

32. A simple and effective temporary sign which prevents people tripping over the rope; enlists co-operation; explains why, and is low enough not to interrupt the scenery. National Park Service.

33. A very small sign (about 1 in.) on laminated plastic, in exact scale with its purpose: to direct visitors to a confined passage in an Aberdeenshire castle. They must pass within a couple of feet of it and it is fixed to the wall at eye level. Message is in keeping with situation. National Trust for Scotland.

34. Panorama engraved on aluminium at an overlook in the Yosemite Valley. The sign is fixed low at wall level and is sited beyond the boundary. In this position neither it nor visitors can obstruct the view beyond it. National Park Service.

35. Signs can be simply duplicated by branding on timber. Aarhus City Forest.

**Trails (36 – 42)**

36. A bicycle trail in Holland. Given well-drained soil, a thoroughly compacted and reasonably smooth gravel surface is all that is needed for a bicycle trail. This type might be well suited to the drier eastern and southern counties.

37.

38.

*Leaflet dispensers.* Leaflets are often given away free. If a wall safe is needed it should be built into an existing wall whenever possible. Special erections tend to look incongruous and are expensive (38). Where a special wall has to be built to house the safe it is probably better to make something more of it, e.g. by adding a bench (37). But there is always a danger that artefacts of this kind will suburbanize the countryside.

39. The provision of direction finders at viewpoints is becoming popular. There seem to be unexpected pitfalls in the design of plinths. If stone is used, it will look best if it is similar to that in the immediate surroundings. Here incongruously sophisticated dressed ashlar is seen in juxtaposition to a random rubble wall. Both are of local stone.

40. The beginning of a trail need not be grand. A humble shed can answer well and has the advantage of being much less intrusive than a new shelter. The notice is fixed on to the shed rather than on a separate post.

41. A nature trail and a field study centre on a power station site. Nature Conservancy and Central Electricity Generating Board.

42. Sign on motor trail (see page 67). National Park Service.

## Access Roads and Car Parks
### (43 – 57)

43. Wheel track road, 7 ft. 6 in. wide overall. This most attractive type might be used much more with passing places as needed.

44 (*below*). Concrete kerbs and ill designed walls suburbanize their surroundings and undo any efforts which may also have been made in the design of a reservoir.

45. Car parks can look a lot worse empty than full. A recent British example.

46. Contrast with (44). Roads of this kind are as important to the
quality of the countryside as its buildings or scenery.

47. Wherever numbers and terrain make it possible this kind of car park is the best and cheapest. Forestry Commission.

48. A Dutch car park where the scale is broken down by planting within the parking area; the gravel surface is pleasantly textured.

49. Zigzag edge to a car park on open downland marks parking bays and gives a less rigid line. Note cars parked on grass: driveway only is gravel. (Aarhus City Forest Park).

50. Log kerb to car park. Post marks pathway. (Colonial Williamsburg)

51. Cars screened by traditional wall and prevented from parking on verge by boulders. Wall is set back from road so sight-lines are not critical and an opening in scale with the countryside is possible. (National Trust Car Park, Ullswater.)

52. Stumps in the grass effectively prevent parking.

53. Slate edge to a Westmoreland car park. Note chippings surface.

54. A car park on lower ground can be effectively screened by a wall only about four feet high. Such siting is particularly valuable in treeless country. (National Trust for Scotland).

55. Grass reinforced with hollow concrete blocks as a parking surface. Cologne.

56. Layby overlook along the newly-formed reservoir at Tryweren.
(Landscape consultant: Frederick Gibberd.)

Boulders act as markers at edge. Their bold scale and character are
completely in keeping. Other 'paraphernalia' here could wreck the
scene.

57. Timber guard-rail on the Blue Ridge Parkway (National Park
Service). Timber is completely in character with its surroundings. Used
in U.S.A. only for places where traffic is slowmoving.

58. A nature trail through dunes to show a sunken forest. (National Park Service).

59. Note the board - walk, thoroughly ship-shape in design and execution; allows the natural features to 'win'. National Park Service: Fire Island, New York.

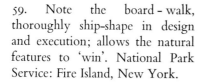

60. A timber stile in non-timber country. The stile is higher than the bank in which it is set and instead of crossing the stile, the bank itself is clambered over. Result: its free ends (possibly not made good when the stile was erected) are collapsing. One has already gone so the path skirts the stile which was intended to serve it.

61. Duckproof stile. (The Wildfowl Trust, Slimbridge.) The tread of the step is made of a shoe scraper so acts like a cattlegrid, being too uncomfortable for ducks to bother to negotiate it.

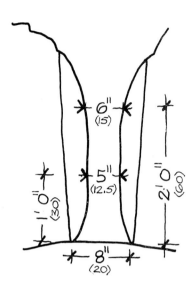

Access to the countryside means an enormous increase in the possibilities of gates being left open (62 and 63). Traditional stone stiles of the Yorkshire Dales which allow a human to pass but not a sheep. A new interpretation of this idea could be very useful elsewhere.

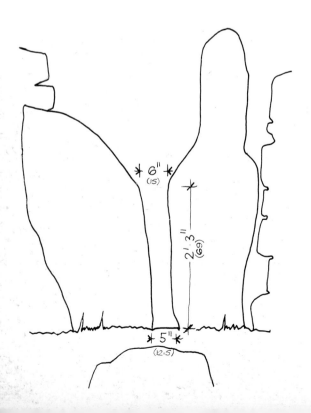

*Foot suspension bridges* are almost always both marvellous to look at and exciting to cross. The course of a river in its wooded valley is defined without intrusion. For spans over 80 ft. they are often the most economical type.

64 and 65. Cwm Coch Bridge (designed and constructed by Mr. R. J. Hope for Radnorshire County Council).

66 and 67. Biblins Bridge
(designed by the
Forestry Commission).

68. A traditional piling causeway recently constructed in the Amsterdamse Bos. This allows for the seepage of slow moving water but not for much change in level. There is no obstruction of the view.

69. An elegant bridge without a handrail across a quiet backwater in Holland.

**Picnic Sites (70 – 78)**

70. A picnic grove in British Columbia. The tables, which are about
10 ft. apart, are grouped near a forest shelter. Each makes a nucleus for
a separate picnic in a sociable atmosphere.

71. Well sited picnic tables on the edge of a clearing. Tables do not block the view of the river nor do they interrupt the glade, but dustbins do from ground level. (British Columbia Provincial Parks Branch).

72. Home comforts
for fishermen.
The Netherlands.

73. A boulder or old log can make
a comfortable backrest for a pull-off
picnic place on a quiet road.
Cheaper and more in character
than a bench and table.

74. Cut logs can make useful picnic
furniture. Like other small artefacts
they look better when tied into the
landscape by something bigger;
trees or outcrops of rock are useful
visually and for shelter.

75. Logs used as benches are more in scale and character with their surroundings than any park bench would be. Snowy Mountains, New South Wales.

76. Picnicking along the Thames clearly illustrates the attraction both of water and of settling on the edge of the meadow. Only when all the edge is taken do cars park in the middle.

77. *Water points*. Drinking jet housed in a keg. Note box used as step. Colonial Williamsburg.

78. Water standpoint in nineteenth-century cast iron housing. Car Park, East Lothian.

## Camps (79 – 88)

79. Banks divide the site and give shelter to caravans. It would be interesting to see the effect on the ground of a more angular treatment similar to that of the fields and plantations beyond. (Yellowcraig Camp Site, Caravan Club. Architects: Morris and Steedman.)

80. At ground level this camp ground gives no sense of being on the edge of a residential area. (Forestry Commission: Forest of Dean.)

81. Tents pitched informally among dunes on numbered camping pitches. Access is by foot only: gear is brought in by trolley. (Kennermenduinen National Park.)

82. Dustbin compound. (Caravan Club, Castleton.)

83. Fire station combined with water waste disposal. Cold water supply taps are mounted on rear of wall. (Caravan Club, Castleton.)

84. Electric razor point outside a camp office evidently gave satisfaction on this small site in Jutland.

85 (below). Camping at high densities on a very well run site in Germany. Four pitches appear in this photo. The washing in left foreground is hung from the guys of a neighbouring tent.

86. Floodlighting lamps can be hidden from view and well protected by this method used in Stuttgart.

Lights on camp sites and footpaths should be low and robust.

87. Lights path through woodland to an open air theatre. Light points do not compete with trees and are not noticeable in daylight. National Park Service.

88. Lights in a Dutch camp. Points are supplied in each box from which campers can take mains electricity for individual tents and vans.

## Lavatories and Camp Wash Units (89 – 94)

89. Wash rooms in a German camp provided choice of conventional basins, and taps to wash under running water. This example works well. Top of column housing taps takes tooth mugs. Rim of bowl 8 ft. (244 cm.) dia., 2 ft. 6 in. (76 cm.) above floor. Six taps, 4 ft. 8 in. (142 cm.) above floor. A socket for a hairdrier was provided in this washroom. Note hooks for sponge bags.

90. Outdoor washing on a Belgian camp. This economical plan worked well largely because the wash basins were sheltered by shower units and planting. Basins were used by all ages of both sexes.

91 (left). For washing under hot running water a wall-mounted spray mixer tap is economical in use of water and allows washer plenty of space. A bowl bracketed clear of wall with no taps or plug to trap dirt is easy to clean. (Messrs. Adamsez Ltd.)

92. W.Cs. without seats are now being installed in women's lavatories in America and Europe. Bonne-femme closet. (Messrs. Adamsez Ltd.)

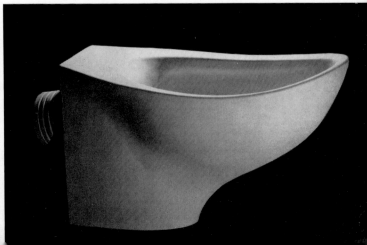

93. Lavatory block lit by high level windows and roof lighting. Trim timber-clad building for the National Trust. (Architect: Philip Jebb.)

94. Door detail, typical of Danish construction. Note quality of lever handle and self-closing hinges and simplicity of boarded door. A design which will stand rough treatment; unlikely to provoke vandalism, on layby lavatories where it is used. This example is from chemical closet emptying point on a campsite. Note sign.

**Buildings (95 – 109)**

95. Geodesic dome developed by David Stabb. (Spandrel Domes Ltd.)
Frame: aluminium with Elastomer junctions. Skin: terylene coated
with silicone. Diameter: 40 ft. Useful where large unobstructed floor
area is needed with minimum ground loads.

96. Cabins for an educational camp. Four sleeping spaces, each with its own veranda, four beds to each are grouped around a central fireplace. (Land between the Lakes Scheme. Tennessee Valley Authority.)

97. Prefabricated Chalets (Vic Hallam Ltd.) sympathetically sited in a woodland glade.

98. Tea and coffee shop (Forestry Commission, Forest of Dene). Bold scale and robust character is in keeping with woodland. Deep porch has benches at each side. Totem poles in foreground are useful decoys for name carvers.

99. Shop and lavatories at Queen's View, Perthshire. Note use of fall of ground with lavatories at lower level and one way pitched roof in sympathy with fall.

'Scotlog' construction with plain timber walls internally and externally. (Perth County Council from sketch scheme by Moira and Moira.)

100. Bus shelter erected by the Parish Council, Svendborg, Denmark. This structure, clad in reinforced polyester resin laminate is scarcely noticed in the country landscape. The colours of the countryside are taken up by the translucent sheeting: it seems as inconspicuous as a bubble. Shelters of this material could be useful on picnic sites and trails.

101 (*left*). Plate glass screens are commonly erected in Holland as windshields. They could be useful in the U.K. This, protecting the outdoor tables of a restaurant, is 5 ft. 5 in. (165 cm.) high; sill, 2 ft. 11 in. (89 cm.) above pavement. Glass is removed in winter. Perspex, fibre-glass, etc. would probably not withstand sand blasting of surface.

102. A sheltered, sunny covered way or porch can be useful at first floor or ground level. This timber-framed balcony has given satisfaction for several hundred years. (Tretower Court, Breconshire.) Such verandas could provide pleasant places for people to foregather outside information centres, camp offices and other recreational buildings.

103. Timber buildings are at their best when thoroughly well detailed and in no way folksy. This Visitor Center is clad in diagonal cedar boarding which is stopped short of the ground at plinth level. The surrounding gravel strip protects the building from mud splashing and solves the problem of mowing close to the wall. (Fort Raleigh, National Park Service.)

*Forestry Commission Observation Towers.* These towers are popular with photographers and naturalists. See page 173.

104 and 105.
Cannock Chase
(on a fire tower
base).

106 (*below, right*). Grizedale.

107. Custodian's hut. (Ministry of Public Building and Works). Small timber buildings produced by industrialized building systems such as this by Vic Hallam Ltd., can be attractive, both visually and economically. Like all other service buildings, these need careful siting, preferably among trees.

108. Souvenir shop at Møns Klint, Denmark. A large timber shelter with a generous covered area outside the shop proper has been constructed by the car park. No additional kiosks are allowed. It is in scale with the space and, sited low, does not jar with the splendid coastal beech woods which the visitor has come to see.

109. Camping shelter in the Yosemite National Park (known as a house-keeping unit).

## Pools (110 – 114)

110. Laying the plastic sheet for a polythene lined pool. (British Visqueen.)

111. Edge detail of the same pool at Birmingham University, designed by Casson and Conder.

112. Timber piling edge detail (timbers may also be tied back into the bank by steel guys secured to a horizontal rail).

113. The finished job (Landscape architect: Mary Mitchell).

114. This pool lies only a few hundred yards from the seashore but people prefer it to the open sea. Apart from the practical advantages of the water being warmer and safer, it gives a sense of enclosure lacking on most North Sea beaches. The bridge, for which there is no real necessity, greatly increases the attraction of the pool and gives it two more 'edges'. Kennermenduinen National Park, Holland. (Dr. Roderkerk.)

### Marinas and Boat Harbours (115 – 120)

115. An artificial island in a popular lake in Holland gives people an objective for a sail. Designed to give maximum shoreline (edge) and to provide shelter whatever the direction of the wind.

116 and 117. Shore berthing can save enormous expense in the construction of boat harbours. Two quick methods of launching: (1) Fork lift and trailer (Fairey Marine Ltd.); (2) Drott Travelift. (Conveyance and Fork Trucks Ltd.)

118. Cresta Marina, Newhaven. A good example of use of a previously
down-at-heel site. Note size of area taken by dinghy park.

119. Port Hamble (Architects: Raglan Squire and Partners in association with Leslie Bewes, A.R.I.N.A.). Trim floating pontoons connected to shore by hinged bridges.

120. Long Beach marina, California. Contrast with the traditional boat harbour. Note area of car parks.

## Litter (121 – 133)

121. Open mesh bins without linings look hideous; wind and birds scatter contents. Closed domestic bins with conventional lids are too much trouble to use. The lid must be replaced properly if it is not to blow away.

122. Camp site litter rack: works well with minimum fuss.

123. Mesh screened by timber slats
(lay-by near Maribo, Denmark).
See sketch below.

124. A paper sack protected by
wire mesh can look ship-shape *if
the mesh is small enough*, as in this
Danish example.

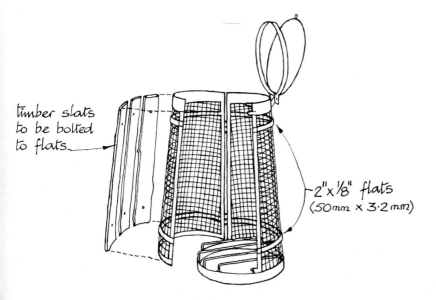

timber slats
to be bolted
to flats

2″ x ⅛″ flats
(50mm x 3·2mm)

125. Partial guarding is little use.

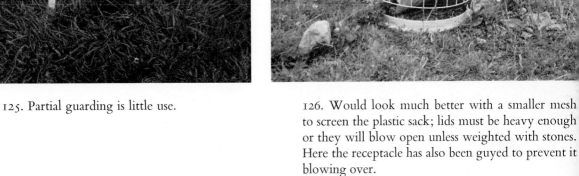

126. Would look much better with a smaller mesh to screen the plastic sack; lids must be heavy enough or they will blow open unless weighted with stones. Here the receptacle has also been guyed to prevent it blowing over.

127. A bracketed receptacle is more practical and easier to maintain if fixed to a stout post. Conveniently sited. Hampshire County Council.

128. Oil drums (with plastic liners) can make good looking litter bins. Here a dual-purpose defeats that object; the drum should be bolted to a stout post.

129. Receptacles with fixed tops through which litter is 'posted'. (P.R.S.I. layby unit. Messrs. Palfrey).

130 (*below, right*). Concrete pipes painted or plain, have been used by some county councils. They look best if painted white and work best where some form of liner with a smaller opening through which the litter can be posted is fitted. Sturdy proportions are good. If made to work, they can look better than many of the conventional 'sack-holders'. Perthshire County Council.

131. A very well chosen picnic place; litter receptacles mar view; they might be withdrawn from cliff edge and be equally accessible.

132. Ingeniously designed Dutch litter bin. Snag: its method of opening is not obvious. This means that on laybys, etc., it may be ignored or damaged. New objects whose function is not immediately obvious encourage vandalism.

133. A keg used as receptacle on an historic site. The keg can have a liner. Colonial Williamsburg.

134. The take-your-litter-home campaign causes a problem for willing campers (and picnickers) who do not happen to use organized sites, simply because they may not be going home for some time. Large packages of litter deposited in a layby bin create a headache for local authorities. A refuse truck on a strategic site, like this in Glencoe, provides an answer, but it too creates its own emptying problem for its owner. National Trust for Scotland.

# Brief Bibliography

Advisory Council on Public Sanitation: *Roadside Lavs—A Preliminary Guide to Local Authorities. Loos and Laybys.*

Barrett, John: *A Plain Man's Guide to the Path Round the Dale Peninsula.* Pembrokeshire National Park, 1966.

Beazley, Elisabeth: *Design and Detail of the Space between Buildings.* Architectural Press, 1960.

Brawne, Michael: *The New Museum.* Architectural Press, 1965.

British Visqueen Limited: *Water Storage.* 1967.

Bulletins of Information—Premier Congrès International A.I.T. Loisirs et Tourisme: *Amsterdamse Bos. The Hoge Weluwe National Park 1966. The Kennemerduinen National Park. Loenermavh & Loenensebos. Open Air Recreation & Rural Development. Roadside Picnic Sites. Staatsbosbeheer.*

Canaperia, Prof. G. A.: *Camping Hygiene.* Council of Europe, Strasbourg, 1961.

Caravan Sites and Control of Development Act, 1960.

Caravan Sites and Control of Development Act, 1960 Model Standards.

Chaney, Charles A.: *Marinas.* National Association of Engine and Boat Manufacturers, Inc., U.S.A., 1961

Christian, Garth: *Tomorrow's Countryside.* John Murray, 1966.

Consumer Council: *Living in a Caravan.* H.M.S.O., 1967.

Dower, Michael: 'The Fourth Wave'. *Architects Journal*, 1966. 'Planning for Sport & Recreation'. *Sport & Recreation*, July 1964.

Ebert, Dieter: *Das Campingwesen und die Anlage von Campingplatzen.*

The Friends of the Lake District: *Traffic in the Lake District.*

Garthwaite, Peter: *The Forester and the Landscape.* (Forestry Commission Research and Development Paper No. 53) 1967.

Hall, Peter: 'The Great British History Parkway Drive-in'. *New Society*, 3.8. 1967.

H.M.S.O.: *Fixed Equipment of the Farm* No. 7, Cattle grids for private farm and estate roads. No. 8, Farm Gates. *The Traffic Signs Regulations and General Directions*, 1964. *Countryside in 1970.* Proceedings of Study Conferences 1963 and 1965.

Koninklijke Nederlandsche Toeristenbond: *Picknickplaatsen.* 1966.

Loewenthal, David: *The American Way of History.* Columbia University Forum, Summer 1966. *Is Wilderness 'Paradise Enow'* Columbia University Forum, Spring 1964.

O

# Brief Bibliography

Loudon, J. C.: *Encyclopaedia of Gardening*.

Lynch, Kevin: *Site Planning*. Massachusetts Institute of Technology, 1962.

Lapage, Wilbur F.: *Successful Private Campgrounds*. U.S. Forest Service Research Paper, 1967.

Ministry of Agriculture, Fisheries & Food: *Water for Irrigation*, H.M.S.O., 1967.

Ministry of Housing and Local Government: *Caravan Parks*. H.M.S.O., 1963. *New Life for Dead Lands*, 1963.

National Audubon Society: *Trail Planning and Layout*.

National Caravan Council: *A Manual of Caravan Park Development and Operation*, 1966.

National Park Service: *The Park Practice Program: Design, Guidelines, Grist, Trends, Park & Recreation Structures*, 1938. *The Interpretive Planning Handbook*, Appendix I (not published).

Nature Trails and Forest Walks and Guides (too numerous to mention).

Netherlands Staatsbosbeheer *Technische Mededlingen and Recreatie*, 1964.

Orrom, Martin: *Recreational Use of Forests in Holland*. Forestry Commission Research and Development Paper No. 48. *Recreation in British Forests*. Paper read to Commonwealth Forestry Conference, India, 1968.

Roderkerk, Dr. E. L. M.: *Recreatie, Recreatieverzoging en Natuurbescherming in de Kennemerduinen*.

Rogers, Taliaferro, Kostrisky, Lamb: *National Capital Region Sign Study, 1966*.

Scottish Development Department: *Survey and Planning Proposals for Tourism*. H.M.S.O., 1964.

Sunset Books: *Swimming Pools*. Lane Books, California, 1959. *Decks for Outdoor Living*. Lane Books, California, 1967. *Cabins and Vacation Houses*. Lane Books, California, 1967.

Tilden, Freeman: *Interpreting our Heritage*. University of North Carolina Press, Revised Edition, 1967.

The Timber Research and Development Association, Ltd.: *Timber Fencing and Gates for Housing and other Buildings. Timber Fencing and Gates for Agriculture and open space purposes*.

*T.P.I. Journal*, November, 1967: 'Recreation'.

Turner, Barbara: *Open Spaces Open to the Public in Hampshire*. Hampshire County Council, 1966.

U.S. Department of Agriculture: Forest Service: *Developing a self-guiding Trail in the National Forests*. 1964. *How to Build a Farm Pond*. 1949.

U.S. Department of Health, Education and Welfare: *Environmental Health Guide for Travel, Trailer Parking areas, Mobile Home Parks*.

Whiteman, W. M.: *Caravans and the English Landscape*. The Caravan Club of Great Britain and Ireland.

Wilson, Raymond: 'Mobility'. *Architectural Design*, May 1967.

# Index

Page numbers in *italic* type refer to diagrams in the text

*Index*

Water Resources Act, 177
Wildfowl Trust, 171–3; plates 6, 7
Windshield, 101
Worboys signs, *see* Signs
Worboys, Sir Walter, 49

Wright Brothers Memorial, *see* Information Centres

Yorktown Battlefield, *see* Information Centres